Understanding Global Slavery

The publisher gratefully acknowledges the generous contribution to this book provided by Sally Lilienthal.

Understanding Global Slavery

A Reader

Kevin Bales

UNIVERSITY OF CALIFORNIA PRESS

Berkeley / Los Angeles / London

University of California Press
Berkeley and Los Angeles, California

University of California Press, Ltd.
London, England

Library of Congress Cataloging-in-Publication Data
Bales, Kevin.
    Understanding global slavery : a reader / Kevin Bales.
        p.   cm.
    Includes bibliographical references and index.
    ISBN-13 978-0-520-24507-5 (pbk. : alk. paper)
    ISBN-10 0-520-24507-5 (pbk. : alk. paper)
    1. Slavery.   2. Slave labor.   3. Forced labor.   4. Prostitution.   5. Slave
trade.   I. Title.
HT867.B38   2005
306.3'62—dc22   2005002967

Manufactured in the United States of America

14   13   12   11   10   09   08   07   06
10   9   8   7   6   5   4   3   2

The paper used in this publication meets the minimum requirements of
ANSI/NISO Z39.48–1992 (R 1997) (*Permanence of Paper*).

To Larry DeBord

Contents

Illustrations and Tables

Figures

Maps

Tables

Acknowledgments

Special thanks to Reed Malcolm, my editor at the University of California Press, and to Bonita Hurd for excellent copyediting. Lisa Matthews Miller was invaluable in working out the kinks in the manuscript and as a researcher. Camilla Brown and Eden Hegwood plowed through an early version and improved the flow. Jeff Howarth, the librarian at Anti-Slavery International, was so very helpful in finding just the right images and needed facts. At Free the Slaves, the Director of Outreach and Technology, Jacob Patton, provided intellectual as well as technical guidance. Burkhard Dammann has been a valued coexplorer of human trafficking. Sometimes a conversation will open a new way of seeing. I can think of several such discussions that fed ideas into this book — chats with Martin Albrow, Lorena Arocha, Alexis Aronowitz, Amelia Becker, Greg Carr, Lou DeBaca, Mike Dottridge, Robert Hadfield, Adam Hochschild, Paul Holmes, Win Jordan, Given Kachepa, Hazel May, John Miller, David Ould, Vivek Pandit, Monica Peruffo, Roger Plant, Samantha Power, Christopher Rowley, Amar Saran, Cristina Tallens, and Pippin Whitaker spring to mind. The Croft Institute for International Studies at the University of Mississippi was a great base of operations; many thanks to its director, Michael Metcalf, and to Glenn Schove and Evelyn Hurdle.

CHAPTER I

Understanding Slavery Today

For Meera the revolution began with a single rupee. When a worker from the Sankalp organization found Meera's unmapped village in the hills of Uttar Pradesh, India, he found the entire population was enslaved through debt bondage to work in stone quarries. The men and women hammered and pried rocks from the earth; the children hauled the rocks in baskets. Children as young as five worked in the pits making sand by smashing stones with a hammer. The dust, flying rock chips, and heavy loads meant that many villagers suffered from silicosis and damaged eyes or backs. These villagers were enslaved in order to make a substance so common, and that costs so little, that only by using slaves could *handmade* sand be profitable.

Calling together a few of the women, the Sankalp worker proposed a radical step. If ten women would agree to set aside a single rupee a week to form a credit union, he would help them put their savings in the local bank and arrange a loan of seed money.[1] In India, small-scale credit unions such as these are known as "self-help groups." In time, the first group was formed and the rupees slowly mounted up. After three months, enough money had been saved that the group decided to pay off the loan that held one woman — Meera — in bondage. The landlord and moneylenders were surprised that she had been able to pay off her debt, but they were not worried. Sometimes it happened that a relative from outside the village might send a gift, or an inheritance might provide enough to pay off a debt bond. Since the original debt holding a family might have been contracted two or three generations before, such repayments are seen as a windfall by the landlords. With the local economy completely under their control, the landlords and moneylenders know they only have to wait for a crisis — a serious illness or the need to pay for a funeral — to drive a family back to them for another loan.

Once a family has taken a loan, they are trapped. Make no mistake, these loans are not like the mortgages we have on our homes or the payments we make on our cars. Under the most common system of bondage in South Asia, work does not repay the debt. When a person borrows from a landlord, that person, his or her family, and all the work that all of them are capable of is simply *collateral* against the loan. Until the debt is repaid, the moneylender owns the family and everything they grow or produce. If the landlord owns all their productive output, is it possible to repay the debt? In a word, no. And so the debt is passed on from husband to wife, father to son, through the generations. The control of the landlord is total, and if he is unsatisfied with his returns, a child can be taken from the family and sold. In Meera's case, with the whole village under their thumbs, the landlords and moneylenders were unconcerned that she had paid her debt; she would be theirs again soon enough.

Freed from her enslavement, Meera shifted to piecework, selling loads of sand directly to the wholesaler, and she began paying larger amounts into the credit union. In another two months, enough money had been saved to free another woman, and she also began to deposit larger sums from her increased income. The following month a third woman bought herself out of bondage.

At that point, a dramatic change came over the self-help group. After a lifetime of slavery, the other members, seeing that freedom was possible, declared themselves free and renounced their debts. Once they saw that Meera and the other women could live in freedom, could work and provide for their families, bondage lost both its threat and its security for them. It was a profound realization and a revolutionary step. The landlords, who had been happy to have the cash that paid off the debts of two or three slaves, now faced revolt. For the landlords and moneylenders, the threat was immense: if the system of collateral debt bondage was dismantled, their power and profits would evaporate. The landlords moved quickly against the women. A gang of thugs was sent to rough them up and drive them from the quarries. Several women were injured, but they stood firm. With backing from the Sankalp worker, they fought to defend their new freedom.

At one point the main landlord came to the village to threaten the women and force them back to work for him. "He told me, 'Even if you die, I will drag your body out of the ground and make you work,'" one of the women said. For this landlord such a revolt was inconceivable — was he not of the upper caste? Hadn't his family controlled these villages for generations? Weren't these people Kols, a tribal group below even the lowest castes? For perhaps the first time in his life, the landlord found that his assumed superiority counted for nothing. The landlords tried to cut the women off from the wholesalers and from the quarries where they worked, but the women made their own deals with the wholesalers and found new areas to quarry. Working together, the women came through. Soon they began to help women in other villages start credit unions. In less than a year, the whole village was freed, and the funds building up in the credit unions were used to equip a simple open-air school for the children who had been freed from the quarries.

Less than fifty miles from the quarries, the land turns flat and fertile. Here, without the help of microcredit, freedom can be difficult for an ex-slave. When I first met Baldev in 1997, he was plowing. His master called him "my plowman." Baldev's father and grandfather had also been bonded to his master's family, held against a debt passed down through the generations. Two years later I met Baldev again and was surprised to learn that he had freed himself from debt. But he had not freed himself from bondage. He told me:

> After my wife received this money [from a relative], we paid off our debt and were free to do whatever we wanted. But I was worried all the time — what if one of the children got sick? What if our crop failed? What if the government wanted some money? Since we no longer belonged to the landlord, we didn't get food every day as before. Finally, I went to the landlord and asked him to take me back. I didn't have to borrow any money, but he agreed to let me be his *halvaha* [bonded plowman] again. Now I don't worry so much; I know what to do.

Lacking any preparation for freedom, Baldev reenrolled in slavery. Without external support, his emancipation didn't last.

Understanding Slavery, Understanding Freedom

To many people, it comes as a surprise that hereditary debt bondage and other forms of slavery persist into the twenty-first century. Every country, after all, has made it illegal to own another human being and exercise total control over that person. And yet there are many people like Baldev — by my estimate, around 27 million people in slavery today. (Please see chapter 5 for an explanation of how this estimate was made.) If slaveholders no longer own slaves, how can they exercise so much control that, sometimes, freed slaves deliver themselves back into bondage? This is just one of the puzzles of modern slavery.

It is important to explain that collateral debt bondage — the complete control of any person because of a debt — is specifically outlawed in India. Meera and the women of her village had no legal obligation to pay back the sums they "owed" to the moneylenders and landlords. In fact, they were breaking the letter of the law when they did repay their "debt." But in the countryside, among the illiterate and systematically oppressed, this law in unknown. The world's great web of television, radio, and the Internet has yet to reach these villages. Their reality is bondage; no other way of thinking is permitted. Clearly, the landlords have no interest in allowing their bonded workers to know their rights. When the workers have been bonded for generations, when they know no other reality but slavery, when their masters constantly reinforce their inferiority and the preordained nature of their bondage, it can be frightening to contemplate "disobedience." The bonded worker is more likely to see resisting the landlord as an act that will threaten the livelihood of his or her family than as an act of liberation. Freedom, being unknown, is hard to imagine. The choices available in freedom are completely alien to these bonded workers. To help these families to freedom means opening their eyes to the reality of their bondage and the possibility of freedom.

For some slaves, the first step out of bondage is to learn to see their lives with new eyes. Their reality is a social world where they have their place and some assurance of a subsistence diet. Born into slavery, they cannot easily redefine their lives outside the frame of enslavement. For other slaves — those who have been enslaved after living in freedom — it is not usually necessary to think their way to freedom. Their challenge is to overcome the crushing violence, the stunned shock, of the total control over their lives.

Rethinking slavery does not happen just with individuals; it also occurs within populations. The way slavery came to be seen as a violation of human rights is based on this rethinking — in the public mind, within religions, and in law. How the understanding of slavery was transformed in the public mind over a period of centuries is the subject of chapter 2. A larger question is how to bring about such a transformation today, when the problem is not apathy or indifference to the continued presence of slavery, but ignorance of it.

The waning years of the twentieth century and the early years of the twenty-first have seen an explosion of interest in and work on modern slavery, yet this work has just scratched the surface. In the early 1990s, when I began to search for funding to carry out research on slavery, foundations that I thought might support my work could not imagine the need for it, since "slavery ended long ago." Fortunately, between the emergence of a generation of young activist-scholars and the pressure that outrage over international human trafficking has brought to bear on governments, public awareness and support for research and antislavery work has mushroomed. Yet while we come to understand that slavery is all around us, even in America and Europe, we are in the dark when it comes to the most basic questions of who, how, how many, and where. These questions are crucial not just for the slaves but for all of us. For if the path to freedom is not as smooth as we can make it, if it leads only to lives of continued exploitation, then the problem is not solved; it is merely postponed.

To see how freedom can be a hollow victory, look at the United States. While Americans can be justly proud of Abraham Lincoln's 1863 Emancipation Proclamation, it simply did not go far enough. Remember that, at first, the proclamation applied only to those slaves *behind enemy lines,* where the power of the document could not reach. With the end of the American Civil War, freedom came to all slaves, but *only* freedom, and that was a great wrong. Slavery is theft — theft of a life, theft of work, theft of any property or produce, theft even of the children a slave might have borne. In America, for generations, the lives and sweat of men, women, and children had been stolen. The debt owed to ex-slaves was tremendous. Their productive labor had built a whole society — it had raised great plantations out of the wilderness — and had created beauty, sustenance, shelter, apparel, and wealth. In return, slaves endured abuse, sexual assault, violence, and the selling away of their children or spouses or parents and were given just enough food to keep them working. Here was a debt that could not be repaid to the millions who had died in slavery, and it was a debt to the living that was denied or ignored.

No Freedom without Forgiveness?

After the Civil War, there were calls from ex-slaveholders for compensation for the billions of dollars' worth of slave "property" they had lost when slavery ended. Given the enormous cost in lives and property the war had already exacted, these calls were ignored. Meanwhile, nearly 4 million ex-slaves also waited, if not for restitution or compensation, then at least for the tools to rebuild their lives. The federal government's Freedmen's Bureau, with its successful education programs, and the potential formula of "forty acres and a mule," could have transformed millions of destitute ex-slaves into economically autonomous families.[2] But the bureau was quickly shut down, and the mule and the forty acres never materialized. Today, we have learned that exactly such a mixture of education and a livelihood can bring stable freedom and citizenship to ex-slaves. Yet after the death of Lincoln, as the Southern elites reasserted their influence, and as many Northern politicians redirected their energies to other issues, no such support came for the freed slaves. The result of this neglect has reverberated into our own lives.

Perhaps no other country in the world so dramatically demonstrates the consequences of a botched emancipation. America has suffered, and continues to suffer, from the injustice perpetrated on ex-slaves. Generations of African Americans were sentenced to second-class status, exploited, denied, and abused. Without education and basic resources, it has been difficult for African American families to build the economic foundation needed for full participation and well-being in American society. Today there are laws that call on criminals to make restitution for what they have stolen, for the damage they have inflicted. No such restitution came for the stolen lives of millions of slaves.

At the end of the American Civil War, nearly 4 million ex-slaves were dumped with little preparation into the society and economy of the United States. Today some 27 million slaves exist in the world. If we can end slavery in this generation — which is a real possibility — do we really want the next four, five, or twenty generations to face the problems of emancipation gone wrong? Our aim in ending slavery cannot be the creation of a population whose suffering and anger spills out over the decades. Helping freed slaves achieve full lives is one of the best investments a government or society can make. We know the alternative: that way lies Jim Crow and a horrible waste of human potential. It also gives birth to anger, retribution, vengeance, hatred, and violence. In fact, one of the most profound, and unanswered, questions about slavery and freedom is this: even if there is restitution, how can there be forgiveness?

Those who have suffered enslavement may say that this is a crime beyond forgiveness. It is no momentary act of violence, no crime of passion, but a systematic brutalization and exploitation that can stretch out over generations. And it incorporates the most horrible crimes known — torture, rape, kidnap, murder, and the willful destruction of the human mind and spirit. It is exploitation, injustice, and violence in their most potent forms all rolled together. The damage slavery does and has done is inestimable, and that includes the damage done to minds deeply injured by enslavement.

The minds injured by slavery include those of the slaveholders. By dehumanizing others in order to enslave them, slaveholders dehumanize themselves. Those of us with little direct experience of slavery find it hard to feel any concern for the slaveholder, but many of those who have lived in slavery recognize the damage slavery does to the master as well. A community that allows slavery in its midst is sick to its core. For the ex-slave to grow as a citizen, that sickness must be treated, especially because many freed slaves continue to live in the same area where they were enslaved. Ex-slaves and their former slaveholders may see each other regularly. If injustices are allowed to fester, it will be impossible for either to move on. In America, the ugly sickness of slavery reemerged in segregation, discrimination, and lynch laws. In part, this was because most Americans sought to ignore the legacy of slavery. The immediate needs of freed slaves were not met in the years following 1865, and Americans since then have attempted to draw the curtain over the past, to let bygones be bygones.

We can see a parallel in postapartheid South Africa. Faced with the large-scale, horrific murders and torture of the past, many people in that country argued that collective amnesia would best serve the reconstruction of a truly democratic state. But Desmond Tutu explained, "Our common experience in fact is the opposite — that the past, far from disappearing or lying down and being quiet, is embarrassingly persistent, and will return and haunt us unless it has been dealt with adequately. Unless we look the beast in the eye we will find that it returns to hold us hostage."[3] In America that beast has been on the prowl for more than a hundred years and has evolved into new forms of discrimination, recrimination, and injustice. Putting down that beast is one of America's greatest challenges. Ensuring that that same sort of beast never grows up when slaves are freed today is a challenge for the whole world.

To help governments enforce their own antislavery laws, to find the best ways to liberate slaves, and to ensure that freed slaves build new lives and that communities overcome the sickness of slavery, means building a sound understanding of what slavery is today and where it is going tomorrow. We cannot solve a problem we do not understand. The aim of this book is to explore some of the fundamental and underlying ideas about slavery in order to help that understanding grow.

Same Slavery, Different Packages

With only a handful of people around the world working to gain an understanding of slavery, the picture is sketchy. What's more, every time someone fills in a few more strokes, the picture gets a little clearer but also a little more complicated. We tend to see slavery in simplistic terms, but it is as complex as any human relationship can be, especially one shaped in different countries by culture, religion, and social change. At the moment, we really are like the blind men with the elephant, each describing just one part of the beast, with only the slightest idea of the actual shape of the whole animal. This book is about bringing together a set of ideas that explore slavery today, and what we can learn from past instances of slavery. Virtually every person wants to live in a world without slavery, but in our fight against slavery our tools are few, our resources scarce, and our knowledge piecemeal. The chapters of this book aim to fill in some of the holes and to save us from reinventing wheels that were assembled in the antislavery campaigns of the past. But it is important, before taking up those ideas, to review the work of investigators who are shining light into the dark corners of contemporary slavery.

One thing researchers do know is that slavery is evolving and seems to be increasing in raw numbers. The past few years have seen the discovery of new forms of slavery. Researchers, journalists, and activists around the world have documented human trafficking in eastern Europe, debt bondage in South Asia, and short-term "contract" slavery in Brazil, as well as "classical" slavery in North Africa put to new uses. Organizations as diverse as the American Central Intelligence Agency, the Vatican, the United Nations, and Amnesty International have turned their attention to slavery.

Slavery is not always easy to recognize, sometimes because the outer "shell" of slavery hides its inner reality. But what is the basic reality of slavery? It is a simple yet potent truth that slavery is a relationship between (at least) two people. Like the other common and patterned relationships that humans have, slavery takes various forms and achieves certain outcomes. The outcomes of slavery tend to be similar across time and cultures, the forms less so. The outcomes of slavery are exploitative: theft of labor resulting in economic gain for the slaveholder, use of the enslaved person as an item of conspicuous consumption, and the possible sexual use of an enslaved person. Any particular slave may fulfill one, some, or all of these outcomes for the slaveholder.

While the outcomes of slavery tend to be similar, the forms of enslavement are more varied. There are core attributes that define slavery, but these attributes are embedded in a wide variety of forms reflecting cultural, religious, social, political, ethnic, commercial, and psychological contexts. The mix of influences for any particular slave and slaveholder may be unique, but they follow general patterns reflecting the community in which the slavery occurs. Part of the challenge of understanding slavery both historically and today is to find the underlying attributes shared by all forms of slavery and to analyze and understand the various forms slavery can take in any particular case. Across time and across different countries, the extreme differences in the forms of slavery mean that the underlying nature of the slavery relationship — the attributes that mark it as slavery — can be obscured. Religious justifications, "willing" participation, token payments, the apparent signing of a contract, and any number of other layers of meaning, rationalization, or explanation can be used as part of the way a community explains and rationalizes slavery in its midst.

Today, the core attributes of slavery remain the same as they have always been. They are the same attributes that described a slave in the past: the state of control exercised over the slave based on violence or its threat, a lack of any payment beyond subsistence, and the theft of the labor or other qualities of the slave for economic gain. All slavery shares these attributes, though there can be occasional exceptions, such as gifts or remuneration beyond subsistence. The key and central attribute, the core, of slavery, however, is the violent control of one person by another.

Slavery has always been about violent control, but modern slavery differs in three important ways. First, slaves today are cheaper than they have ever been. The cost of slaves has fallen to a historical low, and they can be acquired in some parts of the world for as little as ten dollars.[4] This means that they are no longer a big capital purchase, like livestock or equipment. Slaves today are more likely to be seen as disposable — something you use and then throw away when it is no longer useful. Second, slaves are now held for a shorter length of time. In the past, slavery was usually a lifelong condition; today it may last just a few years or even months. Third, today slavery is globalized. This means that the forms of slavery in different parts of the world are becoming more alike. The way slaves are used, and the part they play in the world economy, is increasingly similar wherever they are located. These changes have come about very quickly, occurring, for the most part, in the past fifty years. This new "outer shell" of slavery has grown so quickly that we have trouble seeing the big picture of modern slavery. To see better, we need the help of researchers studying today's slavery where it lives.

Sketching the Big Picture

We can start with looking at what researchers are finding out about slavery at the individual level. Around the world people are looking closely at the lives of slaves and helping them to achieve their freedom. What have they learned that can help us? One of the first things they recognize is the role that poverty and vulnerability play in driving people to slavery. While slavery may be linked to religion in one country, to caste or "race" in a second country, and to gender in yet another country, it always reflects differences in economic and social power. Slavery is no longer based on broad categories of "race." Slavery is fundamentally a question of power and specifically the power to use violence. It is no revelation that some people use power to immorally or illegally enrich themselves. A pertinent question for us to ask is why some people are so vulnerable to this abuse of power that they can be enslaved.

Vulnerability is key to slavery, but not all the vulnerable become slaves. That fact alone generates an important question: Why are some vulnerable people enslaved and others are not? If we can answer that question, perhaps we can learn how to best protect people from enslavement. Of course, with respect to some of the poor the answer is clear — they are not worth enslaving. There are millions of vulnerable people who are, from the perspective of the slaveholder, not fit to be slaves. The elderly, the infirm, and the very young are almost never enslaved. Those in the market for slaves seek health, strength, and youth. But, of the young, healthy, and strong, why are some enslaved and not others? At the broadest level, we can say that those enslaved lack both the personal and financial resources and the social and governmental protections to prevent their enslavement. At the local level, however, the answer quickly gets complicated, and many of the answers are both partial and tantalizing. A quick look at the trafficking and enslavement of children in West African demonstrates this.

THEIR BODIES WASH UP ON SHORE
IN THE MORNING . . .

In 2001, Monika Parikh, a researcher for Free the Slaves, traveled to Lake Volta in Ghana. Her aim was to explore rumors of children being enslaved in the fishing villages there. Lake Volta is one of the world's largest lakes and, in the past, has been a source for fish for both the national and export markets. In recent years overfishing has meant a drop in fish stocks. The resulting economic pressure has pushed some fishermen to use children as workers rather than pay adult wages. These children, some as young as three, work long hours mending, setting, and pulling nets; cleaning and smoking fish; and rowing the fishing boats. The greatest danger comes when they must dive deeply into the lake to retrieve snagged nets. The fishermen tie weights to the children to help them descend more quickly. Much of the work goes on during the night, and in the dark depths the children get tangled and trapped and then drown. A local official stated, "The bodies of children wash up on the shores of our village, but the police typically attribute the deaths to drowning, a natural cause." If not drowned outright, the children suffer from shock when forced down into water that is too cold for diving.

When Parikh was able to speak with some of the enslaved children, she found them hollow eyed, gaunt, and grim. They reported that they were fed fermented corn and cassava flour, but only sparingly. Two little boys reported eating some of the little fish they had netted, but for this their master had beaten them with a cane. If sick or injured, the children receive no care or treatment. Exhausted and staggering from lack of sleep, they often hurt themselves in their work. While most of the enslaved children are boys, some girls are used as well for domestic work and to sell the fish in the market. Like other trafficked girls in Ghana, they are likely to be sexually abused as well.

The children come to this enslavement with the cooperation of their parents. Fishermen visit villages in the surrounding countryside in order to recruit children. With schooling hard to obtain and family incomes around the starvation level, parents sometimes agree to let their children go in order to gain the two hundred thousand cedi (about twenty-eight dollars) offered as an "advance" on their child's labor. Normally, the fisherman promises that another four hundred thousand cedi will be paid to the parents over the next year. Once the children have been taken away from their home villages, the reality of slavery descends. Fishermen, when asked, state that they have "bought" the children, and once they reach Lake Volta, their treatment of them makes this assertion clear.

For all the horror these children suffered, a happy ending to this story is unfolding. After Parikh completed her research, she circulated it to a number of local and international agencies. A local relief organization began to work directly with the children; meanwhile, the International Organization for Migration (IOM), a branch of the United Nations, began to bring their resources and expertise to bear. With a large grant from the U.S. government, the IOM set many of the children free and reunited them with their families. To prevent recurrences, the IOM helped the fishermen move into other types of work if they promised to stop enslaving children. Once the children had been returned home, their families were also helped to find ways to increase their incomes, thus relieving some of the pressure that drove them to "sell" their children in the first place. To date, more than a thousand children have been freed, and the nature of the fishing industry on Lake Volta has been transformed.

The rescue of the fishing children shows that real progress can be made when economic alternatives are developed for both those who would enslave and those who are vulnerable to enslavement. Removing the pressures that tempt some people to exploit workers is important. More important is aiding the families that are vulnerable: helping them get the education, income, and skills that protect them from slavery. The lesson of Lake Volta is also important because it shows that the enslavement of children in West Africa can be stopped — a crucial point because the enslavement of children is widespread and deep-rooted in the region. It is a practice that Anne Kielland understands better than most.

THE SLAVEHOLDER'S APPRENTICE

If we are the blind men examining the elephant, Anne Kielland is an expert on the toes. A Norwegian who speaks flawless French and English, she has spent long periods in the villages of West Africa coming to grips with why and how the children of that region are trafficked into slavery. In 2000, together with Roger Ouensavi, Kielland interviewed more than forty-seven hundred households, representing over 11,500 children, in the country of Benin. Kielland's study is the largest, most complete study of child trafficking and child labor migration ever done.[5] Like most good research, the results immediately brought basic assumptions into question.

It was assumed that trickery and false promises were being used to get parents to allow their children to go to the cities where they could be enslaved. There was a common belief that three factors were driving that traffic: poverty, boredom, and ignorance. It was assumed that the poorest, most destitute families would be the most vulnerable, simply because they were the most likely to take the chance that a child might actually get work abroad and send money home. It was also assumed that in the smallest rural villages, where there was little to do, children and teenagers would be the most willing to take a chance on working abroad if it meant getting to the bright lights of a city. Finally, it was assumed that parents and children would not take recruiters' bait if they knew how likely it was that the experience would end badly. All of these assumptions, which may be true elsewhere, were only partially true in Benin.

A crucial point is that trafficked children are just one thread in a more complex story of children moving around their own country and migrating between countries in order to find work. According to the research, not all children who left home were enslaved: some got jobs, made money, and came home in triumph. Their success, however, helped set the scene for the exploitation of other children. Kielland and Ibrahim Sanogo explain:

> The children in most of the cases agree to go. They have seen children who have returned to the villages having been paid in kind, in form of a radio or a bicycle. They are impressed by such wealth, and when the intermediaries [recruiters] return, new recruits will be eager to travel in order to get the same things. In a few cases children do well and come home to the village with modern commodities, and in even fewer cases they can afford to build a nice house for the parents, showing the entire village how well they have done. Unfortunately, the children normally come back as poor as they left or they don't come back at all. Girls who have been in domestic service often return pregnant. . . . It resembles a lottery. The grand prize is tempting, and the winner gets a lot of attention. Unfortunately in the case of child labor migration, the price of the ticket is human, fragile, and extremely vulnerable.[6]

Within the African context, where children are expected to make a significant contribution to the family economy from an early age, and the transition from childhood to adulthood is not a clearly defined event, it is not unusual or remarkable that children are made to work. Added to that is the custom of "placing" children with relatives who might provide a better life for them, often in what might be thought of as an apprenticeship. This may seem alien, even cruel, to Americans and Europeans, but it is important to remember that, in the early nineteenth century, this was absolutely normal and common in both Europe and the United States before the institution of mandatory and universal primary education. The end of such "placements" in Europe and North America came just over one hundred years ago. In Africa today, many villages have little or no schooling available, and the alternative of sending a child to the city to learn a skill and earn much-needed money can be appealing. The tragedy comes when human traffickers, concealing their aim of enslavement, take advantage of this system and convince parents and children that a golden future awaits.

Poverty, boredom, and ignorance were found to have an effect on this process, but in unexpected ways. The better-off families of the poorest villages were the ones most likely to send their children away to work, confounding the idea that this placement was some sort of last resort when a family faced destitution. In Benin, better-off families actually used their resources and connections to get their children out of the poorest villages, hoping for a chance of a better life.

HOW YOU GONNA KEEP THEM DOWN ON THE FARM, AFTER THEY'VE SEEN TV?

Assumptions about boredom driving children into risky work turned out to be backward. While villages with daily markets were found to have fewer children leaving, those with their own soccer teams and televisions saw *more* children go. Playing on soccer teams seems to cause young people to identify with the big teams in the cities, and it holds up the possibility of enjoying, or even participating in, big-time sports. In a curiously contradictory effect, soccer, the very activity that most holds the attention of rural children, also helps them to see and yearn for life outside the village. Television has much the same effect. As a window through which children see the world — the cities, the wealth, luxury, excitement, and glamour outside the village — television helps prepare children and parents for the blandishments of recruiters and traffickers.

Finally, it was assumed that if parents really understood the risk their children were facing when they left home, they would not let them go. If a village had a place where information about trafficking and migration was handed out, if there were groups that met regularly where such topics could be discussed, then surely parents would learn and children wouldn't be put at risk. Once again, the results were mixed. It turned out that exactly the places and groups that could warn about the risks of trafficking could also spread the word about "successful" children; they may have even served as recruitment grounds. When the international movement of children was decreased through public education, then the within-country placement of children into jobs increased. Having organized women's groups in a village decreased the amount of in-country movement of girls, but this increased the amount of international traffic, the very type that is most dangerous. Only public education through press and radio uniformly slowed the outflow of children.

If we are trying to keep vulnerable people out of slavery, what can we learn from Anne Kielland's studies? First and foremost is that we have to look for answers appropriate to the people at risk. From the outside we might view the traffic in children in West Africa simplistically: it is wrong; it must be stopped. Up close we see it is the criminal exploitation of a much larger, culturally accepted use of child labor to support families. Sometimes getting people out of slavery is about kicking in doors and helping them to freedom. But in this case the solution is most likely to be a matter of making sure families don't need to send their children off to work, and establishing universal and mandatory education — the fundamental basis for economic growth and social development.

Why Aren't Governments Doing More?

To establish universal and mandatory education, not just on the law books, but also in reality, takes government will and resources. Many governments in the developing world lack both, and sadly the rich and powerful governments are partially to blame. The investments our governments make in the Southern Hemisphere are too often focused on developing those countries as trading partners and selling them weapons. Weapons are the last thing these countries need, but as the guns flow south, the money gushes north. Every year, the countries of Africa, Asia, the Middle East, and Latin America spend about $22 billion in the international arms market.[7] The estimated cost of providing primary education to every child on the planet who currently lacks it is less than half that amount. The powerful countries are getting richer on this trade; the United States, Russia, France, Britain, and China together sell almost 90 percent of the weapons delivered to poor countries. The volume of this production is almost beyond comprehension. For example, every year about three pieces of ammunition, bullets, bombs, mortar shells, and so forth are produced for every man, woman, and child on earth. They are added to an existing stockpile that could kill every human being many times over. There are a lot of inhuman and vicious examples of bad government and business policy. But when we know that basic education keeps children out of slavery, and when we know that just half the money the developing world spends on weapons in one year would provide that basic education to every child, how can there be a choice?

However, the solution requires more than education alone. Ignorance supports slavery, but there is another pillar helping to prop up bondage. Around the world, slavery grows where corruption disrupts the rule of law and makes the vulnerable open to violent control. Not surprisingly, there is a link between corruption and the flooding of poor countries with guns. The U.S. Department of Commerce reports that the arms sector accounts for one-half of all the bribery cases it records.[8] The guns flood in, and the cash flows to corrupt politicians. They, in turn, create a web of crime and violence using those weapons. Down at the village level, an honest policeman can't compete with heavily armed criminals, and taking a bribe worth a hundred times his monthly salary is the safest thing to do. The result is that, when the criminals with guns show up, the poor are defenseless: they can be harvested as slaves.

Corruption and the arms trade are just two of the ugly factors that keep national governments from doing the right thing. Many countries of the developing world have excellent antislavery laws. Enforcing those laws is another matter. In India, Vivek and Vidyullata Pandit have been helping people gain their freedom from debt bondage for nearly thirty years. India has an excellent law on debt bondage, one that provides funds to all freed slaves to help them make a new start. Getting access to those funds should be as easy as presenting the freed person to a local official and documenting their bondage. To help protect newly freed slaves, the law mandates an immediate cash-in-hand payment to cover food and shelter. This is crucial since many slaves escape with just the shirts on their backs. In reality, obstacles are thrown up at every step, and even when a grant is approved for the person, the money may never come. Corruption and government indifference is so deep that, Vivek told me, "we just don't bother with government anymore; we know that it will take more effort than it is worth to get any help from the government for the people we help to freedom." Without government cooperation, the Pandits have helped thousands of people gain freedom. If the government had been doing everything its laws promised it would do, who knows how many thousands more would now be free? But while India has an excellent antislavery law, it also spends a lot of money on arms, including an active nuclear weapons program. Couldn't some of those funds be used to deliver basic education and to help freed slaves build new lives?

Even with the lunacy of pouring money into weapons while citizens starve and children go uneducated, it doesn't take a revolution to set slaves free. In many countries in the developing world, slaves can be helped to freedom at a low cost. A good example of this is the work done by the Sankalp organization in northern India, the group that helped Meera to freedom, as described at the beginning of this chapter. If you add together the annual wages of outreach workers, their transportation costs to rural villages, the cost of organizing and guaranteeing seed money and maintaining the microcredit unions, the cost of keeping the Sankalp office ticking, and so forth, and then divide that sum by the number of families they help to freedom in a year, the result is about $35 per family. So, for the price of a nice lunch or a pair of blue jeans, a family goes from slavery to freedom. None of that money goes to pay off the illegal debt that holds the family in bondage, or into the hands of criminals to buy slaves' freedom. What it does include is the cost of helping villagers to organize themselves and know and safeguard their legal rights. It helps families get control of the means to earn an independent living. Freedom may be precious, but it doesn't have to be expensive.

Determining the cost of freedom is important, because governments run on money. Knowing what it will cost to end slavery in a country makes it possible to build an effective strategy for eradication. The good news is that the balance of costs and benefits of ending slavery makes it a great investment. Let's assume that the $35 figure for liberation and a new life applies to slaves all over the world, not just in India. What would be the price of ending all slavery? If there are 27 million slaves — our best estimate — then ending slavery on the planet would cost $945 million. That's a lot of money. Or is it? Compare it to the price of the new system of roads and tunnels that the city of Boston, Massachusetts, began constructing in 1991, a project known as the "Big Dig." This system of streets and tunnels will cost an estimated $10.8 billion, more than ten times the price tag of freedom. In fact, in the Big Dig, the cost of construction mistakes, errors, and overruns alone is more than $1 billion. I'm not criticizing Boston here, but attempting to draw some comparisons that make sense. The citizens of Boston are paying for the Big Dig through their taxes and tolls. Imagine the citizens of single city deciding to underwrite the costs of ridding the world of slavery. It's amazing to think that, financially, it's possible. To look at it another way, there are about 281 million people in the United States, if they all took a share, the cost of ending world slavery would be $3.37 per person. Freedom is not just affordable, it's a bargain.

These cost comparisons are important because they show that money is not the barrier to ending slavery. They demonstrate that, with political will and a fairly small amount of input, eradication is possible. Of course, it is true that freedom for many slaves may cost more than $35. If the human traffickers linked to organized crime gangs are to be caught and punished, the price will be high. These criminal networks are notoriously hard to crack. But even if the cost of global freedom were to double or triple, it would still be a drop in the economic ocean of the world economy. But if that's the cost, what's the benefit? What do we get for the money spent to free slaves? Wouldn't freeing them just dump millions of ex-slaves into national economies, all expecting a hand out? The simple answer is that freedom isn't just a bargain: it is a great investment.

Priming the Pump

What do slaves do when they can earn their own money? To put it simply, they buy stuff. They buy more and better food, medicine, tools, books and school supplies for their children, clothes, furniture — everything needed to build a decent life. Freed slaves work hard to buy these things, things they've never had, things they've dreamed of giving to their children. They become what a slave can never be: a consumer. Slaves may make a lot of money for slaveholders, but they are a drag on a country's economy. They contribute only a little to national production; they buy nothing in a country's markets. Their work is concentrated at the lowest end of the economic ladder, in basic, low-skill jobs that are dirty and dangerous. Slaves work both ineffectively and as little as they can, and who can blame them? The value of their work is stolen and pocketed by criminals, who are more likely to spend it on booze, drugs, and fancy consumer items than on necessities. Economically, except to these criminals, slaves are a waste, an untapped economic resource.

In freedom, these new consumers become engaged in the economic cycle. They work, they produce, they earn, they spend, and they use their resources to build better lives for their children. One estimate of the profits made from slaves by criminals is $11 billion a year.[9] Compare that to the $20 billion that would be earned by freed slaves, assuming that they did no more than reach the poverty line of $2 dollars a day. For poor countries, doubling the earning and spending of slaves would be a small but important improvement in the national economy. If you compare all countries according to the strength of their economies and the number of slaves they have, the picture is clear — the more slaves, the weaker the economy.

If there is a vicious cycle of weapons sales, corruption, and slavery, there is also a positive cycle of freedom, education, productivity, and economic growth. This is why freedom is such a good investment for governments. Unlike buying weapons, which generate enormous costs in destruction, injury, and death, paying for freedom generates business and consumption and increases tax receipts. The arms trade is worse than pouring money down the drain: it is an investment in catastrophe. The cost of freeing slaves is just the opposite. It generates stability, reduces crime, builds the economy, and creates citizens. Of course, some arms sold won't be used to maim, kill, and destroy, but will be stockpiled; they represent funds locked away gathering dust. Equally, some freed slaves won't make it. Some will fall back, some will need support for years, and some will turn to crime. In short, in freedom they'll act like the rest of us. But however you cut this pie, freed slaves are an asset to the local, national, and world economies.

When Meera and the other people of her village gained their freedom and, with Sankalp's help, obtained a lease to government land that they could quarry, there were two immediate economic outcomes. The first outcome was that the children of the village stopped working and went to school. This opened up jobs for adult workers, including the job for a teacher hired by the village. In many developing countries, the number of working children is about equal to the number of unemployed adults. The second economic outcome was that Meera and the villagers did what the slaveholders never did: they paid the government for their leases and paid taxes on their income. The slaveholders often mined illegally, without permits, on land set aside as national forest preserves. These villagers now dig in areas designated as appropriate for mining. The slaveholders destroyed the forests and wrecked the environment. The freed villagers use quarrying to create watersheds and then plant new trees. Slaveholders stole money and natural resources from the state and evaded taxes. Freed slaves are building a community that pays its own way, contributes to the tax base, and renews the environment. It will be some years before we can calculate the "profit" generated by their freedom, but the basic economic equation is clear — freedom brings economic growth and stability.

Blood and Earth

The destruction of forests by the slaveholders in northern India is just one example of the enormous cost of slavery. It is a burden all of us have to face, no matter where we live, no matter what we do. The simple fact is that, around the world, slaves are being used to destroy the natural environment. And in another vicious cycle, that destruction generates more and more slaves. This link between environmental destruction and slavery is one that we are just beginning to understand, but the shape of the problem is clear.

Everyone knows about the destruction of the Amazon rain forest. Around the world, forests are disappearing at the rate of 150 acres a minute (two football fields every second). In Brazil over 5 million acres of forest are lost each year.[10] We tend to imagine smoking bulldozers smashing trees and big corporations buying up the land. The truth is worse in many ways.

Binka Le Breton is an Englishwoman who has lived and worked in Brazil for years. She describes some of the many forms of slavery in that country:

> Rubber tappers in the state of Acre still live in perpetual debt to the traders who buy their rubber in exchange for the bare necessities of life. Child prostitution flourishes in the remote gold mines of the interior, as well as in the big cities. Across the central and northern states of Brazil there are charcoal burners working twenty-four hours a day under the most inhumane conditions burning the soles of their feet and coughing their lungs out, while deep in the Amazon men labor away cutting and burning the forest in a new version of the ancient evil of debt slavery.[11]

Except for prostitution in the big cities, all these types of slavery mean environmental destruction. The poor are lured to jobs that are, literally, at the end of the road. At the edge of the great forests, they are put to work, often at gunpoint. Their job is to clear the forest, sometimes burning the trees in rough ovens to make charcoal. Slaves wield the axes and stack the wood for burning. Meanwhile, the indigenous people, the forest dwellers, are driven away, often at gunpoint. Their livelihood is lost, and they begin the descent into destitution and vulnerability. In time, they are ripe for enslavement and the cycle begins again.

In other countries there are slightly different versions of the same tragedy. In India, dam construction forces subsistence farmers from their land. Like the government payments due freed bonded laborers, promised compensation for their land is rarely paid. One dam currently being constructed on the Narmada River will submerge 245 villages and displace two hundred thousand people.[12] Pushed off their land, these small farmers cannot just start farming somewhere else; the surrounding land is already taken. Soon, as their resources run out, as illness touches their families, debt becomes their only alternative. In rural India this means slavery through debt bondage. In bondage, like the people in Meera's village, they can be put to work on land that is "available" — in the national forests or other protected areas. Here they cut the trees and dig quarries, and more of the natural world is destroyed.

This is one more cost of slavery. As already noted, the criminals that destroy the lives of slaves care just as little for our natural world. Ruthlessly squeezing profits is the rule, and it doesn't matter if it is a person or a forest that bleeds. The cost is borne by local communities first, then by governments, and then by all of us who have to live on a planet that is quickly and surely degrading. The productive capacity of the forests is lost — to local farmers and to the national and world markets. Economically, the loss is severe. A 1989 article in the prestigious journal *Nature* gave this comparison of the economic value of one hectare (about two acres) of Peruvian rain forest: $6,820 per year if intact forest is sustainably harvested for fruits, latex, and timber; $1,000 if clear-cut for commercial timber (not sustainably harvested); and $148 per year if used as cattle pasture.[13] Here too the slaveholders make a quick buck and everyone else loses.

Now What?

The shape of the economic costs and benefits of slavery and freedom is beginning to emerge, but like all businesses slavery varies enormously from place to place. This book is about questions as well as answers, and another question to add to list is: How does the economic equation of freedom play out in different countries and with different sorts of slavery? When we have an answer to that question, planning liberation will be easier.

Funding that liberation already looks as if it might not be too expensive, and all of us have an interest in helping out. One of the most shocking facts about slavery for people in the United States and Europe is that we are using slave-made products every day. Cotton, chocolate, sugar, steel, even some of the metal in cell phones, may be tainted by slavery. The total volume of these slave-made ingredients is actually very small. Only a tiny fraction of the world's cotton or cocoa or steel has slave input. The problem is that it is almost impossible to know which shirt or candy bar or chair carries slavery into your home. The criminals using slaves sell their produce into the market like everybody else, and it flows into the global commodities market and mixes with goods from free workers. While criminals may justify their use of slaves by pointing to economic pressures to reduce labor costs, they rarely if ever pass the savings from slavery to you, the consumer. The slaveholder pockets the market price for his slave-made goods — a price set in a market that reflects the presence of free workers. So, if slaveholders are feeding on our purchases, it would seem that we should just stop buying those goods. In fact, this may be exactly the wrong thing to do.

The revulsion we feel when we consider that we are eating something or wearing something that comes from slave labor is strong. Our reaction is to push that crime away from us, to distance ourselves. The last thing we want to do is support slaveholders in their crime. Yet for every criminal using slaves to grow cocoa or cotton or sugar, there are hundreds or thousands of farmers producing the same crops without using slaves. Great agribusinesses are also involved, and so is every size of farm in between. Small farmers in the developing world have enough problems competing against the vast subsidies given to U.S. and European agribusiness; if the consumers turn against them as well, the result could be destitution and even enslavement. So, while our disgust tells us to boycott, the truth is that boycotts can hurt the innocent more than the guilty. We think of ourselves as consumers. We want to vote with our dollars in the marketplace for the things we believe in. But this problem can't normally be fixed at the point of purchase.

The point of purchase is the last stop in a long line from, for example, the farm to you. Cotton grown and picked with slave labor piles up at the cotton gin with all the other cotton for processing. Packed into bales, the ginned cotton, now a mixture of "free" and "slave" cotton, moves to a factory for carding, spinning, and weaving. That factory may be in another country or even another continent. Spinning, this cotton is mixed with cotton from still other sources. The thread, and the cloth woven from that thread, may have only the smallest fraction of slave-grown cotton in it. The next stop will be a mill where the cloth is dyed or printed, and then it moves to the factory where it will be cut and sewn into, say, a shirt. From there, it travels to another location to be packaged, and in time, crossing another border or two, it reaches a wholesaler, who sends it to the retail shop where you find it on the rack. Behind that shirt are the truck drivers and salespeople, the seamstresses, the mill and factory hands, the gin workers, and the transport workers who drove the raw cotton to the gin. At the beginning of the chain are some farmers and a handful of slaves. Along this chain, some of the workers are paid well, some are exploited but paid something, and some aren't paid at all. Boycotting that shirt can hurt them all.

The place to stop slavery is not at the cash register, but where it happens — on the farm, in the sweatshop, or in the quarry. The thirty-five dollars you avoid spending — by boycotting a shirt — is worth little or nothing to the fight against slavery. The slaveholder has already made his profit on the front end, and if a boycott leads to a collapse in cotton prices, the slaveholder just moves the slaves to another job, or dumps them, or worse. Meanwhile, boycott-driven unemployment puts other farmers and mill hands at risk of enslavement. A boycott is a blunt instrument. Sometimes it is exactly the right tool, but often it carries the risk of creating more suffering than it cures. Sometimes the immediate and obvious answer isn't the right one. Fortunately, another approach is more effective. If companies work with antislavery groups, take responsibility for their product chains, and establish systems that root out slavery at the farm gate, then the slavery comes out of the product at its source. To take the slavery out of cotton or cocoa or any other product, you have to set slaves free and bust the criminals that enslave them. You also have to crack the system feeding slavery into the product chain, otherwise some criminals will just suck more people into slavery. Once they are freed, ex-slaves need support to build independent stable lives. Here the circle closes and the way ahead becomes clear. The thirty-five dollars you might spend on a shirt is the cost of a family's freedom in northern India. Don't stop buying shirts; but start investing in freedom.

One crucial tool that consumers and citizens require to fight slavery is knowledge. Modern slavery is still little understood in both its details and its broad themes. The ugly, violent, fundamental truths of slavery we understand, but not the many faces it takes or the many roads to freedom. This book is about building an understanding of slavery, its history, its effect on each of us, and its many forms. The chapters that make up this book were each produced as an independent work exploring one of the facets of slavery. Some touch on history in the hope that it will shed light on today's puzzles. Some chapters explore our basic ideas about what slavery is and how it fits into our moral, political, and economic world. Other chapters explain how human trafficking and the demand for trafficked people shape modern slavery. One chapter asks how we can measure slavery when it is a hidden crime. All these chapters push at the edges of our understanding of modern slavery and its consequences. It is my hope that this book will be used as a toolbox. If we want to end slavery, we have to understand it, and that will take thousands of us thinking, imagining, collecting information, analyzing it, and building answers.

CHAPTER 2

Slavery and the Human Right to Evil

The Slave Master Next Door

Because my work concerns contemporary forms of slavery, I am often asked about the "evil" of slaveholders. Most people, when they confront the shocking realities of modern slavery, seek to understand it by defining the actions of slaveholders as evil. "How can anyone use violence in such a regular and dispassionate way merely for economic gain?" they wonder. Indeed, the cases of horrific abuse, even torture, that abound in my own research are enough to send one searching for a way to disassociate oneself from slaveholders. Young men from Mali are enslaved on the cocoa plantations of the Ivory Coast; those who try to escape are whipped, and some are killed. Teenage girls are locked into brothels in Thailand, used by ten to fifteen men each night, and then dumped when they contract HIV. How can I, and a slaveholder capable of such cruelty, both be called human? For many people, the answer to this question is to define the slaveholder as different from a "normal" human being: the slaveholder is evil.

In fictional accounts of slavery, this process of redefinition is common. Consider, for example, the slaveholder and slave trader depicted in *Uncle Tom's Cabin,* whose name became synonymous with evil: Simon Legree. While this stereotype may in some way comfort us, defining a slaveholder as evil becomes much more difficult when we meet actual slave masters. Researching slavery and meeting slaveholders in many countries has convinced me that we must explore (though not accept) their own self-definitions. In all my research, only one slaveholder ever struck me as personifying evil. This man, a pimp in a provincial, working-class Thai brothel, was violent and cruel in his management of the concentration camp that was the "Always Prospering Restaurant." He was, however, not the person who owned the slaves he controlled, he was just an employee. He was the personification of the violence needed to enslave someone, but in many ways he was just as disposable and replaceable as the enslaved prostitutes.

Almost all the actual slaveholders I have met and interviewed were family men who thought of themselves as businessmen. Pillars of the local community, they were well integrated socially, well connected legally and politically, and well rewarded financially. Their slaveholding was not seen as a handicap, except, possibly, in communication with "outsiders" who, they felt, misunderstood the local customs of business and labor. Part of my work has been to explore slavery from their perspective. It is important, for example, to demonstrate the economic underpinnings of contemporary slavery, to show how one might engage in the business of slavery. This perspective allows us to see possible points of intervention. It can also draw the discussion of slavery away from outrage over its evil, because, while any reasonable person defines the act of one person enslaving another as evil, no slaveholder enslaves people just to do evil. The very act of slavery may be perceived as evil or not evil by both slave-holders and slaves. What I explore in this work is how our definitions of human rights are bound up with our ideas about evil. I demonstrate how acts move through a process of being redefined as evil, and how that attribution of evil then leads to a privileging of victim's perspectives. Those perspectives undergo a further process of codification, ultimately emerging as "human rights." To understand this process better, we can turn to modern slavery for examples. But first I must explain what I mean when I use the word *evil*.

Evil Defined

It is important to note that I am not raising theological questions about evil. It is also important that I state clearly my debt to the work of Roy Baumeister, the psychologist whose exploration of evil in human relations provides key insights leading to an understanding of evil with respect to human rights.[1] While concentrating on the role of evil in an understanding of human rights, we can define evil as deliberate actions taken by people that harm other people. Indeed, most of those actions that we routinely and easily define as evil are violent actions: torture, murder, and slavery.[2]

If we take as our starting point the idea that evil is located in deliberate actions that harm other people, then we also have to distinguish between evil actions that *actually* occur and what Baumeister has termed "the myth of pure evil." In many cultures, including modern Western culture, there is an extensive mythology, supported by the media, of people and actions that are defined as pure evil. Pure evil is marked, he says, by eight attributes, most of which are also found in popular perceptions of slavery.[3] Recasting these attributes as applying to slaveholders, we see in the list below that they hold true for fictional representations, as well as common perceptions, of slavery, which I have illustrated in parentheses:

1. The evil person intentionally inflicts harm on people (the slaveholder regularly brutalizes his slaves).

2. Evil is driven by the wish to inflict harm merely for the pleasure of doing so (the slaveholder sadistically enjoys whipping slaves).

3. The victim is innocent and good (the slave did nothing to deserve slavery).

4. Evil is the other, the enemy, the outsider, the out-group (the slaveholder is not like us and belongs to a group that we could never and would never belong to).

5. Evil has been that way since time immemorial (slavery has always taken this basic form: total violent control and violation).

6. Evil represents the antithesis of order, peace, and security (enslavement means violence, disruption, destruction of families, and a total lack of security).

7. Evil characters are often marked by egotism (the slaveholder believes himself to be superior to the slaves).

8. Evil figures have difficulty maintaining control over their feelings, especially rage and anger (the slaveholder's rage is part of the terror endured by the slave).

For the most part these attributes are myths, as we shall see when we explore slaveholders' views and actions. On the other hand, Baumeister points out, the last two, high self-esteem and poor self-control, while central to the myth of pure evil, are more likely to be found in the reality of evil actions than the first six are. At the same time, the first six best convey the sense of the myth of pure evil: "A force, or person, that seeks relentlessly to inflict harm, with no positive or comprehensible motive, deriving enjoyment from the suffering or others . . . [, and who] maliciously and gratuitously seeks out unsuspecting, innocent victims from among the good people of the world."[4]

By separating the myth of evil from the realities of evil, Baumeister enlarges our understanding of the perpetrator's view of the "evil" act. Not surprisingly, victims and perpetrators view the evil act differently. In fact, along several dimensions of perception — time, space, and intensity — the victim and perpetrator interpret evil acts, especially violent acts, in dramatically different ways. Slaveholders and slaves demonstrate this clearly. For the slaveholder the enslavement of a worker is simply a small variable among many in a much larger economic equation. For the slave, enslavement is a fundamental state of being.

The definition of any action as evil is, in part, determined by its social and political context. For example, many Germans, including the Catholic archbishop of Freiburg, viewed the Nazi SS troops as the most respectable of all soldiers, and their entry requirements meant that they had impeccable backgrounds in social and legal as well as genetic terms. Yet as the troops who manned the concentration camps, they have become a personification of evil. Slavery has also existed within many contexts, operating in many different forms, for most of recorded history. Later I explore further the question of social and political context, but first it is necessary to use the history of slavery to illustrate the ways that different perceptions of evil may change over time into accepted human rights.

Evil and the Definition of Human Rights

A key assertion that I illustrate in this chapter is that the expansion of the concept of human rights is based on the privileging and then codification of the *victims'* definitions of evil. If evil is in the eye of the beholder, then many harmful actions can be differentially defined as evil or not, depending on perspective. What especially marks the relationship between evil and human rights is that, within an intellectual context often decried as increasingly relativist on moral questions, there is an ongoing reification of certain definitions of evil. This reification is important in the protection of human rights and dignity, but it is not helpful in the investigation of a phenomenon such as slavery, since the perspectives of slaveholders are

often ignored or dismissed. On the other hand, slavery is especially useful in viewing this process of reification because slavery has been defined
and redefined many times over the ages.

Slavery has been with us since the beginning of recorded human history. When people began to congregate in Mesopotamia around 6800
B.C., they built strong external walls around their towns, suggesting a situation of raiding and war. Sumerian drawings in clay that survive from
4000 B.C. show captives taken in battle being tied, whipped, and forced
to work. Papyrus records from 2100 B.C. record the ownership of slaves
by private citizens in Egypt. Slavery seems to predate both laws and
money. The first record of the price of a slave dates from the period when
slavery had been around for about two thousand years: the price paid was
eleven silver shekels. Not long afterward, slavery as a business enterprise
took off: a record of a slave-raiding expedition from Egypt shows that
1,554 slaves were captured in Syria. About one hundred years after that,
around 1790 B.C., the first written laws introduced the legal status and
worth of slaves. The basic idea in these Babylonian codes, that slaves were
worth less than "real" people, is repeated again and again through human
history for nearly four thousand years. The ancient code is gruesomely
clear: a physician making a fatal mistake on a patient, for example, is
ordered to have his hands cut off, unless the patient is a slave, in which
case he only has to replace the slave.

This code regulated slavery; it did not define it in moral terms. In it,
slaves were protected from the worst forms of abuse but were treated as
property, or chattel. Precisely how the slaves of the ancient world perceived their situation we will never know; their views are not recorded.
But we do know that at times their objection to enslavement, their perception of it as unacceptable, was strong enough to lead to them to run
away (an act covered in all slave codes) or even to revolt. Likewise we
know that some people in the ancient world did perceive slavery as evil.
Milton Meltzer notes that, around twenty-one hundred years ago, two
Jewish communities, the Essenes and the Therapeutae, rejected slavery as
evil. But he also points out that, "to condemn slavery as powerfully as
these two sects did was extraordinary for that time. No one else in antiq-
uity seems to have advanced that far. Not until certain radical Protestant
sects appeared many centuries later did the world hear slavery denounced
so sweepingly."[5] That said, Roman laws became progressively more
humane regarding the treatment of slaves in the first century A.D. This
change reflected a philosophical view that held slavery to be against
"natural" law. Roman jurists, basing their ideas on the philosophy of the

Stoics, suggested that, while slavery was universally practiced, it was also contrary to nature.

Over time the moral definition of slavery was irregularly debated. The expansion of the Roman Empire led to a vast slave trade. With the contraction and fall of Rome, slavery diminished in proportion to the population held in serfdom, but the official view of slavery put forward by the church changed little. "Slavery," said St. Augustine, "has been imposed by the just sentence of God upon the sinner." Only the church's decree that Christians should not enslave other Christians in war (non-Christians were still eligible) worked to diminish the number of slaves in Europe. William the Conqueror allowed the enslavement of Britons to continue after 1066, but forbade their export to the slave markets of Europe. Two hundred years later Thomas Aquinas pronounced slavery to be morally justifiable and economically necessary — a stance still repeated by contemporary slaveholders.

The number and perception of the status of slaves varied with political and natural events. The Crusades opened up new Eastern populations to European enslavement and vice versa. The expansion by force of the Byzantine Empire flooded Constantinople with slaves, just as the Roman expansion had earlier glutted the slave markets of Rome. In time, Genoa, Venice, and Verdun-sur-Meuse became major slave markets, especially after the decimation of the European workforce by plague in the thirteenth century. Slavery became central to the economy of Tuscany, fading only with the decline in supply that came with Turkish control of the Eastern slave trade. The position of the church throughout this period was to condemn sales of Christians and to prohibit the buying of any Christians by Jews, but it accepted slavery as an institution. When the European empires began to expand into Africa and the Americas in the fifteenth century, the church continued its support of slavery in both policy and trade.

As the sixteenth century saw the growth of the transatlantic slave trade, it also heard new voices raised against slavery. In the beginning these were feeble and few in number, mere pinpricks against the lucrative trade. But by the seventeenth century, while these voices were still a tiny minority, themes were developing that would grow into a more general redefinition of slavery as evil. One indication of this change in thought was the influence and popularity of Aphra Behn's work *Oroonoko, or the History of a Royal Slave* (1688), in both published and theatrical forms. English poetry of the eighteenth century is shot through with denunciations of slavery, and the first moral tracts against slavery published by Quakers appeared at the beginning of the 1700s. These tracts and related agitation led, in 1758, to Quakers in the American colonies and in Britain condemning both the slave trade and slaveholding. It was a harbinger of change. Hugh Thomas quotes a prominent Bostonian of the time: "About the time of the Stamp Act [1765], what were only slight scruples in the minds of conscientious persons, became serious doubts and, with a considerable number, ripened into a firm persuasion that the slave trade was *malum in se*."[6] In 1767 Quaker activity brought, for the first time anywhere, a proposed law against slavery into the Massachusetts legislature. The bill failed, but the potential for the codification of a human right to freedom was established.

Academic philosophy often runs far ahead of political practice, and as the ideas of the Enlightenment spread, so did an academic redefinition of slavery. Adam Ferguson, a Scottish professor of philosophy, argued in 1769 that "no one is born a slave; because everyone is born with his original rights."[7] In the same period, commentaries on law by the famous English jurist William Blackstone put forward similar arguments on the inherent nature of human rights. Continued activism by Quakers, now taking the work against slavery outside their own religious society, included the organization of "little associations" against slavery in the middle American colonies and, ultimately, the first society dedicated to abolition in Philadelphia. These little groups laid the groundwork for the sharp debates over slavery that followed the American Revolution, and slavery was legally abolished (with various reservations) in many of the Northern states by 1804. A change in moral perception is hard to measure, but it is possible to identify moments when a sufficient critical mass of belief is achieved. Thomas sees one such moment occurring in 1786–87: "The climate in Britain with respect to the slave trade was now transformed in a special way."[8] In that year, Quakers formed the Committee for Effecting the Abolition of the Slave Trade and began the process of transforming abolition into an international movement. I explore this movement in more depth in chapter 4.

The moral thrust of that international movement — its redefinition of slavery as evil — is clear. Two moments in its history demonstrate this process. On July 4, 1829, the abolitionist William Lloyd Garrison, then twenty-four, made his now famous speech in Park Street Church in Boston. In it he laid down the framework for the abolitionist movement to come. Abolition had to be a moral endeavor, he argued, since only "an aroused public conscience could persuade legislators to withdraw protection from slavery."[9] With a few exceptions the argument fell on deaf ears, and little immediate activity resulted. But holding to that line, Garrison and others built a movement, a human rights campaign that would alter the popular definition of slavery. Twenty-five years later, speaking in New York's Broadway Tabernacle, he reiterated the same position that slavery was evil, and that it must be viewed from the perspective of the slave. But this time he was cheered regularly, and the *New York Times* reprinted the entire speech the next day. Two years later, in 1856, the poet Walt Whitman described the struggle for the national conscience in this way: "No man knows what will happen next, but all know that some such things are to happen as mark the greatest moral convulsions of the earth."[10]

"Moral Convulsions" and Human Rights

The various abolitions of legal slavery that occurred in the nineteenth century reflect Whitman's "moral convulsions." In most cases a sufficient number of electors reached the decision that slavery was no longer morally supportable. The path to this decision was made possible by a shift in the focus of attention on the part of the decision makers. The general view of slavery changed from the economic focus of the eighteenth century to the moral, or victim, focus of the nineteenth. The histories of these movements and their tactics are echoed in later struggles for the recognition of other human rights. The agitation, boycotts, armed struggle, and political maneuvering of the antislavery movement were repeated in the antiapartheid movement, for example. If we widen our view to other human rights and note the parallels in their evolution, we see that they also represent the legitimizing of the perceptions of the victim. In this way the United Nations' Universal Declaration of Human Rights (UDHR) of 1948 is a list of evils we are (guaranteed to be) allowed to perceive. It is an official recognition of the primacy of the perceptions of the victim over the perpetrator and especially over the power of states; and it carries an implied commitment to act on this perception.

Yet the UDHR was originally aimed at protecting individual victims against the evils committed by perpetrators who were nation-states. It is part of the ongoing process of redefinition that, in addition to an increase in the number of acts defined as evil, the list of types of actors that can be categorized as violators of human rights is also becoming more varied. Allowing other actors, especially transnational actors, to be seen as perpetrators directs our perceptions toward new vehicles for evil. For example, in the current process of redefinition, transnational companies, the World Trade Organization, and the International Monetary Fund are all asserted to be evil perpetrators. The campaigning organization Corporate Watch UK, for example, uses this slogan: "The earth is not dying, it is being killed, and those that are killing it have names and addresses."[11] The controversy being played out mirrors that of the past. Just as businessmen of the nineteenth-century English textile industry argued that they were not responsible for the slavery that raised the cotton that fed their mills, today World Bank executives argue that their job is to alleviate poverty and they cannot be held responsible for the effects of speculation in world markets. The farmer in the developing world may announce himself or herself to be a victim of economic structural adjustment programs, but International Monetary Fund officials cannot perceive that an evil act has been committed. The round of assertion, denial, moral denunciation, righteous retort, public appeals by both sides, and ultimately, redefinition, continues.

What has altered in this process is that it has also undergone the transformation of globalization. Martin Albrow describes globalization as being, in part, "the active dissemination of practices, values, technology and other human products throughout the globe."[12] As a researcher who has heard the words (in English) "Universal Declaration [of] Human Rights" come from the mouth of a non-English-speaking, illiterate farmworker in rural India, I can attest to the dissemination of this set of values that privileges the perceptions of the victim. But what did this phrase mean to the farmworker? I can have no certainty of what it meant phenomenologically, but his denunciation of actions by his landlord as evil is an indication — especially since, in this place, these were actions thought of in the recent past as traditional or normal.

Hearing, Seeing, and Speaking Slavery Today

For much of history, slavery was seen as a reasonable, legally sanctioned action reflecting a divinely ordained order, perceived as firmly in ancient Babylonia as in Alabama in 1820. Baumeister puts it this way: "Evil is but rarely found in the perpetrator's own self-image. It is far more commonly found in the judgments of others."[13] Evil is in the eye of the beholder. In northern India I spent time among enslaved agricultural workers and their slaveholders. The workers were enslaved through debt bondage,[14] as described at the beginning of chapter 1. In the form of debt bondage practiced in India, families endure being owned by the landlord without such ownership being legal. The level of control is so high that violence is rarely necessary. One bonded laborer explained to me: "We have always lived here. I do not know about before my grandfather, but he said we have always lived here. My grandfather was *halvaha* [a plowman] to the landlord, and later my father was also his *halvaha*. They were both bonded by debt, my father by his father's debt, I don't know about my grandfather's debt. It's a regular thing. Kol people like us have always been bonded to Brahmins like my master. That's the way it has always been around here."[15] This is a family that lives constantly on the edge of starvation, whose children will never attend school, a family with no freedom of movement, whose members risk violence if they defy the system. However, the minor government official who is the slaveholder, their landlord, sees their state as benign:

Of course I have bonded laborers: I'm a landlord. I keep them and their families, and they work for me. When they aren't in the fields, I have them doing the household work: washing clothes, cooking, cleaning, making repairs, everything. After all, they are from the Kol caste; that's what they do, work for Vasyas [people of a higher caste] like me. I give them food and a little land to work. They've also borrowed money, so I have to make sure that they stay on my land till it is paid back. They will work on my farm till it is all paid back. I don't care how old they get — you can't just give money away!

Anyway, they're doing fine. Look, with the grain I give them and the land, they are getting a lot more than the official farm labor rate of sixty-seven rupees a day. I don't mind giving them so much, because, since I am a Labor Department official, I don't have to pay any bribes to anyone. If I wasn't, I would have to pay the police just to keep my own laborers. After all, there is nothing wrong in keeping bonded labor. They benefit from the system and so do I; even if agriculture is completely mechanized, I'll still keep my bonded laborers. You see, the way we do it I am like a father to these workers. It is a father-son relationship; I protect them and guide them. Sometimes I have to discipline them as well, just as a father would.[16]

The different perceptions of slavery shown in these two quotes are very clear. What the slave perceives as an all-encompassing state that cannot be changed, the slaveholder sees as simply part of the business of farming, with the added altruistic opportunity to "be like a father" to members of a lowly caste. The slaveholder also subdivides the rights of the slave. The right of the slave to fulfill basic human needs for food, clothing, and shelter are met through their bondage. The loss of status rights — freedom of movement, expression, and so on — are seen by the slaveholder as one of the prices paid by the slave for the support of his or her needs. By further conceptualizing the slave as childlike or subhuman, the slaveholder moves the slave into the same category as other beings that are not allowed status rights: animals, infants, criminals.

These different perceptions have rarely been compared in studies of slavery. Nor are they as simple as the example above might suggest. Depending on the legal status of slavery, the imputation of evil to the act of enslavement varies along two continua: the official and the personal. When slavery was legal, most slaveholders could assert that their actions were not evil because they were not illegal. But legal slavery also allowed slaveholders to enslave others *even when* they saw their own actions as evil. Scattered through the antebellum American South were slaveholders who believed slavery to be morally wrong although it was legally right. Most of these slaveholders, however, were unwilling to act on this conviction, believing that their livelihood, as well as the stability of the economy, depended on slavery. For many people in the nineteenth century, slavery was a "necessary evil." They were practicing what Baumeister calls "instrumental violence," an evil act as a means to an end. And as was the case for these ambivalent slaveholders of the past, Baumeister states, the "defining criterion of instrumental violence is that the perpetrator would be willing to abandon violence if he or she could achieve the same goal without it."[17]

At the same time, when slavery was legal, slaveholders expended significant effort in an attempt to destroy the slaves' perception of slavery as evil. They tried to convince the enslaved persons that their status as slave was not the result of evil actions against them, but was a status determined by higher powers for good reasons. Reading through the life narratives of ex-slaves collected in the United States in the 1930s, there is little indication the masters were ever successful in this. Individual ex-slaves allowed that certain masters were good men who treated them well; the ex-slave Julia Baker said of her master John Dabney that he was "a good master and treated his slaves right."[18] But none seem to have doubted the inherent wrongness of their enslavement.

With contemporary slavery it is much more likely that enslavement will be generally defined as evil. Even the Indian landlord quoted above knows debt bondage is illegal and thus implicitly recognized that other people might think it evil. Despite the high level of control exercised over slaves today, they too are more likely to know that their enslavement is illegal and to perceive it as evil. This knowledge points to one of the great tensions within the master-slave relationship: the attempt by the master to destroy the perception of evil in the victim. Force, violence, and mind control are used to convince slaves to accept their enslavement, and this establishes the mental bonds that make slaves so much easier to control. When slaves begin to accept their role and identify with their master, their enslavement is total. This requires that slaves stop seeing slavery as evil. They must not see their enslavement as a deliberate action taken to harm them, but as part of the normal, if regrettable, scheme of things. Put another way, if evil is in the eye of the beholder, then the slave is pushed to take on the viewpoint of the perpetrator or slaveholder.

A good example of this is the change in perception that occurs among many of the young women enslaved and sold into prostitution in Thailand. Arriving at a brothel from a sheltered childhood, they have little idea of what it means to be a prostitute. Their initiation into slavery normally takes the form of rape and assault. Shattered, the young women are in shock, and from there they must find a way to live as a slave:

> In the world in which they live, like the world of the concentration camp, there are only those with total power and those with no power. Reward and punishment come from a single source, the pimp. The girls often find building a relationship with the pimp to be a good strategy. While pimps are thugs, they do rely also on means to control other than violence. They are adept at manipulation, at fostering insecurity and dependence. They can be kind, at times, and they can treat a girl with affection in order to increase her pliability and her reliance on them. Cultural norms have also prepared the sex slaves for control and submission. A girl will be told how her parents will suffer if she does not cooperate and work hard, how the debt is on her shoulders and must be repaid. The need to submit and to accept family responsibility will be hammered home again and again. Thai sex roles are clearly defined and women are expected to be retiring, non-assertive, and obedient, as the girls hear repeatedly. Their religion, too, supports this manipulation. Thai Buddhism asserts that everyone must repay the karmic debt accumulated in past lives with suffering in this life. Such beliefs encourage the girls to turn inward, as they realize that they must have committed terrible sins in a past life to deserve their enslavement and abuse. Their religion urges them to accept this suffering, to come to terms with it, and to reconcile themselves to their fate. As a result the girls become willing slaves, [trusting] and obedient.[19]

Slavery, for these young women, is redefined, possibly as a duty or a job, but in some way that makes them compliant.[20] This requires, in part, extinguishing the idea that it is evil. If they are to accept the rule of the pimp and their own enslavement, they must try to diminish their view of themselves as a victim who has been wronged. They must begin to see their enslavement from the point of view of the slaveholder. Because the power is virtually all in the hands of the pimp, their shared social reality is a moral economy heavily weighted toward his viewpoint. This in turn shapes any social transaction defining their different roles and perspectives.

These different points of view are important in understanding the evolution of human rights as well as the history of slavery. An important step, possibly the key step, in the social and legal evolution of the human perception of slavery was its redefinition as an evil act. This redefinition did not happen all at once but over decades, if not centuries. Consider the American movement to abolish slavery in the nineteenth century. It was, above all else, a moral movement designed to convince the populace that slavery was evil. The assumption was that, if slavery came to be generally perceived as morally wrong, then that perception could be translated into legislation. Yet after many years of campaigning, the movement convinced few politicians. Even the leaders who accomplished the ultimate political abolition of slavery were ambivalent about slavery. Lincoln told Horace Greeley in late 1862 that, "if he could save the union without freeing a single slave, he would do it."[21] And long after emancipation, a significant proportion of the white population, North and South, continued to believe that the African American population deserved only second-class citizenship if not enslavement. The specific act of slavery had been redefined as evil, but not the other acts that "naturally" kept African Americans "in their place." The evolution of the perception of acts like legal segregation — from political and economic necessities to serious social evils — further illustrates the link between social definition and human rights.

The emergence of what we call human rights is in fact the process of redefinition of certain acts as evil. If evil exists in the eye of the beholder (almost always the victim), and if the public perception of that evil evolves, the outcome will be a set of rights emerging as a counterbalance. Of course, some actions can be redefined over time in the opposite direction, as not being evil. Suicide comes readily to mind as an action that was once defined as evil, but that is now seen as regrettable, a cause for intervention, but not generally as a deliberate action based on an evil motive. Current controversies concerning homosexuality are an indication of the struggle involved in its ongoing public redefinition as not evil. What helps us to understand the evolution of human rights is that they arise from differential perceptions of evil.

It is also true that the definition of an act as evil may come from a third party (neither the perpetrator nor the victim). This is important in our consideration of human rights because it introduces the question of cultural relativism. The process of defining an act as evil may depend more on the process of emotional imagination or sympathy by outsiders than it does on the expressed perceptions of the victims. It is the nature of many "evil" acts that their perpetrators try to secure the compliance of their victims, including by silencing any sense of violation. The public response to slavery shows this. The campaign against slavery has its greatest number of supporters in countries where slavery is not practiced. At the same time, some Westerners argue that much debt bondage is little different from the "wage slavery" endured by factory workers. In countries where slavery is practiced, I have heard both views expressed by educated local people. Those who press for a universal application of human rights codes argue that there is something sufficiently common in the human condition that the exercise of sympathy for anyone held in bondage is legitimate and appropriate. Cultural relativists, on the other hand, argue that, given the internal validation of each culture, it is inappropriate to engage in this sympathetic response and to condemn an indigenous cultural expression. In any event, the globalization of the concept of human rights — the redefinition of certain acts as evil, and thus the ascendancy of the victim's perceptions — raises a number of implications and questions.

Implications and Questions

One implication is that the globalization of human rights is, in some cases, the globalization of Western concepts of evil. Debates rage, however, over the relevance of human rights. One side argues that human rights are universal, and the other that they are simply Western constructs being forced onto indigenous cultures. In this debate, different groups break down the articles of the UDHR into the categories "acceptable in my culture" and "unacceptable in my culture." Thus many Muslim states, while accepting much of the UDHR, reject the provisions concerning freedom of thought, religious belief, and expression (Articles 18 and 19). What this debate often misses, in its competing "official" positions, is the diversity of views represented by both victims and perpetrators. The expressed views of some Muslim states, for example, do not have total internal endorsement. If there is a resolution of this debate, it will be in the popular and general assessment of good and evil, benefit and damage. But as we have seen, that assessment changes over time.

A further implication is the globalization of complicity. In the past an individual's complicity in large-scale evil tended to be restricted to the nation-state. Complicity was a measure of a person's responsibility for acts carried out by the government. The last thirty years, for example, have seen a wide-ranging deliberation concerning the complicity of the average German in the evil acts of the Nazi government. Today the individual's complicity in perceived evil may be connected to transnational perpetrators, and an individual's participation in movements against evil can be transnational as well. A globalized system of human rights implies that a violation anywhere requires responses from everywhere. Because we can know about violations in almost any part of the world, and because our actions can have some effect on the continuation or termination of those violations, we are potentially implicated. If rights are taken seriously, then their protection cannot begin and end at national borders. The result is an interesting twist on the biblical explanation of evil: that with the knowledge of right and wrong comes the fall from innocence, and we become culpable for what we do or fail to do. Today the combination of a more highly sensitized public human rights consciousness with globalized communication enhances our awareness of evil and informs us of its stunning pervasiveness. At the same time, that extension of human sensitivity, and of global networks to lift up the human condition, could be called a saving grace.

But if this is true, it also leads us toward an unlikely utopia. The extension of the definition of evil to more and more acts, and thus the extension of protection against those acts, suggests a future in which any intentional harm is prohibited. At this point we revisit the question of severity. If there is a universal right to perceive evil, and if every act perceived by a victim to have been an intentional act of harm is evil, then the UDHR might be reduced to: "the right not to be harmed in any way." Yet this is unrealistic for two reasons. First, where are the limits of severity? Second, is the perception of the victim to be privileged even when the severity is slight? Given the propensity to define an action as "not evil" when one is a perpetrator, at what point should the perpetrator's views be given weight? It is a fundamental question: What are the limits of human rights?

This is a question beyond this chapter, but I can still suggest a way that it might be resolved. Within the refinement and extension of human rights, the question of evil can be addressed in two stages. First, we must continue to ensure the right of victims to express their perception of evil and their right to act on it. This, in turn, requires the creation of protected spaces and the development of methods of healing psychological damage.

Second, especially in the case of borderline acts of harm, we should promote active mediation between victims and perpetrators. Its aim should be to bring perpetrators to the realization of the evil of their actions, and victims to an acceptance of the humanity (if not the perceptions and motives) of their perpetrators. A result of such mediation over time could be a consensus on what constitutes evil in the construction of human rights. The value of such a consensus is that it gives us a new opportunity to act. It leads to the realization, for example, that intervention to end slavery must provide alternative economic opportunities and reconciliation for both slaves and slaveholders.

CHAPTER 3

No One Shall Be Held
in Slavery or Servitude

*A Critical Analysis
of International Slavery Agreements*

You'd Think It Would Be Obvious . . .

Most historians of slavery don't know how lucky they are. The majority of scholars concerned with slavery focus on the eighteenth and nineteenth centuries, the legal slave trade of the period, and its aftermath. For these scholars, the historical period can be clearly demarcated by the legislative moments when the slave trade or slavery itself was abolished within states or empires. The scholar of contemporary slavery enjoys no such clarity. Slavery as a social and economic relationship has never ceased to exist during recorded history, but the form that it has taken and takes today, as well as its definition, has evolved and changed. Not surprisingly, legal definitions have often failed to keep up with this evolution. While it is true that legal slavery has been generally abolished, the public tends to believe that this means the activity of slavery has disappeared as well.

Today a renewed interest in slavery is highlighting the discrepancy and confusion of the many definitions of slavery used by international bodies, national governments, and scholars. This chapter traces the development of slavery definitions in international agreements from 1815 to the present to show how the concept of slavery has become increasingly confused. My aim is to generate a more dynamic and universal definition of contemporary slavery from theoretical models and substantive examples. I examine, in relationship to this definition, the practices defined as slavery in order to separate slavery from other similar human rights abuses. A clearer definition of contemporary slavery will allow for more effective study of and legislation against it. A first step is to review definitions of slavery found in international law.

Understanding Slavery Definitions in International Law

What follows is an overview of the ways in which freedom from slavery has been defined in international law as a fundamental human right.[1] I highlight this in particular because, although freedom from slavery has been seen as essential, and is subject to some of the strongest sanctions of the international community, none of the more than three hundred laws and agreements written since 1815 to combat first the slave trade and then slavery have been totally effective.

Those who began the abolitionist movement in the late eighteenth century took as their first goal not the abolition of slavery as an institution, but the ending of the international slave trade. The 1815 Declaration Relative to the Universal Abolition of the Slave Trade (the "1815 Declaration") was the first international instrument to condemn it, and one of the abolitionist movement's first clear achievements.[2] The early attempts to redress slavery established duties to prohibit, prevent, prosecute, and punish anyone engaged in the slave trade. The goal was to eliminate slavery by imposing an obligation on each state to make the slave trade a crime. In the aftermath of the Napoleonic Wars, a large number of agreements were made, both multilaterally and bilaterally, containing provisions prohibiting slavery and the slave trade in times of war and peace.

When the League of Nations was established in the aftermath of World War I, slavery was lodged clearly within its mandate. The league actively sought to eliminate slavery, and international attention focused on the elimination of slavery and slavery-related practices under the league's leadership,[3] though opposition by, and quarrels among, the colonial powers often slowed its efforts. Colonial interests also prevented strictures against forced labor from being more firmly included in the Slavery Convention of 1926 (discussed below). The league's work on the elimination of all forms of slavery helped to convince the world that the rights of individuals constituted a legitimate part of international law. Until that time, international law mostly dealt with the relationships between sovereign nations. The United Nations took over this role after World War II, and slavery was firmly established as a violation of basic, internationally recognized human rights. Early work of the UN included updating the Slavery Convention made by the League of Nations. It is now a well-established principle that the "prohibition against slavery and slavery related practices have achieved the level of customary international law and have attained '*jus cogens*' status."[4]

Customary international law is the general practice of states; over time it becomes binding law. The Statute of the International Court of Justice identifies "international custom as evidence of a general practice accepted as law."[5] *Jus cogens* rules are the highest norms of international law, and they function as potent rules of customary international law somewhat similar to an international constitutional law.[6] The International Law Commission in a report to the General Assembly of the United Nations acknowledged that the "prohibition against slavery is one of the oldest and best settled rules of *Jus Cogens*."[7] The right not to be enslaved is an absolute right recognized and upheld by international law, and no state can derogate from its obligations in this regard. In confirming that "a state may not reserve the right to engage in slavery, to torture, to subject people to cruel, inhuman and degrading treatment or punishment," the Human Rights Committee of the General Assembly, too, endorsed this view.[8]

The practice of slavery has therefore been universally accepted as a crime against humanity. Furthermore, freedom from enslavement is considered a basic and fundamental human right, and "all nations have standing to bring offending states before the Court of Justice."[9] In international law, slavery, slave-related practices, and forced labor constitute

(a) a "war-crime" when committed by a belligerent against the nationals of another belligerent

(b) a "crime against humanity" when committed by public officials against any person irrespective of circumstances and diversity of nationality

(c) a common international crime when committed by public officials or private persons against any person.[10]

Furthermore, the International Court of Justice ruled that the protection from slavery is one of two examples of "obligations *erga omnes* arising out of human rights law."[11] These *erga omnes* obligations are owed by a state to the international community as a whole. It has been clearly and categorically established that slavery is an international criminal offense irrespective of whether a government has ratified the relevant agreements.

The Evolution of Slavery Definitions in International Agreements

Over the last hundred years, the definition of slavery has been expanding, broadening to include more and more activities. Its definition has been controversial since the beginning of the abolition process, and the international community's inability to agree on a clear definition has not helped promote the eradication of slavery. The process of defining slavery has caused controversy in two ways: first, there are arguments about which practices should be categorized as slavery and thus designated for elimination. Second, because definitions have often obliged governments to carry out particular actions, there has been confusion about how to best accomplish the eradication of different forms of slavery. This last question has been especially problematic, since the relevant Conventions have treated slavery as an institution that can be outlawed, but its actual eradication requires social and economic remedies in addition to legal ones.

If any part of the United Nations or other international body is to be effective in addressing slavery, development of an international consensus on what practices constitute slavery would be helpful. If it is defined in a way that includes phenomena across the breadth of social injustice or human rights violations, then the word *slavery* becomes diluted and meaningless. An overly broad approach in turn leads to a diffusion of the effort to eliminate slavery, which means that the resources dedicated to eliminating slavery are spread thinly across many areas, some of which may be less clearly linked to the core types of human bondage. A brief review of slavery as defined in the international instruments will identify and clarify the categories of practices included within its current definition.

SLAVERY CONVENTION OF 1926: A FIRST DEFINITION OF SLAVERY

The first definition of slavery appearing in an international agreement is in the Slavery, Servitude, Forced Labor and Similar Institutions and Practices Convention of 1926 (the "Slavery Convention of 1926") agreed on by the League of Nations.[12] This Convention was adopted on the basis of recommendations by the Temporary Slavery Commission, which was established by the League of Nations in 1922. Article 1(1) sets out the definition of slavery as "the status or condition of a person over whom any or all of the powers attaching to the right of ownership are exercised."[13] The Slavery Convention of 1926 also prohibits all aspects of the slave trade. The slave trade "includes all acts involved in the capture, acquisition or disposal of a person with intent to reduce him to slavery; all acts involved in the acquisition of a slave with a view to selling or exchanging him; all acts of disposal by sale or exchange of a slave acquired with a view to being sold or exchanged, and, in general, every act of trade or transport in slaves."[14]

Describing Forced Labor and Ownership.   While Article 1 of the Slavery Convention of 1926 may appear to be relatively restrictive in its definition of slavery, Article 2 requires countries ratifying the Convention "to bring about, progressively and as soon as possible, the compete abolition of slavery in all its forms."[15] Recognizing that one of these forms was closely linked to the forced labor practices common under colonial administrations in the 1920s, the Slavery Convention specified that "forced labor may only be exacted for public purposes," and required states parties "to prevent compulsory or forced labor from developing into conditions analogous to slavery."[16]

The various forms of slavery had been officially listed and partially defined in a work prepared by the Temporary Slavery Commission in 1924, which was subsequently approved by the Council of the League of Nations. In addition to defining enslavement, slave raiding, the slave trade, and slave dealing as illegal, the commission also defined the following:

1. (c) Slavery or serfdom (domestic or predial);[17] . . .
2. Practices restrictive of the liberty of the person, or tending to acquire control of the person in conditions analogous to slavery, as for example:
   (a) Acquisition of girls by purchase disguised as payment of dowry, it being understood that this does not refer to normal marriage customs;
   (b) Adoption of children, of either sex, with a view to their virtual enslavement, or the ultimate disposal of their persons;
   (c) All forms of pledging or reducing to servitude of persons for debt or other reason.[18] . . .
4. System of compulsory labor, public or private, paid or unpaid.[19]

Understanding the 1926 Slavery Convention.   It should be noted that these are essentially pragmatic definitions based on examples of existing practices, rather than an attempt to find the common attributes of the different manifestations of the relationship known as slavery. Much of the subsequent confusion concerning what is and what is not slavery springs from this separation of the practical and the conceptual. Seeking to reflect the realities of current criminal activity, political interest, and public concern, the League of Nations set out definitions designed for legal enforcement but did so through a process of negotiation and compromise. The diplomats engaged in this process were also mindful of national interests, and the definition reflects this. The result is a definition highly reflective of its historical context; it includes a list of examples of slavery that was designed by diplomats with an eye to legal enforcement. This definition has been adopted by scholars and activists and applied to changing forms of slavery, but it has failed to provide the analytical clarity required.

References to *"any* or all of the powers of . . . ownership" and "abolition of slavery in *all* its forms" (emphasis added) in the first two articles of the Slavery Convention had the effect of covering not only traditional types of slavery but also the other forms of slavery referred to in the report of the Temporary Slavery Commission.[20] The same League of Nations Assembly resolution that approved the Slavery Convention confirmed the league's interest "in securing the progressive abolition of slavery and conditions analogous thereto," thereby establishing the foundations for international interest in "conditions analogous" to slavery. It also commented on forced labor, suggesting "it should not be resorted to unless it is impossible to obtain voluntary labor."[21] This in turn set the scene for consideration of forced labor by the International Labor Organization — an organization parallel to the League of Nations — and the adoption, four years later, of the Convention on forced or compulsory labor in 1930.

While the 1926 Slavery Convention outlawed slavery and associated practices, it did not establish procedures for determining the existence of slavery in the countries signing the Convention, nor did it create an international body that could evaluate and pursue allegations of violations. Despite these omissions, the league, through international pressure and publicity, did help convince governments such as Nepal (1926) and Burma (1928) to abolish legal slavery within their borders.[22] It should be noted that in some countries, as in Burma, these laws actually compensated the slave owners for their loss but made no provision for restitution to the freed slaves. Beginning in 1931 the league established committees of experts to consider information about slavery, but the work of the second of these, the Advisory Committee of Experts on Slavery, was ended by the outbreak of World War II.

In the 1920s and 1930s there was increased public concern in Europe and North America about the issue of "white slavery," and a series of international conventions were adopted concerning the trafficking in women for prostitution.[23] These abuses were not mentioned in the 1926 Slavery Convention or dealt with by the various committees of experts on slavery, although the first of the international conventions on trafficking in women referred in its title to the "white slave trade." The title demonstrates the difficulty faced in the 1920s in separating contemporary forms of slavery from historical forms. The experiences of the seventeenth to the nineteenth centuries had fixed in the Western mind the idea that slavery was an institution in which *black* people were *owned* as property. (This idea still has currency and resilience.) For that reason trafficking in women was given a racialized definition as the *white* slave trade, and relationships characterized by violent control and economic exploitation, but without benefit of legal ownership, were termed "practices similar to slavery."[24] This chapter argues that these aspects — violence, control, and economic exploitation — are central to understanding contemporary slavery.

THE UNIVERSAL DECLARATION OF 1948: SERVITUDE IDENTIFIED

Following the establishment of the United Nations, its General Assembly in 1948 adopted the Universal Declaration of Human Rights (the "Universal Declaration"), Article 4 of which states, "No one shall be held in slavery or servitude; slavery and the slave trade shall be prohibited in all their forms."[25] This provision confirmed the international community's opposition to servitude and to all forms of slavery. The newly established UN also reviewed the existing League of Nations Conventions to determine which might be continued within the UN framework. In 1949, the Ad Hoc Committee of Experts on Slavery stated that there was "not sufficient reason for discarding or amending the definition contained in Article 1(1) of the Slavery Convention 1926."[26] This committee did, however, point out that the definition in the Slavery Convention of 1926 did not cover the full range of practices related to slavery, and that equally repugnant forms of servitude, such as the extensive forms of debt bondage present in the Indian subcontinent, should be prohibited. It also stated that a passive commitment to abolition was inadequate, and that national authorities should take "positive measures of international assistance in eliminating the economic and social causes of slavery."[27] The committee, therefore, recommended that a supplementary convention be drafted to cover practices analogous to slavery, including many of the practices outlined in the Slavery Convention of 1926, such as serfdom, debt bondage, and forced labor.

THE SUPPLEMENTARY CONVENTION OF 1956: SERVILE STATUS DEFINED

The Supplementary Convention on the Abolition of Slavery, the Slave Trade, and Institutions and Practices Similar to Slavery of 1956 (often referred to as the "Supplementary Convention" or the "1956 Convention") extended and broadened the definition of slavery put forward in the 1926 Slavery Convention. The provisions of Article 1 oblige states parties to abolish certain institutions and practices analogous to slavery that create the circumstance of "servile status."[28] These include:

(a) Debt bondage, that is to say, the status or condition arising from a pledge by a debtor of his personal services or of those of a person under his control as security for a debt, if the value of those services as reasonably assessed is not applied towards the liquidation of the debt or the length and nature of those services are not respectively limited and defined;

(b) Serfdom, that is to say, the condition or status of a tenant who is by law, custom or agreement bound to live and labor on land belonging to another person and to render some determinate service to such other person, whether for reward or not, and is not free to change his status;

(c) Any institution or practice whereby:

   (i) A woman, without the right to refuse, is promised or given in marriage on payment of a consideration in money or in kind to her parents, guardian, family or any person or group; or

   (ii) The husband of a woman, his family, or his clan, has the right to transfer her to another person for value received or otherwise; or

   (iii) A woman on the death of her husband is liable to be inherited by another person;

(d) Any institution or practice whereby a child or young person under the age of 18 years, is delivered by either or both of his natural parents or by his guardian to another person, whether for reward or not, with a view to the exploitation of the child or young person or of his labor.[29]

Article 1 of the Supplementary Convention consequently clarified that state parties should seek "the complete abolition or abandonment" of the various form of slavery and slavery-like practices "where they still exist and whether or not they are covered by the definition of slavery contained in Article 1 of the Slavery Convention signed at Geneva on 25 September 1926."

Analyzing the Supplementary Convention of 1956. Sections (c) and (d) of the Supplementary Convention concern unfree forms of marriage and child labor. These sections indicate two important themes in the construction of definitions of slavery. First, they demonstrate the tendency of international bodies to widen the definition of slavery as time passes. By designating unfree forms of marriage and child labor as institutions analogous, or similar in certain respects, to slavery, they opened the door to allowing other relationships, situations, and institutions to be classified as "forms" of slavery. In time, this category would include phenomena as diverse as prostitution, incest, and the sale of human organs. Second, by including unfree forms of marriage and child labor, and to a lesser extent debt bondage, the Convention introduced a new area of ambiguity. This ambiguity hinges on the concept of consent and the location of consent within cultural boundaries. This is best seen in section (d) on child labor. Depending on how the word *exploitation* is defined, it could describe the apprenticeship of a seventeen-year-old to a skilled craft worker.

The Supplementary Convention of 1956 augments but does not replace the definition of slavery in the Slavery Convention of 1926. Although there have been concerns that slavery may need redefinition in light of the changing social and economics conditions, the combined definition in these two Conventions has remained in place. The UN has made occasional restatements; for example, in 1983 slavery was said to be "any form of dealing with human beings leading to the forced exploitation of their labor."[30] In spite of those restatements or additions, the definition of slavery in the international legal context has not been altered essentially since 1926, although slavery has been repeatedly prohibited by numerous later international conventions.

THE COVENANTS OF 1966: UNFREE LABOR

It took nearly twenty years for the obligations set out in the Universal Declaration to be given international legal clout by the introduction of two binding covenants.[31] The International Covenant on Economic, Social and Cultural Rights (the "Economic, Social and Cultural Covenant") and the International Covenant on Civil and Political Rights (the "Civil and Political Covenant") were adopted in 1966. The latter covenant has been more widely ratified than the former, and it has a mechanism whereby an individual whose rights have been violated can make a claim directly to the Human Rights Committee in accordance with the Optional Protocol to the Civil and Political Covenant.[32]

The two covenants contain provisions relating to slavery and its prohibition. Article 6 of the Economic, Social and Cultural Covenant recognizes the right to work, "which includes the right of everyone to the opportunity to gain his living by work which he freely chooses or accepts."[33] Article 7 and 8 of this covenant set out certain conditions and rights that must be upheld and protected by governments, such as fair wages and equal pay for work of equal value and the right to form and join trade unions.

Analyzing the Civil and Political Covenant of 1966. Article 8 of the 1966 Civil and Political Covenant prohibits slavery and servitude, using words similar to those of the Universal Declaration of Human Rights. This provision constitutes one of the inalienable rights (even in times of public emergency) under the covenant in accordance with Article 4(2), indicating the importance attached to the abolition of slavery. The only difference from the terms of the Universal Declaration is that the covenant's prohibition against servitude is set out in a separate section.[34] Article 8 also contains a provision that prohibits the use of forced labor, subject to certain limited exceptions.[35]

THE INTERNATIONAL BILL OF HUMAN RIGHTS

The Universal Declaration; the Economic, Social and Cultural Covenant; the Civil and Political Covenant; and the Optional Protocol to the Civil and Political Covenant have together become known as the International Bill of Human Rights, as they set out the basic fundamental human rights that must be protected and upheld under international law. The International Bill of Human Rights does not contain definitions of slavery, servitude, or forced labor, however. When applying the International Bill of Human Rights, the international community must look to the definitions that exist in other international instruments.

THE ROME FINAL ACT
AND THE ANTI-TRAFFICKING PROTOCOL

A recent reference to slavery in an international instrument is in the Rome Final Act of 1998, which established the International Criminal Court.[36] Enslavement is deemed a crime against humanity that falls under the jurisdiction of this court. Enslavement is defined as "the exercise of any or all of the powers attaching to the right of ownership over a person and includes the exercise of such power in the course of trafficking in persons, in particular women and children."[37] This definition is largely the same as the first definition adopted by the League of Nations over sixty years ago, but it has an added, specific reference to trafficking.

The explosion in the trafficking in human beings that followed the end of the cold war, led to a section being added to a new United Nations Convention that is still in the process of being ratified. This is the 2000 United Nations Convention against Transnational Organized Crime, and its Protocol to Prevent, Suppress and Punish Trafficking in Persons, Especially Women and Children. The latter is customarily known as the Anti-Trafficking Protocol. The international body recognized that a transnational crime, such as trafficking in persons, required a transnational solution, and that globalization and new technologies had created new opportunities for criminal organizations just as they had for legitimate businesses. One of the key aims of this Convention and the Protocol to Prevent, Suppress and Punish Trafficking in Persons, Especially Women and Children is to standardize terminology, laws, and practices. For the first time, the international community, in this Protocol, has agreed on a standard definition of trafficking in persons: "Trafficking in persons is the action of: recruitment, transportation, transfer, harboring, or receipt of persons; by means of: the threat or use of force, coercion, abduction, fraud, deception, abuse of power or vulnerability, or giving payments or benefits to a person in control of the victim; for the purposes of: exploitation, which includes exploiting the prostitution of others, sexual exploitation, forced labor, slavery or similar practices, and the removal of organs. Consent of the victim is irrelevant where illicit means are established, but criminal law defenses are preserved."[38] In this definition of human trafficking, slavery is included though undefined, but the concept of violent control is made explicit.

SUMMARIZING THE DEFINITIONS IN THE CONVENTIONS

Table 1 lists and summarizes the definitions of slavery and slavery-like practices as they appear in the international instruments since 1926. This review illustrates the fact that views of slavery in international conventions evolved and became confused over time. In 1926 the notion that a person exercised rights of ownership over another led to the example of forced

TABLE 1. Summary of the Evolution of Slavery Conventions

Slavery Convention	Definition/Declaration Regarding Slavery
Slavery Convention (1926)	Slavery is defined as "the status or condition of a person over whom any or all of the powers attaching to the right of ownership are exercised." "Forced labor" is added to the definition: States should "prevent compulsory or forced labor from developing into conditions analogous to slavery."
Universal Declaration (1948)	"Servitude" is added to the definition: "No one shall be held in slavery or servitude; slavery and the slave trade shall be prohibited in all their forms."
Supplementary Convention (1956)	"Servile status" is added to the definition: Practices that create the circumstance of servile status should be abolished: debt bondage; serfdom; unfree marriage; the exploitation of young people for their labor.
Economic, Social and Cultural Covenant (1966)	Freedom to choose work is added to the definition: This recognizes "the right of everyone to the opportunity to gain his living by work which he freely chooses or accepts."
Rome Final Act (1998)	Trafficking is added to the definition: Slavery is redefined as "the exercise of any or all of the powers attaching to the right of ownership over a person and includes the exercise of such power in the course of trafficking in persons, in particular women and children."

labor in colonial settings being added as a situation that could develop into a practice analogous to slavery. In 1948 and 1956 the ideas and practices related to "servitude" and "servile status" were added. Whereas *The Oxford English Dictionary* (1991) defines these terms using the word *slave* or *slavery,* international legislators consciously avoided defining servitude and servile status as slavery. In 1966, the issue of unfree labor was addressed. By 1998, the definition of slavery had returned to its original 1926 version, but with the addition of the practice of trafficking in persons.

How do we make sense of these definitions? Human rights activists and researchers use them as guides in their work, but a close examination shows that these definitions suffer from internal disagreements and a lack of clarity. The answer is to be found in examining the main characteristics of slavery. This will clarify the phenomenon of slavery and provide the basis for a more useful definition of contemporary slavery.

Analyzing the Main Characteristics of Slavery in International Agreements

DEFINING OWNERSHIP AND THE LOSS OF FREE WILL

A common theme in all the agreements concerning the abolition of slavery and slavery-like practices is the concept of ownership.[39] The fundamental characteristic of many of these practices is that they curtail freedom of movement and freedom to make decisions, as well as many other fundamental freedoms. That is, many of these practices deprive victims of their free will. It is understandable that, in identifying slavery, the international community recognized as a central issue the concept of ownership, pursuant to which the enslaved individual loses all control over his or her own life and labor. The wording of the Slavery Convention of 1926 is ambiguous as to whether this concept of control must be absolute in nature — that is, whether enslaved persons totally lose their ability to exercise their free will. It can be argued that the use of the phrase "any or all of the powers attaching to the right of ownership" was intended to give a more expansive and comprehensive definition of slavery, one including not just the forms of slavery involved in the African slave trade but also many slavery-like practices.[40] An international treaty must be interpreted in accordance with its ordinary meaning and in the light of its object and purpose, taking into account, among other factors, relevant rules of international law applicable in the relations between the states that sign the treaty.[41] It is clear that the aim of the Slavery Convention of 1926 was to eliminate all forms of slavery, however they arose, given slavery's severe and often irreversible effect on individuals.

The concept of ownership has resulted in slaves sometimes being described as "chattels." Traditional slavery is often referred to as "chattel slavery" because the owners of such slaves had the right to treat them as possessions, like livestock or furniture, and to sell or transfer them to others. Slavery as a form of legal ownership of a person is extremely rare today. The criterion of ownership may obscure some of the other characteristics of slavery associated with the complete control one person may exert over another, characteristics implied by the Slavery Convention's wording: "any or all of the powers attaching to the right of ownership."

It is clear that identifying the nature of the relationship between the slaveholder and the slave, as well as the conditions under which the slave is held, is crucial to identifying and understanding what actually constitutes slavery. To accomplish this requires a consideration of certain conditions, including the following:

1. Does an individual have freedom of movement and choice of work, and if not, what restriction are placed on this freedom?

2. Does an individual have control over his or her own productive capacity, personal belongings, and earnings?

3. Has an individual given informed consent, and does this person have a full understanding of the nature of the relationship between him- or herself and the other person(s) involved?

The economic exploitation and loss of free will that are inherent in slavery are often accomplished through the threat of violence and accompanied by ongoing abuse. For this reason violence also becomes a key identifying attribute of slavery. The bonded laborer whose family has been enslaved for generations against a falsely accounted debt, the child kidnapped and locked into a workshop, the woman forced into prostitution — all have lost the elements of choice and control in their lives. This loss is normally enforced by violence, whether the entity taking it is an individual or a state.

DEFINING UNFREE LABOR AND VIOLENCE OR THE THREAT OF VIOLENCE

The use of intimidation, coercion, or force is frequently cited as a reason for categorizing particular forms of exploitation as slavery. Thus, we must ask whether economic imperatives — a need for money or income — constitute a form of force. The question is raised in various contexts, but chiefly in relation to the trafficking in women and their exploitation in prostitution. Some argue that certain women and men enter prostitution voluntarily and should not therefore be categorized as victims of slavery. Others argue that the women and men concerned enter prostitution only because of a lack of alternative sources of income, and that these economic considerations — combined with institutionalized discrimination against women — result in a lack of income-earning opportunities, forcing them to resort to prostitution. Evidently, this type of force is different from the threats of physical violence by pimps or others to which many prostitutes are subjected, though once a person becomes a prostitute the two types of force can be brought to bear on him or her in combination. Also difficult to categorize is the pressure of discrimination to which women practicing prostitution (whether they enter prostitution voluntarily or involuntarily) are subjected, and which keeps them from leaving prostitution. Although such pressure is different from the coercion that may have led them into prostitution in the first place, it is a very real force, one that prevents them from changing their occupation.

These questions apply to more than just prostitution. For example, some bonded laborers potentially could escape by leaving the community in which the person responsible for their bondage (their "employer" or slaveholder) has influence. No obvious physical barriers prevent them from leaving. Economic and social considerations, however, along with not knowing what might happen to them and their families, influence them not to leave. Laws and rules set out by well-meaning officials of international organizations do not always neatly cover the circumstances they are meant to address. The dynamic nature of the master-slave relationship demonstrates the adaptability of both the victims and the perpetrators of slavery. Thus, slavery is a social phenomenon that can be better understood with the help of social scientific concepts and theories.

Slavery and Social Science

CAPITALISM AND SLAVERY

Two types of social theory that help explain slavery are those that deal with economic and cultural aspects of social relations. Economic explanations, from both a Marxist and a neoclassical perspective, examine the development of capitalism in rural areas of the Third World, where slavery is more prevalent. They argue that the process of developing a capitalist mode of production is a process of liberation: liberation from the land and liberation from an employer or slaveholder. In this view, the worker becomes free to sell his or her own labor power as a commodity. Political transformations generally accompany the creation of a working class and bring pressure for better wages and working conditions. This view argues that enslaved people are not free to sell their own labor power as a commodity; they are economically exploited by their holders and are held under threat of violence. Slave labor as sometimes used in rural areas in the developing world stalls the political transformations that generally accompany the proletarianization of the workforce. It also reimposes authority over a workforce where a proletariat already exists.

From this economic perspective, slave labor can perform the same role attributed to technology in the class struggle: capital can use slave labor to bring down the cost of paid labor, to discipline paid labor to accept less, or to substitute for paid labor. In precisely the situations where political consciousness begins to develop, capital can shift the balance of power by using slave labor to restrict labor mobility.[42] This can include importing enslaved workers, such as bonded laborers, or converting free workers to enslaved workers. In this sense, the labor power of the enslaved person becomes the property of the slaveholder. It is a commodity over which the slaveholder has complete control. A free laborer can enter or withdraw from the labor market at any time, but a slave cannot. He or she cannot sell his or her own labor power and thereby commodify it. This is true whether the period of enslavement is fixed, temporary, or indefinite.[43] This socioeconomic explanation of slavery can help inform certain aspects of slavery as a social relationship, but not other sociocultural factors.

SLAVERY AND ALIENATION

The slaveholder holds the labor power of the slave, but the slave is also owned or controlled in a much more basic way by the slaveholder: the slave's own life is held by the slaveholder. This has led some writers to focus on the cultural aspects of the social relationship of slavery. Orlando Patterson, one of the best-known writers in this field, defines a slave's status as a form of "social death," to encapsulate the radical way in which the life of the slave is held. When people become slaves, he says, they become "natally alienated"; that is, they effectively lose their cultural, social, and personal history and future, and their slave status is created or socialized only in relationship to the slaveholder.[44] This exists for as long as they are slaves, whether their enslavement lasts for a few weeks or a lifetime. The idea of social death and natal alienation can be described with reference to the situations of actual slaves. A Mauritanian slave has stated, "My master separated me from the father of my children and forbade us to marry; he cut me off from any contact with the world outside his house."[45] The instance of a person's enslavement in the charcoal industry in Brazil has been described this way: "From this moment[,] the worker is dead as a citizen and born as a slave."[46]

BUT IS IT REALLY SOCIAL DEATH?

The concept of social death highlights the essentialism and totality of enslavement, but it begs certain questions. The effect of enslavement on the life of the slave shares certain characteristics the effect of immersion on the lives of inmates in total institutions, such as concentration camps. Elie Wiesel, for example, discusses the resocialization of inmates of Nazi concentration camps: the dissolution of their personalities, the fading from memory of their previous lives, the invention of a new being tailored to the demands and context of the camp.[47] Like slavery, life in a concentration camp was a state marked by the loss of autonomy, a lack of free will, and subjugation to extreme and violent control. But could inmates in such camps truly be said to be socially dead? Slavery is, after all, a social and economic relationship between (at least) two people. It may be marked by an extreme imbalance in power, by ongoing exploitation, and by the potential for violence, but it remains a relationship understood and recognized (if not agreed to) by both parties. From historical slavery comes extensive accounts of the interdependence of slaves and masters and of the sometimes rich and caring relationships that grew between them.[48] In Mauritania in 1997, David Hecht found an Afro-Mauritanian walking hand in hand with a White Moor dressed in matching robes. They told him that they were master and slave as well as best friends.[49] It may be that the concept of social death works best when *social life* is defined as existing in a state of autonomy and free will, but autonomy varies enormously in human relationships. Slavery may occupy one end of the continuum, a relationship marked by the least amount of autonomy, but it remains a social relationship.

Two other factors prompt questions about the concept of social death. The first is the difference in psychological and social adjustments to enslavement by people of different ages. Having interviewed a number of slaves, I find it worth noting that those who have been enslaved from a very early age often show an acceptance of slavery and a willingness to define themselves in relation to their masters. They tend to have a clear idea of their location in the social universe, as "belonging" to a certain family or individual slaveholder. Yet that state holds within itself a social and personal history, one that slaves will easily recount when asked. For example, recall the reply given in chapter 2 by the bonded laborer in India who said, "We have always lived here. I do not know about before my grandfather, but he said we have always lived here."

People who are enslaved as adults, on the other hand, carry with them the memory of their former state. This memory often becomes the emblem of their desire for freedom. Having known some form of freedom, they are unlikely to accept a view of themselves as socially dead, but instead see themselves as abused, coerced, and controlled against their will. Given these self-definitions, we can assert that neither those enslaved as children nor those enslaved as adults cease to be social beings.

The second factor that prompts questions about social death concerns the length of time a person is enslaved. Contemporary slavery is marked by temporary enslavement. Given that a social life exists before and after the period of enslavement, and that family ties may be disrupted but are rarely lost or forgotten, it is difficult to support a diagnosis of "natal alienation," in spite of Patterson's assertion that temporary slaves are equally "socially dead." This form of alienation might be characteristic of slavery that entails the complete legal ownership of one person by another, with the concomitant transformation of the slave into portable property. But enslavement does not require ownership, only control, usually achieved through violence or its threat. Slavery existed as a social and economic relationship before it was legally defined and has continued to be one since becoming outlawed.

Defining Slavery

Slavery is a state marked by the loss of free will, in which a person is forced through violence or the threat of violence to give up the ability to sell freely his or her own labor power. In this definition, slavery has three key dimensions: loss of free will, the appropriation of labor power, and the use or threat of violence. Applying this definition to many practices, we can see that, while a number of them have the elements of slavery and are often defined as such, they do not have all three aspects and, therefore, in this definition, do not constitute slavery. Table 2 identifies practices that have been officially defined in international agreements as forms of slavery, and it assesses them based on the three variables of our definition.

THE THREE DIMENSIONS OF SLAVERY

In white slavery, forced labor, debt bondage, child prostitution, forced prostitution, and sexual slavery, all three aspects of our definition are present. Prostitution, forced marriage, and the work demanded of some migrant workers can be manifested as slavery under certain conditions.[50]

TABLE 2. Practices Defined as Forms of Slavery
in International Conventions

√ = *present in the practice;* ✕ = *not a necessary condition
of the practice;* √/✕ = *sometimes present, sometimes not*

Practice	Loss of Free Will	Appropriation of Labor Power	Violence or the Threat of Violence
White slavery	√	√	√
Forced labor	√	√	√
Debt bondage	√	√	√
Child prostitution	√	√	√
Forced prostitution	√	√	√
Sexual slavery	√	√	√
Abusive treatment of migrant workers	√/✕	√/✕	√/✕
Prostitution	√/✕	√/✕	√/✕
Forced marriage	√/✕	√/✕	√
Apartheid	√/✕	✕	√
Incest	√/✕	✕	√
Organ harvesting	√/✕	✕	√/✕
Caste	✕	✕	√
Prison labor	✕	√/✕	√

Apartheid, incest, organ harvesting, caste, and abusive treatment of migrant workers have all been defined as slavery-like practices, but should not be defined as slavery, since the theft of labor power in particular does not occur to the same degree as in the practices already identified as consistent with slavery. The case of prison labor is unique: prisoners have had their free will and labor power appropriated by the state as punishment for committing crimes.

Prison labor is a particularly thorny question, because the accusation that it constitutes enslavement depends primarily on the legitimacy of the government in control and the fairness of its justice system. When people are held against their will without due process, threatened or coerced with violence, and robbed of their labor power — all features of the current situation in Burma, according to the International Labor Organization — then it is reasonable to assess this as a form of state-sponsored slavery. When an inmate of a British prison is voluntarily enrolled in a work project for which he or she is remunerated, this can hardly be described as slavery. Violence or the threat of violence, which heads the third column in table 2, can be present in all the practices labeled as slavery. This may explain some of the confusion stemming from the definitions of slavery in international agreements. Furthermore, in defining slavery, we must recognize that, in some instances, some or all of the three dimensions of slavery may exist in practices we do not define as slavery. The aim of this chapter is to separate the practices where all three dimensions of slavery are always present. These include, for example, instances of debt bondage, forced prostitution, and sexual slavery.

Debt Bondage.   In the 1956 Supplementary Convention, as noted earlier, debt bondage is defined as "the status or condition arising from a pledge by a debtor of his personal services or of those of a person under his control as security for a debt, if the value of those services as reasonably assessed is not applied towards the liquidation of the debt or the length and nature of those services are not respectively limited and defined."[51] In Section 1, Article 1(a), the Convention places debt bondage within the category of practices likely to result in "servile status" and obliges governments to pass laws to abolish it.[52] One of the key areas of misunderstanding in both international instruments and popular understanding centers on that part of the definition that reads: "the value of those services . . . is not applied towards the liquidation of the debt." The confusion arises because this definition notes that the labor power is not applied to the debt, but it does not explain how that labor power is actually viewed and used within the lender-debtor relationship. There are in fact two distinct forms of debt bondage, both meeting this criterion but in different ways. In many cases of debt bondage, the labor power (and indeed the very lives of the debtor and his or her family) becomes *collateral* for the debt. This establishes the trap of bondage. Since all the labor power of the debtor is the collateral property of the lender until the debt is repaid, the debtor is unable to ever earn enough to repay the debt by their own labor. This arrangement is a hallmark of the debt bondage of the Indian subcontinent. In the other common form, the work of the debtor ostensibly may be applied to the debt, but, through false accounting or extortionate interest, repayment remains forever out of reach. In the first form the very nature of the agreement — which transforms labor power into collateral — practically disqualifies the debtor from ever repaying the debt. In the second form, a violation of the agreement — when "the value of those services as reasonably assessed is not applied towards the liquidation of the debt" — traps the debtor.

The definition of debt bondage in the Supplementary Convention also highlights the important fact that requiring the pledge of a person's services to repay a debt becomes abusive if the terms and conditions of such an arrangement are unregulated. This criterion distinguishes between an acceptable arrangement, whereby an individual can work to pay off a debt incurred, and the enslavement of debt bondage. In the former, it is legitimate for a worker to accept credit for whatever reason and to repay this amount by working, so long as the repayment terms are fixed and the capital sum borrowed is subject to no more than reasonable interest rates. In contrast, in a debt bondage situation none of these safeguards exist. The bonded laborer is often at the mercy of his or her employer or creditor, and the terms of the loan or advance are either not stipulated or not followed.

The dominant position of the employer or creditor in such instances increases the risk of and opportunity for abuse. For example, the creditor may be able to adjust interest rates upward or simply add interest without informing the bonded laborer, impose unreasonable charges for food or tools, or make additional advances on wages resulting in increased debt. Ultimately, these conditions mean that the debtor is unable to repay the loan and so must remain bonded for an indefinite period, potentially throughout his or her life. In many cases the obligation is inherited by the victim's children.

In 1924, the Temporary Slavery Commission pointed out that, although the contract is made with the consent of the debtor, "it often happens that the creditor so arranges that his debtor gets more and more into debt, with the result that what was in the beginning only one apparently equitable contract is transformed finally into enslavement for life."[53] In theory, the laborer is bonded for a temporary period; in reality, repayment is impossible.

In some instances, individuals unable to complete all the work to be done are compelled to place a child or another member of the family in bondage too in order to repay a debt or to obtain a loan. This situation perpetuates the cycle of debt from one generation to the next. The practice of placing a child or other family member in bondage is sometimes identified as pawning or pledging. When families remain in debt bondage from one generation to the next, it is generally referred to as chronic bondage.

The evidence of debt bondage received by the United Nations Working Group on Contemporary Forms of Slavery has been collected mainly in rural areas. Indeed, the problem of bonded labor is viewed internationally as "an economic malady" linked to rural unemployment.[54] The International Commission of Jurists Seminar titled "Rural Development and Human Rights in South Asia," held in India during December 1982, concluded that "landless and bonded laborers are among the weakest and most exploited sectors of the rural communities in South Asia."[55]

Debt bondage is not exclusive to rural or agricultural laborers, however; it also occurs in such industries as construction, quarrying, and brick making. The debt that results in the enslavement of the victim can be incurred in many different ways, notably as a result of travel costs, subsistence and housing costs, or through the activities of a recruitment agency.[56] The Supplementary Convention's definition of debt bondage is sufficiently wide to cover the circumstances of many migrant workers, who either borrow money or unwittingly incur costs that employers or agents subsequently tell them they must repay. This predicament can affect both migrant workers who leave their own country to seek work abroad and those who leave their own community to seek work elsewhere within their own country. The definition of debt bondage in the Supplementary Convention was, however, not drafted to deal specifically with the question of migrant workers, as the large flow of international migrants was not such a common phenomenon at that time.

This more recent manifestation of debt bondage experienced by migrant workers is similar to that experienced by bonded laborers who work on their creditors' land. In both instances the victims cannot terminate the contract until the debt is repaid, and they are equally vulnerable to abuse or coercion by their creditors. It has been observed that the connection between trafficking and forced labor practices "is nowhere more clear than in the practice of debt-bondage."[57] The victims are enticed, procured, or kidnapped and taken to their new workplace by an agent or trafficker and must, on arrival, repay the travel and subsistence costs incurred. Often women — under threat of violence, and aware of their total dependence on the creditor or slaveholder in the new environment — are pushed into prostituting themselves to repay this money.

Debt bondage or bonded labor today affects millions of adults and children in their own countries and migrant workers throughout the world. It has been suggested that one reason these practices continue is the economic pressure to maintain competitive export prices.[58] As a result, bonded labor systems continue to operate openly in many developing countries despite legislation prohibiting the practice. They also flourish more clandestinely in industrialized countries, affecting migrant workers in general and illegal migrants in particular. These cases are consistent with the analysis of the role of unfree labor in the process of capitalist development discussed earlier.

In view of the prevalence of bonded labor among the landless in rural areas, some governments may have to reform the existing land tenure sys-tems in order to meet their obligation under the Supplementary Con-vention to prevent debt bondage. The UN's Food and Agricultural Organization (FAO) has for many years assisted in the reform of feudal and semifeudal structures of land tenure and the abolition of debt bondage through the development of credit institutions.

However, debt bondage is now an international phenomenon as well, affecting many migrant workers. The marked increase in international travel for employment opportunities and in the number of refugees has increased the risk of migrant workers being forced to work to repay an agency fee of an undetermined amount — that is, the risk of becoming vic-tims of debt bondage.

"Forced" or "Enforced" Prostitution.   The treaties introduced in the first half of the twentieth century do not refer explicitly to the term *forced prostitu-tion,* but they do refer explicitly to the use of violence and threats. For example, the 1910 White Slavery Convention made it a crime for "any per-son who, to gratify the passions of others, has by fraud or by the use of violence, threats, abuse of authority, or any other means of constraint, hired, abducted or enticed a woman . . . for immoral purpose."[59] The use of some form of coercion or force was anticipated in the 1910 Convention, whereas later treaties, including the United Nations' Suppression of the Traffic in Persons Convention, were less clear about specifying the pres-ence of violence.[60]

This transition reflects the change in attitude toward prostitution, a matter that has remained polarized in recent times. On the one hand are those who believe that there can never be such thing as consensual pros-titution, and that the exploitation of individuals through prostitution in all its forms should be eliminated and the perpetrators punished.[61] On the other hand is the view that only coerced or nonconsensual prostitution should be controlled and prevented by international standards and crim-inal law.[62] Advocates of the first view — that all prostitution is forced — point out that women are forced to become prostitutes because of a lack of money or other financial pressures.[63] In so doing, these advocates attribute an inclusive meaning to the term *forced* in relation to threats of violence, intimidation, or coercion linked to other forms of slavery — although it is clear that a lack of alternative sources of income does con-stitute a form of coercion, especially when the lack of alternatives for cer-tain individuals is due to societywide constraints imposed upon women.

Forced prostitution is usually defined as when a person (normally a woman) is forced through violence or intimidation to engage in sexual acts in return for money or some other payment. The Council of Europe proposed that forced prostitution be defined as the "act, for financial gain, of inducing a person by any form of constraint to supply sexual services to another person."[64] "Constraint" would include the more obvious forms of violence, such as beatings, rape, torture, and threats. It was suggested, however, that "any form of constraint" should be interpreted more widely to include the act of obtaining sexual services from a person "by taking advantage of his/her vulnerability resulting either from his/her precarious or illegal situation, or of his/her position of economic dependence."[65]

As in our definition of slavery, prostitutes are controlled by various methods, including beatings, rape, and torture, to ensure their acquiescence. It is this loss of free will brought about through violence and intimidation that places forced prostitution clearly within our definition of slavery, as well as within the definitions in the UN slavery Conventions, including the Suppression of Traffic Convention. Forced prostitution has been described by one intergovernmental organization as "the ownership of women and children by pimps, brothel owners and sometimes even customers for the purpose of financial gain, sexual gratification and/or power and domination."[66]

There has been a great deal of interest by legal writers and scholars in the concept of forced prostitution and, in particular, the element of control held by pimps over prostitutes. In the words of one such commentator:

> Pimps control prostitutes through:
>
> (1) physical abuse;
>
> (2) physical control of prostitutes' children; with threats to keep the children as hostages if prostitutes leave;
>
> (3) serious threats of physical harm, including murder;
>
> (4) keeping prostitutes in a continuous state of poverty and indebtedness; and
>
> (5) ensuring that they have no freedom to move outside unaccompanied.[67]

John F. Decker, in his work *Prostitution: Regulation and Control*, states that an individual is deemed to be a pimp if he or she "draws another into prostitution and thereafter dictates the daily activities, supervises the manner of operation, . . . expropriates and spends virtually all earnings and otherwise commands influence over that person's life."[68] In fact, in certain circumstances the control may be so complete "that he will have little difficulty actually selling his 'possession' to another pimp."[69] Since the end of the cold war, there has been a dramatic increase in illegal migration. Illegal migrants are especially vulnerable to forced prostitution. Those involved in smuggling illegal migrants take control by retaining passports, using violence, and convincing the victims that they have even more to fear from law enforcement authorities in the destination country. In combination this supplies the power needed to subject someone to forced prostitution.

All the key elements necessary for a practice to fall within the definition of slavery are present in forced prostitution. In the United States, for example, it has been pointed out that "forced prostitution like slavery implicates all of the core concerns of the Thirteenth Amendment — physical abuse, lack of free will, forced labor and social stratification."[70] Forced prostitution can therefore be deemed a form of slavery and found to be within the purview of the prohibition against slavery in the U.S. Constitution. It also falls under the definition of slavery, servitude, and forced labor as set out at the international level. This was made clear as early as 1978, when an observer for the Commission on the Status of Women told the commission's Sub-Commission on Prevention of Discrimination and Protection of Minorities that the commission considered forced prostitution to be a form of slavery.[71]

The United Nations General Assembly adopted the Declaration on the Elimination of Violence against Women in 1993 to increase the coverage already provided in the Convention on the Elimination of All Forms of Discrimination against Women. Article 2 of this declaration provides that violence against women shall be understood to include "trafficking in women and forced prostitution."[72] This reference to *forced* in relation to prostitution in the Declaration on the Elimination of Violence against Women is exceptional in UN standards. In international humanitarian law, however, the prohibition has always been against combatants resorting to force, with a consistent reference to *en*forced prostitution, rather than simply to prostitution per se.

International humanitarian law is the law of armed conflict, both international and internal. The laws relating to armed conflict were codified after World War II in the four Geneva Conventions of 1949.[73] These Conventions deal with the treatment of the wounded and sick in armed forces in the field and at sea and the treatment of prisoners. The Fourth Geneva Convention deals with the protection of civilian persons in time of war.[74] According to this Convention, "Women shall be especially protected against any attack on their honor, in particular against rape, *enforced* prostitution, or any form of indecent assault."[75] It is unclear whether the use of the term *enforced* prostitution in this instance can be distinguished in any way from *forced* prostitution, although this difference in terminology has persisted in international humanitarian law documents. In Additional Protocol I (to the Geneva Conventions relating to the victims of armed conflict), for example, Article 75 lists fundamental prohibitions, one of which outlaws "outrages of personal dignity, in particular humiliating and degrading treatment, enforced prostitution and any form of indecent assault."[76]

Sexual Slavery.   The concept of sexual slavery is less clearly defined than forced prostitution. It is normally treated as a separate and distinct form of sexual exploitation. The implication is that there does not have to be any direct financial gain in sexual slavery. However, since the slave is forced to provide a service that has economic value, this act might be seen to represent the theft of the labor power of the enslaved; but it is better conceptualized as an extended form of rape. Sexual slavery involves one person's absolute control of, or power over, another. The sexual exploitation of individuals through the use or threat of force — sometimes occurring in times of war, armed conflict, or belligerent occupation — places it within the concept of rape. Sexual slavery violates the basic human rights guaranteed by the Universal Declaration of Human Rights.

Kathleen Barry has suggested that sexual slavery occurs within a wide set of conditions. She notes that female "sexual slavery is present in all situations where women or girls cannot change the immediate conditions of their existence; where regardless of how they got into those conditions they cannot get out; and where they are subject to sexual violence and exploitation."[77] In this definition, the key element of this form of slavery is the complete control over the victim. This concept of sexual slavery has been recognized by some national courts. *United States* v *Sanga* offers a clear example.[78] In this case a man compelled a woman to work as a domestic servant for over two years and forced her to have sex with him. The U.S. Court of Appeals for the Ninth Circuit unanimously held that she had been kept as a "virtual slave" contrary to the provision of the Thirteenth Amendment to the U.S. Constitution, which prohibits slavery and involuntary servitude.

The use of sexual slavery in any form during times of armed conflict — in, for example, rape camps such as those seen in the conflict in the Balkans or the "comfort stations" established by the Japanese in World War II — constitutes a grave breach of international law and human rights. Armed conflict increases sexual violence against women, and the UN has instituted specific protective and punitive measures.

Although the fundamental basis of the laws of war has not changed — namely, the balance of military necessity and human dignity — human rights law has become more relevant during armed conflicts. This principle was first recognized in the International Conference on Human Rights in Teheran in 1968, which confirmed that "peace is the underlying condition for the full observance of human rights[,] and war is their negation."[79] Humanitarian law is therefore seen as an effective method of protecting noncombatants from the consequences of war.

The Geneva Conventions prohibit all parties to a conflict from perpetrating "outrages upon personal dignity, in particular humiliating and degrading treatment."[80] "Sexual slavery" is not specifically mentioned in the Geneva Conventions, but this provision, in Common Article 3, has been interpreted to include this type of violation.[81] In addition, Article 147 of the Fourth Geneva Convention, which deals with "grave breaches," prohibits "torture or inhuman treatment . . . willfully causing great suffering or serious injury to body or health."[82] There is no immunity under international law for "grave breaches" of the Convention. Additional Protocol I and II both contain prohibitions against any form of indecent assault, especially assault on women and children.

International humanitarian law has acknowledged that women and children are vulnerable to abuse in times of war and has attempted to redress this problem. While this is not a new problem, sexual slavery is a recent addition to the issues considered in international documents. The UN has discussed sexual slavery in research and reports about abuses in modern warfare.[83] For example, the final report by the Subcommission on Prevention of Discrimination and Protection of Minorities, written by Special Rapporteur Gay J. McDougall and titled "Sexual Slavery in Times of War," points out that detaining women in "rape camps or comfort stations [and] forced temporary 'marriages' to soldiers are both in fact and law forms of slavery contrary to the international standards."[84] In response to the secretary-general's report on the abuse of women in the Territory of the Former Yugoslavia, the General Assembly "strongly condemned the abhorrent practice of rape and abuse of women and children in the area of armed conflict in the former Yugoslavia and reaffirmed that rape in the conduct of armed conflict constituted a war crime."[85]

As has been shown, both forced (or enforced) prostitution and sexual slavery have been repeatedly identified as slavery. By our definition as well, virtually all forms of these two phenomena can be thought of as slavery.

It is not enough to say that prostitution represents a special case because it may exist on a continuum from consensual to forced prostitution; many forms of debt bondage also exist along such a continuum. Given this fact, the question arises concerning why these two particular forms of slavery were picked out for differentiation. The prevalent argument is that this differentiation has occurred for two reasons, one historical and negative, one contemporary and positive. Historically, there has been a reluctance to deal with prostitution within the legal discourse on slavery. The willingness to define most prostitution as consensual, the stigmatization of prostitutes, and the marked ambivalence of (primarily male-directed) law enforcement to prostitution led to its separation from "real" slavery and its toleration in many countries. Past instruments, the 1910 White Slavery Convention being a good example, were attempts to establish a line between unacceptable forms of forced prostitution (especially of white women) and those forms of prostitution that the framers considered normal, acceptable, or inevitable.

More recent and more positive is the position, exemplified by the World Congress on the Commercial Sexual Exploitation of Children in 1996, that forced prostitution is a special case within slavery because its effects on the slave have certain key differences. One key difference is what might be thought of as the transferability of skills. The enslaved agricultural worker can, upon liberation, apply his or her skills as an independent farmer, given the right opportunity. This, in fact, is very often what happens when modern bonded laborers are freed. However, the enslaved prostitute who is freed is extremely unlikely to want to remain a prostitute (though some feel pressed to do so given the stigma attached to prostitution in many cultures). Second, it could be argued that the enslaved prostitutes' need for rehabilitation is generally more profound than that of other freed slaves. All slavery can be a harrowing and traumatizing experience, but the repeated sexual violation amounting to rape that characterizes forced prostitution brings tremendous psychological damage and requires intensive rebuilding of self-esteem and self-worth.

Our assertion then is this: Forced prostitution and sexual slavery must be firmly located as forms of slavery and not be devalued or obfuscated by virtue of the sexual or gendered nature of the exploitation. Further, these forms of slavery must be recognized as requiring special consideration. It is a sad thing to point out that there is no developed field of study or practice that concerns the rehabilitation of freed slaves. But different kinds of slaves need different kinds of rehabilitation upon liberation: children, the sexually brutalized, and the tortured are needful of special care. As international instruments and national laws are further refined, the definition of slavery in all its forms must be linked to recognition of the rehabilitation needs of freed slaves.

No international agreement has been completely effective in reducing slavery. This stems in part from the evolution of slavery agreements, and from the inclination of the authors of conventions to include other practices as part of the slavery definition. Part of the problem has been a confusion of the practices and definitions of slavery. What has been missing is a classification that is dynamic and yet sufficiently universal that it can recognize slavery no matter how slavery evolves. This chapter has attempted to build on theories and examples to clarify the definition of slavery by focusing on an irreducible core of three aspects: the complete control of one person by another, the appropriation of labor power, and the enforcement of these conditions by threats or acts of violence. Many practices identified in international agreements have some but not all of these three aspects; all three are present in traditional forms of slavery, bonded labor, forced prostitution, and sexual slavery.

Effective research on and legislation against slavery is important because slavery affects an estimated 27 million people worldwide, and because slavery is on the increase as many developing countries are forced to compete for income in a global economy.[86] Finally it is important to remember that slavery, like all social and economic relationships, evolves over time. Any definition based on a historical form of slavery will soon lose its power to capture new forms of slavery. Our understanding and our definition of slavery must become as dynamic as the phenomenon itself.

CHAPTER 4

Slavery and the Emergence of Non-governmental Organizations

The Big Shift

One significant change in the nature of political action over the last fifty years is the shift away from established political parties to nonstate, issue-based campaigning groups, and away from nation-state politics to global politics. Before World War II, formal politics tended to take place at the level of the nation-state and within a context of competing sovereign nation-states. Indeed, the nation-state was a defining feature of life in the early twentieth century. In democratic countries, political action normally occurred through the vehicle of ideologically driven political parties competing for power. These parties operated with a bundle of policies and programs. Most of the social and political scientists of earlier periods — Hobbes, Locke, Rousseau, Hegel, Mill, Marx, Weber — assumed the primacy of the nation-state. Only Kant, with his notion of cosmopolitanism, could be considered an exception.[1]

After 1945, nation-states and broadly based political parties continued to predominate, but movements emerged that concentrated on achieving goals that transcended nation-state borders. These movements highlighted such issues as the global environment and universal human rights, issues that had not been adequately taken up by political parties.

The shift away from nation-state-based politics to these issue-based concerns (connected to what Anthony Giddens calls "life politics") reflects a growing awareness among the citizenry that the things which most directly affect our lives often transcend national boundaries and the reach of national political parties and governments.[2] The result has been a decline in memberships in political parties and a tremendous growth in campaigning organizations such as Greenpeace, Friends of the Earth, and Amnesty International and in the peace movement. Note, for example, that the governing political party in Britain, the Labour Party, has around 250,000 members, while the essentially environmentalist Royal Society for the Protection of Birds has over a million members.

State politics and class-based politics are not dead, given the importance of resources generated by tax regimes and politics' effect on a broad range of issues that occur within national boundaries. Organizations concerned with global social and environmental issues, however, are now key players in both national and international forums. They are unlike political parties, in that they are not democratically elected and do not have territorial constituencies. While they have come to resemble governments and business in their bureaucratic organization, their organizational goals are unlike those of states and other nonstate actors. In this chapter I look at the first major human rights organization and campaign and use the history of the antislavery movement to chart the evolution of the organization and the influence of nonstate actors. I argue that bureaucratization has been a key stage in the acquisition of influence, and, further, that the effort to redefine slavery — from an economic issue to a moral one — created an ideological basis that transcended national boundaries.

"The Originator": Slavery and the First Human Rights Campaign

If there is a pathfinder for the development of nonstate actors as a potent force for political change, it is the various incarnations of the antislavery movement. The sheer size of the antislavery movement of the eighteenth and nineteenth centuries is mostly forgotten today. Likewise the reality of this campaign as the world's first human rights campaign (and organization) is rarely remembered. A brief look at the history of this movement can illuminate its origins and the beginnings of its role in addressing human rights.

Greek and Roman philosophers held that slavery was against "natural law," a view echoed by Aquinas, but the first long-lasting group operating as a non-governmental organization with the aim of altering both state policy and public perceptions of human rights was a committee assembled by the British Quakers in 1783. This committee was charged with promoting the total abolition of the slave trade and gradual emancipation. The committee petitioned Parliament and published some antislavery tracts and, in 1786, decided to publish a long essay by Thomas Clarkson, an Anglican and recent Oxford graduate.[3]

The resulting pamphlet was very well received, and Clarkson became a minor celebrity. Clarkson then dedicated his life to building up the antislavery movement, using the fifty thousand Quakers in Britain as the base on which to build. In 1787 the original Quaker Committee on the Slave Trade evolved into the nondenominational Committee for Effecting the Abolition of the Slave Trade, with Clarkson as its secretary. In modern terms Clarkson was the first director of a non-governmental organization for human rights, though at the time there was no simple title for him and he was often referred to as the "originator." What was crucial was that his "vision was of one unified plan of action engaging widespread participation and directed toward destroying the legal basis of a centuries-old commercial enterprise."[4]

The movement built up slowly at first, and Clarkson was equally involved in fund-raising, research, public speaking, and publishing. Fundraising involved soliciting money from rich individuals; research meant spending months interviewing sailors and businessmen in the slave ports of Bristol and Liverpool. The necessary public awareness campaign, during a time without media that reached the majority of the public, was especially arduous. Clarkson would travel up to ten thousand miles by horseback over a period of ten to twelve months in order to speak in hundreds of towns and cities. Possibly the most powerful graphic image he used was the diagram of how slaves were packed on board ship, which the committee had published as a poster — an image that most of us are familiar with today, even if we don't know that it originated with Clarkson (see figure 1). In the process of his campaign, the committee evolved yet again, into the *Society* for Effecting the Abolition of the Slave Trade, and ultimately, in 1824, into the Anti-Slavery Society (which continues today as Anti-Slavery International). This was truly a mass human-rights campaign: note that the Anti-Slavery Society's thirteen hundred local branches generated 5,484 petitions to Parliament in just six months in 1830–31,[5] and that two years later a women-only "monster petition" carried 187,000 signatures.

It is important to recognize that, while this was a large campaign, the key aims of the Anti-Slavery Society were primarily located within the state political system — particularly the enactment of laws — first, to end the slave trade and, second, to emancipate all slaves. The organization's

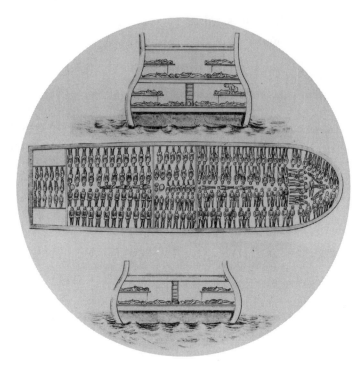

FIGURE I. How slaves were packed into slave ships. Hundreds of thousands of copies of this picture were printed as flyers, leaflets, and posters. This illustration became a central image of the abolitionist movement. Courtesy Anti-Slavery International.

tactical work, however, involved other non-governmental organizations, especially businesses. This was the case with the widespread sugar boycott of the 1790s. An estimated three hundred thousand people in Britain refused to use West Indian sugar at this time,[6] though it is difficult to see any effect on government policy or trade, except for a significant increase in the importation of East Indian (or nonslave) sugar. But whether the organization acted within or outside state politics and policies, a critical dimension of this original human rights campaign was its intention to bring about a shift in values by raising public awareness. Put another way, the key to the success of this campaign was to redefine slavery in the public mind. Whatever philosophers had written, slavery was, to the best of our understanding, for the majority of the population in the eighteenth century an *economic* issue. By the mid–nineteenth century, it was generally seen as a *moral* issue, and the core of this redefinition was the privi-

FIGURE 2. Logo of the British and Foreign Anti-Slavery Society.
Courtesy Anti-Slavery International.

leging of the slave's point of view. For the British antislavery movement,
this is captured in the campaign's other best-known and powerful graphic
image, the chained slave on one knee raising his arms and asking, "Am I
not a man and a brother?" See figure 2.

A Second "Originator"
and a Second Mass Campaign

The history of the antislavery movement may be unique — possibly only
because of its longevity — in its ability to repeat itself. At the end of the
nineteenth century, the role of the researcher-activist in the mode of
Clarkson was taken up by E. D. Morel. Like Clarkson he began his work
independently and then came to a close working relationship with the

Anti-Slavery Society (at that point known as the British and Foreign Anti-Slavery Society). His aim was the exposure and eradication of the widespread enslavement of the people of the Congo. This campaign was important in that it demonstrated that a public could be brought to action over events far removed geographically and over events that directly touched supporters as consumers.

King Leopold II of Belgium, acting in a personal capacity, established the Congo Free State in 1884 and subsequently ran it as a private business. This enterprise was based upon slave labor, and, with the rubber boom at the turn of the century, millions of people were placed under permanent or temporary enslavement. The death toll was horrific; up to 10 million people were killed or died of abuse and disease over a forty-year period.

Like Clarkson, Morel began his research on the quayside. By studying shipping manifests, he came to understand that the "trade" between Europe and the Congo was all one way, deducing that only slave labor could produce such a volume of imports without having any noticeable requirement for goods in the return trade. What was different in the design of this campaign was that effective public media now existed. Using mass circulation newspapers as the primary organs for generating public awareness, the campaign to end slavery in the Congo became what we would now think of as a public relations battle. On one side were the antislavery activists and investigative journalists who fed hundreds of articles to the newspapers. On the other was King Leopold's sophisticated public relations team also generating hundreds of counterstories and, with greater resources, purchasing the cooperation of large numbers of journalists and editors.

In this public relations battle, the antislavery forces had one significant advantage, a new technology that left the public with little choice but to define the colonial exploitation of the Congo as evil: the photograph. Not only could photographs document abuses, they also could be reproduced in newspapers. Mark Twain was a vocal supporter of the campaign, and in one satire he had King Leopold damning "the incorruptible Kodak," the only witness he couldn't bribe.[7] John and Alice Harris, who had been missionaries in the Congo, returned with extensive photographic evidence of the torture and mutilation of forced laborers. They made their photographs into slides and showed them at more than six hundred public appearances over the course of two years. (See figure 3.) It was the early-twentieth-century equivalent of a well-made documentary, shown to a fresh audience each time. After their work with Morel and the con-

FIGURE 3. One of John and Alice Harris's "magic lantern" slides, used in their antislavery public lectures. Courtesy Anti-Slavery International.

clusion of the campaign, the Harrises went on to direct the Anti-Slavery Society for many years.

Conviction vs. Responsibility: The Process of Bureaucratization

So far I have presented the early antislavery movement as the pathfinder for the development of modern non-governmental organizations, particularly those concerned with human rights. But if we are to understand the development of the role of such non-governmental organizations, we must place them within the larger theme of the development of organizations, and especially the bureaucratization process. To discover why non-governmental organizations have more or less influence, power, or ability to alter the activities of states, we should consider their level of bureaucratization as an indicator of these attributes. Max Weber, in his classic work on bureaucracy, explained that, as a form of organization, the bureaucracy is "superior to any other form in precision, in stability, in the stringency of its discipline, and its reliability. It thus makes possible a particularly high degree of calculability of results for the heads of the organization and for those acting in relation to it. It is finally superior both in intensive efficiency and in the scope of its operations and is formally capable of application to all kinds of administrative tasks."[8]

It is interesting to note that the first bureaucratized organizations were nonstate organizations: universities and religious bodies. But the bureaucratization of states and businesses set the tone for modernity as well as created a context in which political action took the form of allegiance to ideologically driven political parties competing for power on broad platforms, as mentioned earlier. The transformation of nonstate actors into their current role as near equals in the interplay of states came about, in part, because of their bureaucratization. This required a resolution of one of the basic tensions within the organization of nonstate actors — the contrast between conviction (the leadership of charismatic individuals) and responsibility (collective leadership following strategic goals).

The early antislavery movement was marked by a mixture of the two, but it maintained its continuity and effectiveness through its bureaucratic structure rather than the personality of Thomas Clarkson. The test of any organization, whether state or nonstate, is its ability to withstand the loss of the leader who personifies the organization's convictions. This was demonstrated when Clarkson suffered mental and physical breakdown in 1793 and retired from most antislavery work for ten years. The committee forming the core of the antislavery organization continued to function, albeit at a reduced capacity, and was ready to mount the major campaigns that followed Clarkson's return in 1804. Similarly, when slavery remained legal in much of the rest of the world after its abolition in most Western countries by the 1870s, the Anti-Slavery Society continued, even if reduced in size. In the 1890s, it provided an organizational structure to support the campaign against slavery in the Congo. Such continuity is crucial to the empowerment of nonstate organizations addressing human rights.

Organizations like Amnesty International are well known for their highly bureaucratic and hierarchical structures. What differentiates these bureaucracies is their aim. While continuity, expansion, and profit remain the goals of states and businesses, human rights bureaucracies add moral aims. They are the reification of conviction within structured responsibility. They also face unique problems because of their moral aims. When these goals are finite, such as the goal to eradicate slavery, it is possible to reach an end. This is antithetical to bureaucratic structure, since bureaucracies tend to be self-replicating and continuous. While businesses can turn to new areas of profit making, and governments to other forms of regulation and oversight, the organization with an achievable moral goal can find itself facing self-determined extinction. In this way the Congo Reform Association withered away after King Leopold gave up control of the Congo, whereas the Anti-Slavery Society continued. Moral aims are also hostage to fortune, in that they are determined in part by the public perception or definition of whether they are achieved. The Anti-Slavery Society spent the 1950s to 1980s in something like standby mode, as it faced a public convinced that slavery no longer existed. It did successfully press for the establishment of a UN working group on slavery and promoted the 1956 Supplementary Convention, but recognition of the organization by the general public was minimal. Its bureaucratic structure and core of supporters (some of them descendents of the original Quaker organizers) kept it afloat. Compare that stability to the collapse of the Campaign for Nuclear Disarmament in Britain at the end of the cold war. While its moral aim of ending the threat of nuclear proliferation and war was far from achieved, by the early 1990s the public was convinced it had been. Given its chaotic (less bureaucratic and hierarchical) internal structure, the Campaign for Nuclear Disarmament could not adapt quickly, or mount an educational campaign to counter this perception, before it had hemorrhaged supporters and resources.

Yet even the bureaucracy with moral aims can adopt the tactical approach of business bureaucracies to threats to its raison d'être. The business with a shrinking market diversifies; a business with an expanding market concentrates and improves its product to remain ahead of the competitors that will be drawn to a growing market. In the 1970s and 1980s, the Anti-Slavery Society, faced with a shrinking "market," diversified into such issues as child labor, female genital mutilation, and unfree forms of marriage while concentrating on slavery. It is instructive that it diversified with hesitation, and that it was quickly surpassed in size by organizations whose missions reflected the economies of agglomeration. If Anti-Slavery International is the custom tailor crafting responses to a key single issue, Human Rights Watch is the department store of moral goals. As public and state awareness and recognition of slavery and human trafficking began to dramatically increase in the late 1990s, Anti-Slavery International also saw the "invasion" of its market. Groups as various as Amnesty International, the Central Intelligence Agency, and the Vatican announced their own investigations of, and policies on, slavery. Diversification is to be expected of any successful organization, for it is indicative of the third main force driving the establishment of powerful nonstate actors in human rights: globalization.

Globalizing Nonstate Organizations

Redefining an issue in moral terms sets out the intellectual justification for a non-governmental organization. The bureaucratization of the group addressing that issue establishes an non-governmental organization with some stability and the potential for continuous operation. But the longevity, size, and power of a nonstate actor depend on the arena in which it operates. Confined within the boundaries of a nation-state, with their range of activity restricted to what the state allows, non-governmental organizations often define themselves in relation to the state both in identity and aim. The nonstate organization before globalization aimed to alter state policies, and its aims usually reached only as far as the national border. Note that the nomenclature still reflects this orientation: it defines these organizations by what they are *not* — non-governmental organizations, nonstate actors, nonprofit organizations. (Imagine referring to governments only as "nontribal entities.")

The process of globalization has created a fertile context for non-governmental organizations concerned with human rights. They are not restricted to nation-state boundaries (except by choice), and most important, their organizing intellectual paradigms center on moral concepts generalizable to all people. The object of their work is normally the alteration of a human activity that transcends cultural boundaries, and their potential market is the world population. Their challenge is to bring about a public redefinition of their issue as a moral issue, not locally but globally.

Much of the writing about the globalization process has centered on changes in businesses and the world economy, but globalization has equally affected nonstate organizations. Two key themes of globalization are the erosion of control by nation-states and the functional integration of dispersed (economic) activities.[9] These characteristics have suited human rights organizations admirably and created a context for potential growth. These characteristics have also fostered nonstate actors that might be thought of as anti-human-rights actors, especially criminal organizations.

For example, these two themes, dispersed economic activity and the loss of governmental control, apply to the newer forms of slavery as well. Slaveholders disperse both slaves and slave-based activities. In Brazil, slaves are taken in densely populated, economically depressed regions and then shipped more than a thousand miles to the fields where they will make charcoal. The charcoal, in turn, is shipped another thousand miles for use in steel mills. In Southeast Asia, women are enslaved in Burma or Laos for use in Thailand or transshipment to brothels in Japan or Europe. Capital from Hong Kong funds the brothels of Thailand; investment from Europe the charcoal operations of Brazil. Slaves from Mali are found in Paris; slaves from the Philippines are found in London and Saudi Arabia; and eastern Europeans, especially women, are dispersed as slaves around the globe. The profits generated by slavery also flow indiscriminately across national borders. Governments (like many individuals) that still conceptualize slavery as a legal status entailing titled ownership linked to the nation-state are at a loss to regulate this trade. It was only in early 1999 that the United Nations met to begin developing new Conventions to address this globalized trafficking in persons.

Organized criminal groups are also globalized nonstate actors of significant scale having an important role in slavery and human trafficking. The United Nations estimates that human trafficking now ranks as the third-largest profit center for transnational criminal groups, after the trade in drugs and in weapons. The number of Russian organizations involved in trafficking is estimated to be between five thousand and eight thousand, involving up to 3 million people.[10] Organizationally, however, these groups are simply businesses, some of them bureaucratic in nature and others centered on a leader. While they operate within a context of increased risks and threats to the stability of the organization, they also work to shorter timescales and are able to achieve goals (profits) quickly. Like other businesses, they do not seek the public redefinition of any issue into moral terms. They also meet challenges and competition through diversification and concentration, and they consciously make the most of transcending nation-state boundaries.

Especially interesting are the nonstate actors that have organized themselves according to moral values but which operate in the gray area between the nonstate actors that are criminal businesses and the nonstate actors that are human rights organizations. The groups in this gray area can become especially potent when they combine criminal means with the high levels of conviction and strategic moral certainty that characterize non-governmental organizations.

The violent attacks on New York and Washington, D.C., on September 11, 2001, demonstrated the power of a nonstate actor of this type. While the U.S. government has worked hard to lead public perception to a moral definition of the al Qaeda organization as evil incarnate, it is, after all, a non-governmental organization with an agenda focused on (according to its own definitions) moral goals. It has also shown itself to be capable of transcending state boundaries and carrying on highly dispersed activities. Likewise it faces the challenge that most human rights organizations confront, the need to convince a sufficient proportion of the global public to redefine certain geopolitical or economic problems as moral issues. Osama bin Laden himself is a leading example of the increased salience of globalized nonstate actors, being the first *individual* to be the recipient of a United States cruise missile attack (as if he were another nation-state) in the late 1990s. The survival of the al Qaeda organization depends on many of the factors discussed earlier: how much it relies on the leadership of a single individual, how it has balanced conviction and ideological fervor with organizational structure and stability, how resilient its bureaucracy is, and whether it can favorably alter a sufficient proportion of the opinion of its chosen audiences. Yet in terms of survival, al Qaeda has one advantage: unlike most non-governmental organizations with a moral agenda, it has worked very hard to design an organizational resistance to attack.

Of course, by using violence as a tactic al Qaeda has removed itself from the general marketplace of nonstate, non-governmental actors. This may also be its downfall, since one result of globalization is that nonstate actors have shifted their focus away from nation-states, and to be successful they must work cooperatively. Violence denies any group access to cooperation with most non-governmental organizations. In the past, non-governmental organizations sought to alter public opinion in order to change the policies of a single government. The early antislavery campaigns are a good example of this. Today the orientation of action is less toward government and more toward other non-governmental or intergovernmental organizations. At the same time, the power of non-governmental organizations with respect to that of governments is dramatically increased. Both the United Nations and many national governments now rely on non-governmental organizations to provide the intelligence and structure necessary to develop policy. The International Labor Organization Convention 183, for example, on the worst forms of child labor, was originated by, and driven to a successful conclusion by, a coalition of non-governmental organizations. Recent policy announcements by the Economic Community of West African States, while apparently authored by national governments, were actually written by non-governmental organization and intergovernmental organization staff. In the United States two coalitions of nonstate actors — the chocolate industry on one hand, and human rights organizations on the other — were parties to a major new Protocol (note the adoption of diplomatic language). The government stood as a guarantor and participant in this case, but it is worth asking how much longer an official blessing will be needed to legitimize such agreements. Indeed, at the meeting establishing the foundation mandated by the Protocol, the role of government as participant was excluded without discussion.

The near future will see struggles as non-governmental organizations seek institutional roles commensurate with their power. Consider the tripartite organization of the International Labor Organization. It was established in the early twentieth century, and its membership is limited to the key actors of that time: governments, employers (businesses), and labor unions. Today much of its work relies on non-governmental organizations, and especially human rights organizations, but none of the three member groups are willing to allow non-governmental organizations full membership.

Non-governmental Organizations and the Eradication of Slavery

This brief review of the evolution of nonstate actors, particularly non-governmental organizations concerned with human rights, leads to a few thoughts about where these organizations might be going. In the work of Anti-Slavery International and its American sister organization, Free the Slaves, I've identified several mechanisms by which slavery might be eradicated. One of these is the elaboration of grassroots organizations that directly liberate and rehabilitate slaves. At the present time, in several countries, such organizations are literally freeing slaves and creating circumstances to ensure that reenslavement is less likely to occur, at a rate far beyond that achieved by state governments. For the most part these organizations have scant local resources and little or no support from the developed world. While most national governments have both the resources and the laws on the books to eradicate slavery, decades of urging them to do so has had little effect. While antislavery organizations will continue to push governments to enforce their own laws, they are also looking for a multiplication of grassroots groups and their effectiveness.

To maximize their effectiveness, they must take on board the lessons of past campaigns and of the histories of non-governmental organizations. In the developed world, we live among and through bureaucracies in the way fish live in water. Bureaucracies are ubiquitous and provide most of our sustenance. It is easy to forget that, in some parts of the developing world, organizations are much less likely to be bureaucratic in nature. For example, recent research in the Ivory Coast by Free the Slaves looked at farmer cooperatives as a possible mechanism for reducing enslavement in the production of cocoa and other commodities. What surprised researchers was that the existing cooperatives could hardly be thought of as functional organizations except in the way they centralized produce for sale: these cooperatives functioned as depots. In sociological terms they met none of Weber's criteria for identification as bureaucracies.[11] This is not to say that cooperatives will be ineffective against agricultural enslavement, only that their work must begin at an organizational level. This requirement is mirrored in the rapid expansion of capacity-building projects being carried out by intergovernmental organizations, non-governmental organizations, and states.

In the effort to reduce slavery, this capacity building takes several forms. One of the most basic is providing a safe space in which grassroots organizations can operate. When governments fail to enforce their own laws against slavery, they also often fail to enforce laws that protect human rights workers, or, indeed, they may actively undermine nonstate actors, to the detriment of the latter. The power of non-governmental organizations in the developed world can extend to protect non-governmental organizations and activists in the Southern Hemisphere. This has been demonstrated historically and in the recent past. In early 2000, Anti-Slavery International worked closely with national non-governmental organizations and grassroots organizations in Nepal to bring about new legislation banning the traditional form of debt bondage known as the *kamaiya* system. Mixed delegations of Nepali, Indian, and European representatives visited all major political actors and state organizations. The overt participation of Anti-Slavery International increased the safety of local actors in a country that still imprisons members of any troublesome opposition group. If there was a significant error in this cooperative approach, it was to underestimate the influence it would bring to bear on the state: the law abolishing *kamaiya* was established by decree rather than legislation, and it occurred much more quickly than expected. As a result grassroots organizations in the countryside were not prepared for the harsh reaction of landowners or the resulting tens of thousands of refugees driven from their homes.

The experience of Nepal is repeated in other countries. While non-governmental organizations tend to view themselves as secondary in importance to states, their influence is often more important in achieving human rights goals. After the knee-jerk reaction by politicians, the planned emancipation of *kamaiyas* in Nepal turned into a refugee crisis. In the United States the passage of the Trafficking Victims Protection Act, in late 2000, also depended on information and guidance provided by non-governmental organizations. After the law's passage, these organizations were called upon to help train law enforcement in its application and to research the best ways to address human trafficking. In spite of the fact that this new law addressed a serious crime, the majority of experts on this issue were located outside the state law enforcement agencies. This fact points to one of the advantages that bureaucratic non-governmental organizations bring to human rights: they are not encumbered by an excess of democracy internally, or by the abrupt changes that can occur in policy and personnel with changes of government. In spite of having a lobbying and advocacy role, most human-rights non-governmental organizations operate *outside* the political system of parties and elections, a characteristic crucial to their job of protecting human rights.

Politics is about winning the support of constituents and voters, and voters are defined by their physical location within the nation-state. Electoral success requires addressing the concerns of voters first, and voters rarely rank the human rights of foreigners above their own material concerns (in their own countries, slaves are politically voiceless). For most politicians in the Northern Hemisphere, there is little incentive to do anything about slavery, as it has neither economic implications nor salience with constituents. A handful of politicians recognize moral imperatives, but these are few.

The job of the non-governmental organization is as it has always been: to bring about a redefinition in public perception. To alter policy requires translating this public redefinition into voter demand. And this, in turn, requires making the issue real to voters and pushing it up their list of priorities. Since most slavery occurs in the developing world, a close working relationship with grassroots organizations is imperative. For the majority of voters, issues require a human face and clear, single-sentence encapsulation, otherwise the issue falls into the pool of concerns too big, too complex, or too distant to worry about. Grassroots organizations provide that face and story. If there is one hopeful note concerning the shallowness of voter response, it is that, in terms of human rights, the political processes of the developed world are less and less important.

Bureaucracies freed of nation-state borders by the process of globalization have wasted little time in building constituencies that transcend the political systems limited by those borders. Transnational corporations and transnational criminal organizations — the bureaucracies whose organizational goals could be maximized by this shift — moved most quickly to do so. But a number of coalitions of non-governmental organizations have sprung up whose organizing philosophical positions give them one advantage over businesses and criminal groups. Businesses and criminal groups must maximize profit, and this inevitably leads them into competition as they expand into new markets. Human rights organizations, too, compete with one another for resources (grant money, supporters), but do so while pursuing virtually identical ultimate goals (the protection and elaboration of human rights). This means that conflict within these organizations is more apparent than real. The squabbling may never stop, but it is a form of communication and negotiation taking place while the organizations generally move forward together. Anyone involved in the Global March against Child Labor would be familiar with both the squabbling and the ultimate achievement of the common goal of a new International Labor Organization convention. On the other hand, the conflict among business groups is more real than apparent, and geniality in interaction masks a willingness to completely destroy (through bankruptcy) a rival bureaucracy.

The future of human rights protection may rest primarily with these non-governmental organizations. The example of the Protocol signed by the chocolate industry and witnessed by human rights organizations is instructive. Two national governments were party to this agreement, but the resources that underwrote it, and the expertise that drove it, came from businesses and non-governmental organizations that transcend the state. In this case the effort at moral redefinition pressed by non-governmental organizations went first to the constituents of the businesses (the consumers) and only secondly to the constituents of the politicians. This helped to overcome a second problem with electoral democracy: its long timescales. In any election, voters can register a single choice only once every two years or so, and such choices are highly restricted and ill defined. Consumers can "vote" many times daily in a clearly specified manner. At times their choice is also restricted, but a consumer's choice not to buy becomes a boycott. The same action by a voter is simply self-disenfranchisement.

This link between business and non-governmental organizations is critical when the human rights violation under consideration is slavery. Slavery is an economic and social relationship between two or more people, one of the oldest of all forms of human relationship. While popular perceptions of slavery focus on its cruelty, the truth is that people are enslaved for economic exploitation, and cruelty is simply a tool used to achieve profits. The total estimated value of slave production globally is about $12 billion. This is a mere drop in the ocean of the world economy, but it is important in that some of this production flows into the homes of consumers in the developed world. Of the world's slaves, only a small minority are engaged in production that feeds international markets, but again, they are important in that their condition opens the door to public awareness. For the consumer in the Northern Hemisphere, a slave child in northern India is simply one of millions of needy children around the world; but a slave child who was forced to weave the rug on the floor of that person's bedroom somehow enters the consumer's field of responsibility.

The historical and present work by non-governmental organizations against slavery points both to the importance of bureaucratization of such organizations in the past and to their increasing transcendence of nation-states in doing human rights work. Over time, settings outside of government have taken on a greater importance in the work against slavery, and today the links between actors in the non-governmental-organization and business sectors are often of greater salience than links with governments. A recent delegation that met with the highest levels of the government of the Ivory Coast consisted of representatives of the chocolate industry, human rights organizations, and the U.S. government. As a member of that delegation noted, the representatives of the chocolate industry were deferred to most often by government officials; and human rights organizations, in spite of their very limited size and resource base, were perceived as a highly significant threat to the stability of the nation-state.

The importance of this is that all actors within the field of human rights must understand the shifting importance and influence of non-governmental organizations and other nonstate actors. The temptation to think inside the boundaries of existing and historical relationships is great, but the relationships — between governments, non-governmental organizations, businesses, and criminal organizations — are evolving as well. The relative power of the latter three is increasing, while the power of governments declines. Those who wish to elaborate and safeguard human rights must understand the fluid nature of these relationships and build both internal structures and external coalitions that take advantage of them.

CHAPTER 5

The Challenge
of Measuring Slavery

We worry that the study of contemporary slavery is more of a proto-science than a science. Its data are uncorroborated, its methodology unsystematic. Few researchers work in the area, so the field lacks the give and take that would filter out subjectivity. Bales himself acknowledges all this. As we debated his definitions of slavery, he told us, "There is a part of me that looks forward to being attacked by other researchers for my interpretations, because then a viable field of inquiry will have developed."

Scientific American

The Challenges

Social science data is notoriously loose and slippery. It primarily concerns the behaviors and attitudes of human beings, who are, as a species, often unreliable, confused, mercurial, and dynamic. As researchers we benefit from the fact that people act out their erratic ways within remarkably stable patterns — the most stable of which are the universal social institutions: government, religion, economics, education, and family. Slavery itself is not a universal social institution, as it has not been found in all societies, but it nearly made the list. In the very recent history of our species (meaning the last five thousand years), it has been a constant. For much of that history, slavery was far easier to measure than it is today. When slavery was commonly accepted as a "natural" social and economic relationship, even governments kept detailed records of slaves and their treatment, an activity later neglected

87

only because of the relative lack of social importance of the individual slaves.

In the twentieth century, slavery was generally criminalized and forced underground. This had direct consequences for the construction of our understanding of it. Its hidden nature, for example, concealed the dramatic changes that took place in its economic character after 1950. In parallel with the population explosion of the same period, slaves became more numerous, as well as less costly. The economic processes of modernization and globalization have pushed significant numbers of people in the developing world into social, economic, and political vulnerability. In this context, when governmental corruption allows criminals to use violence with impunity, slaves can be harvested. High levels of vulnerability have produced a glut of potential slaves, and, obeying the rule of supply and demand, the price of slaves has fallen precipitously. Slaves are now less expensive than at any point in recorded history. Their cheapness is a boon to criminals, and it has altered the ways that slaves are treated and used. These changes mean that, while slavery remains a criminal activity, both the law and researchers are forced to confront new manifestations of slavery.

The criminalization of slavery leads to a number of problems in measuring slavery, as in any other abusive labor practice. The first problem is the basic fact that criminals conceal their activities, often going to great lengths to do so. Second, following a long history of more visible and legal slavery, societies (as well as researchers, activists, and policy makers) have been slow to clearly define what now constitutes slavery.[1] This lack of an agreed-upon definition of the phenomenon under study is a recipe for confusion at best. Third, crime is best understood in its context, but in some places where slavery occurs, it is not thought of as a crime. In regions with relatively stable forms of debt bondage, euphemisms are common. In parts of India, for example, bonded workers who have no freedom to walk away, and who are not paid for their work, are often referred to as "attached workers," a term concealing their actual status. Fourth, without agreed-upon definitions, it is impossible to collect information systematically so that it can be shared and tested. The standards put forward by the International Labor Organization are a useful innovation, but note that these definitions usually have been developed through negotiation within a political process, rather than through a process of analysis and refinement.[2]

The role of politicians in determining how we define the social and economic relationships of slavery points to forces — outside observation and analysis — that shape our working definitions. Ideological, political, moral, and cultural viewpoints are all linked to, and affect our perceptions of, data on abusive labor practices. These views bring controversy to the collection, analysis, and interpretation of information. For example, some governments have a vested interest in demonstrating that there have been few violations of their core labor standards. Meanwhile, some nongovernmental organizations have an interest in demonstrating the opposite. When slavery as an economic activity enters into areas with a high potential for generating moral outrage and controversy, such as prostitution, apparently simple measures become battlegrounds. Many a good researcher has been wounded on that battleground and has retired to pursue other, less dangerous subjects. This loss of good researchers is especially regrettable because the phenomenon under consideration is a rapidly evolving, moving target requiring long-term study. Criminals are inventive. They work in a context of intense competition, they must be flexible, and they must adapt quickly or (at times literally) die. The pace of social research, especially large-scale research, is glacial by comparison.

Criminals, human traffickers among them, came to understand globalization before most of us. Early on, they mounted large-scale operations to traffic and enslave people, utilizing the attributes of the newly globalized world economy. Because the context of globalization is rapidly evolving, the fit between abusive labor practices, such as slavery, and the economy, both local and global, is dynamic. This is important, in part because these are economic activities, albeit criminal, and one dimension of their measurement must be economic. Two key themes of economic globalization are the erosion of control by nation-states and the functional integration of dispersed (economic) activities.[3] As discussed in chapter 4, these characteristics have suited human rights organizations admirably and created a context for potential growth. These characteristics have also fostered nonstate actors that might be thought of as anti-human-rights actors, especially criminal organizations.

The importance of these two themes — of dispersed economic activity and the loss of governmental control — for those who try to gain a better understanding of slavery and forced labor is that both tend to obscure the phenomenon and make the collection of information more difficult. Dispersal hinders the researcher's ability to trace the links between slavery in one place and the economic impetus for that slavery in another. The loss of governmental control also means the loss of a government's means to record and investigate the crime of slavery. That said, both of these negative outcomes of the globalization process — which involve the reduction of information about forced labor — are counterbalanced by another outcome of globalization: the increased flow of human rights information from the global south to the global north.

As noted in chapter 4, certain criminal groups are globalized actors of significant scale who play an important role in slavery and human trafficking. A clear linkage exists between the groups who engage in criminal traffic in drugs, guns, and people, all of which are major profit centers for organized crime. That said, these groups are businesses: some are organized bureaucratically; others are centered on a leader. Operating within a fluid, often risky context, they must adapt to very short time-scales and seek to maximize profits quickly. Like legitimate businesses, they often meet challenges and competition through diversification and concentration, and they consciously make the most of transcending nation-state boundaries. The rapid and dispersed movement of organized criminal groups has outdistanced the data collection systems of most national law enforcement agencies, and international agencies like Interpol spend significant resources getting national forces to share more of their information. Unfortunately, the information on forced labor held by these agencies is normally unavailable to most researchers.

All these difficulties, especially the reality that in researching slavery we are researching a criminal activity, point up the fact that careful definition is necessary and measurement is a challenge. In writing about crime and globalization, Mark Findlay notes that "one of the difficulties associated with accurate contextualization of crime is the diverse manner in which it is represented. This is not simply a problem of distortion or misinterpretation; the basic sources from which crime becomes known are so varied."[4] What follows is a discussion of some of the topics that must be resolved conceptually before we can quantify and measure slavery and other forms of forced labor more objectively.

What Are We Trying to Understand?

At the most basic level, slavery is a social and economic relationship played out in systematic ways. It has patterns of expression; it is grounded in cultures and societies. Many patterns of enslavement have been in use for long periods; however, small or large changes over time in those patterns are to be expected. Slavery has history, which can be a problem if this history leads a researcher to hold preconceived notions about what form slavery takes. In fact, we can no more expect historical forms of slavery in contemporary twenty-first-century societies than we can expect to find nineteenth-century forms and expressions of social class. The economic underpinnings of both have irrevocably altered. Slavery is a relationship between individuals (as is marriage, for example), but it exists primarily within communities and is governed by those communities (also like marriage). The slave-slaveholder relationship is marked by a much more extreme power differential than most marriages. Again, as in the case of marriage, an observer should not expect to view previous historic forms in a contemporary society — people who marry today do not expect their marriages to take the form of marriage extant in the eighteenth century.

Another dimension that must be considered in attempting to come to grips with slavery is that it is conceptualized as a social problem, and virtually all social problems are seen as problematic and controversial to a greater or lesser degree. Fortunately, with slavery, there is a strong consensus that it is a significant problem that does real damage to human beings, and that it should be ended as quickly as possible.[5] In a sense, there already exists what Ann Majchrzak terms a "model that appeals to 'higher-order values.'"[6] What is needed is to build a more precise model of the social problem of slavery as the first step in formulating and testing research questions. Such research questions obviously require measurable variables. Finding measurable variables is difficult with a phenomenon like slavery, which has an essential core but varies dramatically from place to place (and from time to time).

This essential core rests on three factors: the use of violence to control the slave, the resulting loss of free will, and the economic exploitation that normally precludes the slave receiving any recompense for their work. As noted in chapter 3, slavery may be defined in a simple, conversational way — as opposed to the various legal definitions discussed in that chapter — as a social and economic relationship marked by the loss of free will, in which a person is forced through violence or the threat of violence to give up the ability to sell freely his or her own labor power.

This definition has something in common with all definitions of slavery used in both laws and international conventions; it also encompasses most of the forms of slavery covered by them. There have been over three hundred agreements written since 1815 to combat slavery, and many of them defined it. The definition of slavery in international instruments has evolved over time. Consider, for example, the changes that occurred in the twentieth century in just some of the international instruments, analyzed at length in chapter 3.

Some international organizations such as the International Labor

Organization (ILO) have not defined slavery per se. ILO Convention 29 defines forced labor as "all work or service which is extracted from any person under the menace of any penalty and for which the said person has not offered himself voluntarily." This contains the elements of coercion and loss of free will, but it only implies the element of economic exploitation. ILO Convention 105, also concerning forced labor, does not define slavery or forced labor but refers to the UN's 1926 Slavery Convention. ILO Convention 182, concerning the worst forms of child labor, likewise does not define slavery or forced labor, but it does prohibit "all forms of slavery or practices similar to slavery, such as the sale and trafficking of children, debt bondage and serfdom and forced or compulsory labour, including forced or compulsory recruitment of children for use in armed conflict."[7] This follows the trend, noted in chapter 3, of broadening the conceptualization of the issue in policy. In fact, other international conventions expand even further the number of activities identified as slavery. Given that the experts at international agencies find it a challenge to arrive at a uniform definition of an activity that they all agree exists, and that they all agree should be eradicated, then it is not surprising that researchers face a similar challenge in developing ways to measure forced labor or slavery.

Eugene Webb and colleagues, who have done classic work on unobtrusive social research measures, neatly describe this challenge, stating that measures should enjoy "multiple operationism, that is, for multiple measures which are hypothesized to share in the theoretically relevant components but have different patterns of irrelevant components. Once a proposition has been confirmed by two or more independent measurement processes, the uncertainty is greatly reduced."[8] To achieve such triangulation requires determining how slavery fits within each society and community, where it occurs within the social matrix. Given slavery's hidden character, we must also determine how unobtrusive methods and other nonrepresentative methods might be brought to bear. This, in turn, requires us to consider both the levels and units of analysis to be pursued.

Slavery is a social action that generates measurable phenomena at all three levels of social measurement — the individual level (micro), the group or community level (meso), and the societal or aggregate level (macro). That said, slavery is primarily a phenomenon of the meso level. The power differential between slave and slaveholder reflects what is allowed in the community; the economic activity — which is the aim of enslavement — feeds into the local economic base. In many parts of the world, slavery has a relatively overt place in the community. Like prostitution, it may be tacitly accepted and managed by community leaders but officially invisible. Maintaining slavery in the face of illegality requires some community acquiescence or at least ignorance. The location of any community on the continuum between acquiescence and ignorance is strongly related to the level of corruption of local officials. But in any community that harbors slavery, there will be some people, in addition to the slaves and slaveholders, who are aware of it. They will interact with slavery in some way and will have some knowledge of it. This knowledge, and possibly records of that interaction, are data that can be collected.

At the micro level are the narratives of slaves and slaveholders, as well as basic factual information about each. This can be fundamental demographic information or information of some subtlety, such as data gathered on the social psychology of the slaveholder-slave relationship. In the case of slavery, macro-level information is normally composed of aggregations of micro- and meso-level information, as few governments or international agencies are able to collect information that is statistically representative of the slave population. Even the few criminological variables that represent aggregate arrests or prosecutions fail to adequately represent slavery. What may be sought at the macro level are national or regional aggregations of information about labor standards and practices. But what is available, given slavery's universal legal status, are crime statistics that concern labor standards and practices. This being the case, it is important to consider how these data are conceptualized by criminologists.

Researchers studying labor standards and practices linked to slavery face many of the same challenges that criminologists face. To fully comprehend the nature of contemporary slavery, we must gather macro-level, aggregate information. One example, however, demonstrates the difficulty of measuring criminal economic activity. The U.S. State Department estimates that each year about 50,000 women and children are trafficked into the United States as slaves.[9] In mid–May 2002, federal prosecutions of this crime had increased 50 percent over the year before, to 111. The discrepancy between these two figures is what criminologists call the "dark figure" of crime statistics. The "rule of dark figures" is that the gap between actual crimes and reported or prosecuted crimes decreases as the severity of the crime increases. Normally, the crime with the smallest dark figure is murder; bicycle theft, on the other hand, has one of the largest dark figures. What is sobering is that slavery, human trafficking, and other abusive labor practices are crimes of extreme severity, but they have the large dark figures normally associated with misdemeanors. The more reliable measures of criminal activity are the representative population-sample victim surveys regularly carried out in the developed world. These have proven to be the best way to achieve estimates of the dark figures of crime.

Slaves, however, are normally invisible, unsurveyable victims, hidden away because the criminal has total control over them.

Collecting information about them is not, however, impossible. Most exploratory social research faces similar challenges. In the social sciences, there is a way to approach this — to start from both ends and work toward the middle. At the micro level it is possible to begin with qualitative exploratory research that aims at discovering the texture of social interaction. Ideally, exploring a series of individual social interactions or relationships (the slaveholder-slave relationship, for example) in depth will lead the researcher to perceive emerging themes in the nature of these relationships. These themes and other information generated can then be used to build the questions and variables needed for more representative work at the meso and macro levels. At the same time, any information gained at the macro level might help build a contextual understanding that will also inform and guide meso- and micro-level research.

My own research into slavery began in this way — with a close reading of the accounts of individuals who had been enslaved, coupled with an attempt to collect information at the aggregate level. When I felt I had learned what there was to be learned, I began, in 1996, to build case studies exploring the meso level of slave-based businesses, one interview at a time.[10] I chose to use case studies for two key reasons. The first was based on the advice of Robert K. Yin, an authority on this research technique, who writes, "Case studies are the preferred strategy when how or why questions are being posed, when the investigator has little control over events and when the focus is on a contemporary phenomenon within some real-life context."[11] I also chose this technique because it was my aim to make some comparisons between the five countries in which I gathered information. To the best of my knowledge, this was the first time that the same set of guiding research questions had been asked in situations of slavery in more than one place. I am convinced that the global nature of contemporary slavery requires such an approach. It was my aim to gather all possible information on slavery in each country, as well as large amounts of background information on the history, culture, and economics of each country, which could then be fleshed out and illustrated by case studies of specific, slave-based economic activity.

The specific economic activities using slavery that I studied were brick making in Pakistan, agriculture in India, charcoal making in Brazil, prostitution in Thailand, and water-selling in Mauritania. In each country I was testing ideas about slavery's changing economic equation, trying to measure the profitability of these enterprises and the cost of using slaves.

I used the slavery research-guide questions (in appendix 1) to query informants, slaveholders, slaves, government officials, and other respondents. Interviews would often require asking many other questions besides those listed. For example, in Pakistan my co-researcher and I presented ourselves as economists (we both do have degrees in economics) who were seeking to understand the nature of the brick market and to "set the record straight about the realities of the brick business." This required extremely detailed discussions of the various factors affecting the brick business, and sooner or later the talk would come around to the "labor problem." Whenever possible, in all countries and businesses, I tried to let the respondent raise the issue of labor first. My aim was to answer the guide questions for each physical site where a slave-using business was operating to which I could gain access. Not all questions applied to every country or business, but having uniform questions allowed comparisons between geographical regions.

The research had to be exploratory because contemporary slavery is almost completely neglected in the social sciences: there was very little previous work on which to build. The interviews generated a great deal of qualitative information (and some quantitative information) that had to be ordered. I began to conceptualize some of that qualitative data, and much of the aggregate information collected earlier, as ordinal variables. The meso-level research provided portraits of slave-based businesses, their roles in local communities, and the methods of control exercised over slaves. This information was used to test various hypotheses I had developed about the realities of contemporary slavery, but it must be emphasized that these were not statistical or precise tests. My first step was to determine whether several of the factors that I theorized as supporting contemporary slavery were, in fact, present when slavery was observed. This type of hypothesis testing is more akin to work in political science or anthropology than in my own discipline of sociology. It does not provide the reassurance of statistical tests or the opportunity for replication. On the other hand, it follows widely accepted logic in social research which states that, when the object of study is relatively unknown, little understood, difficult to observe, and previously unquantified, then qualitative research is the appropriate first step. Ideally, such qualitative research facilitates the understanding necessary for the construction of measures applicable in broader, more representative, research. While working at the micro and meso levels to develop a more sophisticated understanding of slavery, I began to build macro-level estimates linked to existing macro-level data.

The conversion of difficult-to-measure phenomena into measures that can be statistically manipulated is common in sociology. Many of these phenomena are much less visible than slavery and yet are generally and readily accepted by the public and social scientists. Social class is a good example. The empirical reality of social class as a distinct social group or set has never been demonstrated. It is an ordinal construct of a large number of variables, some "hard," some "soft."[12] Slavery as a variable is also a construct, but a much less complex construct, one that requires only three or four variables to estimate (following the working definition given above). This simplicity may be due to the fact that it originated in emerging societies of some five thousand years ago. These are societies we can only imagine, but which we know did not have the complex social differentiation or extensive hierarchies of modern societies. But if slavery is a construct, how can information estimating it be collected? How can effective measures of slavery and human trafficking be made at the aggregate level?

Assessment of Existing Measures

All the preceding discussion is an elaborate contextualizing exercise aimed at concealing the fact that my own methods of data collection have been simplistic and driven less by epistemological concerns than by practicalities. While it may sound as if I brought the surgical precision of the scalpel to bear on my data, in fact I simply employed the social science equivalent of the vacuum cleaner, sucking up data from every possible source. I began my work at the macro level, by drawing up a large data-collection form, or, in the jargon, a "systematic protocol." My unit of analysis was the nation-state. For each country, I recorded the basic economic and demographic information available from the UN and other sources. Then several research assistants and I began to troop (physically and electronically) through every store of information that might bear on slavery.

REPORTS OF U.S. GOVERNMENT AGENCIES

The State Department's *Country Reports on Human Rights Practices* were useful as background materials but had worrying political influences.[13] The clear discrepancies between, for example, what I had observed on the ground in Mauritania and what the report had to say about that country

gave me pause. The U.S. government has initiated a period of rap-
prochement with the Mauritania regime, and this has led to a willingness
on the part of the U.S. government to interpret the human rights situation in that country charitably. The United States is playing politics with
slavery and with knowledge in exactly the way discussed earlier. This is not
surprising, but it doesn't aid data collection. The State Department's *2001
Trafficking in Persons Report* was not available when I first compiled my
data set.[14] However, it has been useful for the background information
given on the eighty countries listed. The report's system of tiers is an
interesting variable, but instead of actually measuring human trafficking,
it measures the *response* of a given country to trafficking. (This variable is
highly correlated with the sale and movement of slaves from a country.)
The 2002 report included more countries. Information collected by the
Office to Monitor and Combat Human Trafficking, from State Department staff around the world, must surely offer a mother lode of data, but
it is seen as politically sensitive and, to my knowledge, is not available at
this time to other researchers.

REPORTS BY THE INTERNATIONAL
LABOR ORGANIZATION

These reports, too, such as the *Stopping Forced Labour* report, are useful
for gleaning pieces of information that can then be assembled in a coun-
try-by-country data set.[15] However, in many ways, the nonsynthesized,
nonaggregated information generated by the ILO is more useful. The
reports on each session of the ILO, which include the reports of the
Committee of Experts on the Application of Conventions and Resolutions, and of the Committee on the Application of Standards, run to
many volumes and contain the transcripts of reports by country, labor,
and employer representatives. These reports contain large amounts of
obfuscation and justification by countries that have been criticized.
(Sudan, for example, consistently and at length insists that they have
"abduction" not "enslavement.") There is also useful information, but a
great amount of sifting is required to uncover it. Here, too, politics plays
a part: in response to demands — primarily by member states — to reduce
criticism, information is edited before release. I have watched this process
close at hand in the meetings and seen the results in the reports of the
United Nations Working Group on Contemporary Forms of Slavery.[16]
This report presents incidences of slavery around the world that have been
documented by non-governmental organizations and others. The annual

reports of the working group consistently water down this information to lessen any criticism of specific countries. In short, there is much more information to be gained by sitting in the sessions, information that never reaches the official reports. This points up a distinction for researchers: there is a difference between "raw" information available in meetings and the "cooked" version that exists for public consumption.

REPORTS BY EXPERTS

If the United Nations has information more likely to be free of political tampering, it is in the reports commissioned from experts. These are not usually made generally available. One example is the report on vulnerability to debt bondage commission by the ILO Social Finance Unit and prepared by the Institute for Human Development in India.[17] Researchers developed and tested the "Vulnerability to Debt Bondage Scale," which significantly furthers our understanding of this form of slavery. They used aggregated information for agricultural workers and multivariate analysis to test the scale. A second example is the work on child trafficking in West Africa done by the Norwegian child-labor expert Anne Kielland for the World Bank, probably the best research on this topic I have ever seen.[18] Carefully sampled, sensitively carried out, precisely analyzed, it dramatically moves forward our understanding of this phenomenon.

REPORTS BY NON-GOVERNMENTAL ORGANIZATIONS

These reports are a narrower, but rich, source of information. Like the reports of consultants to UN bodies, they often are not generally available, but for different reasons. For a non-governmental organization, "publication" may simply mean making a number of copies on the photocopier. Likewise, since non-governmental organizations are concerned with moving public opinion, the only version of a research report that reaches the public may be a press release. Moreover, with non-governmental organization reports, there is also the need to separate outrage and analysis. While countries often try to diminish reports of labor abuses within their borders, non-governmental organizations are sometimes tempted to overstate the same abuses (though this may also indicate a lack of agreed-upon definitions). Of course, some non-governmental organizations have a long history of careful and precise reporting. Anti-Slavery International is the leader in this, and Human Rights Watch, with its legalistic bent, provides sound information. Smaller and more local non-governmental organizations are more problematic; they are less careful in documenting their assertions — which is not surprising, since they see their job as righting wrongs, not presenting detailed documentation. With all non-governmental organizations, it is most fruitful to speak in person to the staff working on a particular issue to discover what reports are available. This points up the need for a repository of these often informal human rights and labor rights investigations. Well organized and well cared for, the archives and library of Anti-Slavery International in London are a rare exception, as are their publications.[19] Most non-governmental organizations are dealing with today's crises and neglecting the solid information they may have collected yesterday.

A positive step worth mentioning, though one that might not immediately seem positive, is Human Rights Watch's criticism of the State Department's *2001 Trafficking in Persons Report*.[20] The criticism calls for more and more detailed information. LaShawn R. Jefferson, executive director of the Women's Rights Division of Human Rights Watch, states, "It's crucial that each country chapter relay basic information about how many people are trafficked into, through, and from it; the types of forced labor for which people are trafficked; the number of actual prosecutions and convictions for trafficking; and how many state agents have been investigated, tried, and convicted for trafficking-related offenses."[21] This can be very difficult information to gather, especially from embassies and consulates. In many countries, the U.S. government is neither given access to such information, nor allowed to collect it independently. Given that gathering this information requires research infrastructure that may not exist, it is somewhat unfair to expect embassies to discover what national and international agencies are unable to determine. That said, the more attention given to research methods, and the possible influence of political concerns on the reporting of trafficking information, the better. Senator Sam Brownback (R-KS), one of the authors and sponsors of the legislation that established the Office to Monitor and Combat Trafficking in Persons, has also criticized the *2001 Trafficking in Persons Report,* calling for clearer recommendations for sanctions. Undoubtedly, the original mandate of the report, which concentrates on the preventative or remedial programs set up by foreign governments, is part of the problem, and I feel certain that the authors of the report must be frustrated by the narrowness of their terms of reference. Yet the report is a positive step made not two years into a major research and development exercise. Moreover, important new information will come from it, and a public debate on that information has already begun. Over time this exchange can only serve to improve the quality of information — especially if organizations like Human Rights Watch also agree to feed their data into the *2001 Trafficking in Persons Report*.

REPORTS BY NATIONAL GOVERNMENTS

Governmental reports that are immediately useful are not common. Of course, more governments may be carrying out research than is being disseminated. But the resources of governments are so much larger than those of non-governmental organizations that, when they bring them to bear, the results can be fruitful. One example of this is the *Incidence of Bonded Labour in India: Area, Nature, and Extent,* by the Lal Bahadur Shastri National Academy of Administration, in India, one of the most comprehensive studies of debt bondage ever undertaken.[22] The academy is a central training school for social workers; its students were deployed across the country to collect data. The results present a remarkable snapshot of a dynamic situation of debt bondage in India in the late 1980s. Sadly, there has been no follow-up. A second example is the report *International Trafficking in Women to the United States,* by Amy O'Neill Richard.[23] Being able to call on the information and analytical capabilities at CIA headquarters in order to collect data may be the fantasy of many researchers; when it does occur it produces remarkably deep information. The CIA and human rights organizations may seem to be strange bedfellows — or perhaps not, given that human trafficking is both a crime and a potential threat to security. It would be good if other governments and agencies within our own government devoted such resources to research. Of course, they do; but few researchers are likely to see much of it. For example, I have two reports that shed new light on conditions of slavery and trafficking in two countries, but I was given them with the express condition that I not share them with other researchers.

THE WORK OF ACADEMIC EXPERTS

Academic studies tend to be most important in contextualizing and organizing the interpretation of more specific reports on labor abuses such as slavery. Few academics study slavery or trafficking up close.[24] Their work is more likely to be synthetic and interpretive. This is still important, as the great preponderance of factual reports must be lodged within theoretical frameworks. However, it can be discouraging to find a group of extremely talented academics devoting their time to arcane discussions of the ways that one might intellectually subdivide information about slavery (if one ever collected it). I have been drawn into debates on several occasions concerning the precise conceptual differences between feudalism, debt bondage, and indentured servitude, and whether any or all of these are forms of slavery. It is important to understand the past, and the relation between different forms of exploitation, but if these discussions concern contemporary slavery, then they must be grounded in research that tests assumptions and debates against the realities found in the field. Perhaps most exciting is work like that of Jok Madut Jok, a Sudanese historian based in the United States who has written about contemporary enslavement in Sudan; and the work of Binka Le Breton, who lives in Brazil and studies labor exploitation there.[25]

PRESS REPORTS

By far the largest source of information on labor abuses, press reports are utterly without organization. The Listserv called Stop-Traffic generates several news reports per day concerning human trafficking and enslavement.[26] The important point is that journalists are normally recording facts or government statements of facts that do not make up large reports, but that, when aggregated, present larger pictures. The investigative reports of large newspapers are often superior to all but the most extensive academic research. The resources devoted to, and the international travel and investigation behind, a single news story may be wide-ranging. Recent investigations by the *New York Times* have illuminated the links between slave labor in Brazil and its key export products.[27] In its voracious hunger for information, the media also scoops up the work of academics and non-governmental organizations, relaying it to other academics and non-governmental organizations in a way that is much more efficient than that of their own organs.

I have canvassed all these types of sources in order to build up a data set on slavery across countries. Whatever the case, I logged every number, estimate, guess, and suggestion on a separate large sheet for each country (or sometimes, for populous and well-documented countries, I assigned a sheet to each region of a country, to be aggregated later). The result, after nearly three years, was a great hodge-podge, but one that concentrated information and organized it by nation-state. Overlapping this process was the fieldwork that provided case study data; some information collected from secondary sources in the countries I visited was added to the mix. Otherwise, I used the on-the-ground observations, where possible, as a check on the reports logged.

Macro-Level Analysis

After assembling that great hodge-podge, I began the process of analysis and estimation. The information collected for each country had to be judged according to its validity, but of course there was no baseline or benchmark against which to do so. To answer this challenge, I looked to one of the pioneers of sociological measurement, L. L. Thurstone.[28] His seminal 1928 article, "Attitudes *Can* Be Measured," demonstrates that attitudes, though highly fluid, interior intellectual constructs, can be located and measured across a population (at the time, many sociologists believed this was impossible). Thurstone generated the first scales for the measurement of attitudes by calling on experts to judge whether each individual item-statement in an attitudinal scale was, in their opinion, indicative of the attitude concerned, and, if it was, whether they felt it was positively or negatively, weakly or strongly, related to that attitude. He compiled these judgments from a large number of experts — as many as one hundred people from many walks of life — whom he believed would have an educated and reliable viewpoint. I followed much the same procedure, though I was forced to do so with even less focus than Thurstone enjoyed. I canvassed experts with personal knowledge of a country, a region, or an industry, often promising them anonymity. They compared the information I had collected with their own and suggested which points might be exaggerations, which ones might be under- or overestimates, and which ones might indicate the social reality. In the process, these experts often suggested additional sources of information.

Two things helped these experts in their deliberations. One was the working definition of slavery that I had developed, which I believe gets at its irreducible nature.[29] Asking the experts to use this definition meant that, probably for the first time, they were comparing apples with apples. The second helpful bit of information was an estimate, an educated guess really, about the extent of slavery in each country. I have always presented these estimates for what they are: very rough, if informed, guesses. Their usefulness lay in focusing the minds of the experts, giving them a point to consider and challenge. That response led to a refining of the estimates. When I felt I had exhausted both the number and the goodwill of experts that I could find for each country, I adjusted the estimates for each country and began to aggregate them. This aggregation produced the figure of 27 million slaves for the world, using my working definition to determine who would be included in that estimate.

At this point one becomes involved in the history of a number. Being highly appreciative of the old computer programmer's rule of GIGO,[30] I was nervous about going on record with my estimate of 27 million slaves. So why do so? In part because the existing estimates for the number of slaves in the world ranged from the low millions to 200 million. These numbers were wildly divergent and apparently often groundless. I traced one oft-repeated estimate of 100 million back to the person in India who had originally offered it. This person explained that this really was a "top of the head" guess and not based on any aggregation or formal estimation. It had taken hold in the literature because it had been voiced in the context of a meeting within the United Nations. When the report of the meeting included this figure, it was taken as an estimate supported by the UN, which gave it credence. I presumed instead that a rough estimate based on aggregation is better than a wild guess.

I hoped that publishing numerical estimates would lead others to challenge and, more important, test them. There is nothing I would like more than to be proved wrong. (Welcoming criticism tends to make it less threatening, and, realistically, I was sufficiently advanced in my academic career that, if my reckless posting of estimates became a disaster, I could just fade into tenured obscurity.) Remarkably, my estimate was seized upon with alacrity and I found myself described as an "expert."[31] Much more important was the fact that an accepted estimate focused people's minds and altered the public discussion, changing it from a debate over definition to a consideration of responses. This was heartening but worrying. It was heartening because the response was to use the estimate in many informative ways, but worrying because of an often uncritical acceptance of the estimate.

In preparing an article for *Scientific American,* I was able to revisit the estimates I had made and refine them, once again with advice from the experts.[32] I endeavored to expand the number of countries for which I could give an estimate. I also hedged slightly by publishing a range, rather than a single number, as my estimate (see appendix 2 for the table of estimates and ordinal measures). I felt trepidation at publishing these estimates, as I knew how "mushy" (as one *Scientific American* editor put it) they were. And as much as I welcomed correction, new information, and the challenge of debate, I worried that many countries and experts would round on me. In any event, the response was muted. The editor of the Brazilian edition of *Scientific American* felt that I had overestimated the number enslaved there, and offered the official prosecution and conviction rates and the work of an non-governmental organization as evidence. A man in Uruguay wrote to say he had never seen slaves there; and the Estonian government got in touch to ask for more details, as they were facing similar difficulties in estimating the number of people trafficked in the Baltic region.[33]

In order to make my data more usable, I went further out on a limb and, for each country (for which I had any sort of indicative data), assigned a categorical point on an ordinal scale of slavery:

0 = no slavery

1 = very little, occasional slavery

2 = small but persistent amounts of slavery

3 = slavery regularly found in a few economic sectors

4 = slavery regularly found in several economic sectors

Likewise, I assigned to each country a point on a similar ordinal scale of human trafficking, according to the flow of slaves to, or from, that country:

0 = no trafficking

1 = rare cases of trafficking

2 = occasional, but persistent cases of trafficking

3 = regular cases of trafficking in small numbers

4 = regular cases of trafficking in large numbers

Once again, I asked experts to suggest whether I had categorized each country correctly, admitting and agreeing that the ideas of "occasional," "regularly," "small," and "large" were insufficiently defined and imprecise. At this point I appreciated that I was potentially building upon bad estimates to construct worse ordinal or ranking estimates. Worse still, at present, there is no way to know if this is the case or not. Stephen Devereux and John Hoddinott discussed this problem with reference to collecting quantitative information in the developing world: "The problem . . . is that a number 'calcifies' at each stage — from questionnaire to coding sheet to analysis — until it is one of several hundred numbers contributing to the production of a percentage, in which uncertainty over the accuracy of each individual number is buried forever."[34] Their response to this problem is to carefully mix qualitative and quantitative information so that each will help check the other — the triangulation mentioned earlier. This is more difficult when developing a protoscience, due to a sheer lack of research results. On the other hand, as we know, data are everywhere, and sometimes the strategy must be to recombine what is already available and convert the experience and memories of observers into data. At the risk of calcifying numbers, I used qualitative information to help me assign estimates to levels of enslavement and trafficking. Hence my little data set of slavery and trafficking and its use in the following exercise.

A Modest Test

What predicts the amount of slavery in a particular country? Given the general and often anecdotal nature of our understanding, and given the lack of in-depth survey research, it is still fair to say there is a theory of contemporary slavery. This theory has not been formally stated, but it has been described.[35] As seen by many of those working in the field, and based on what evidence exists, this theory points to the importance of population pressure, poverty, environmental destruction, social vulnerability, and government corruption as factors supporting the emergence or continuation of slavery in a country. Of course, many of these factors are related. If a country has a "young" population profile — that is, a large proportion of the population is below the age of eighteen — there can be intense competition for employment and a glut of impoverished unemployed workers. Likewise, there are well-known links between poverty and higher levels of fertility. Further, as already mentioned, a vicious cycle exists in which enslaved workers are used to carry out environmental destruction, which in turn pushes populations into economic and social vulnerability and, thus, into enslavement. Corruption is also known to be linked to poverty, and police corruption is essential if slaveholders are to use violence with impunity to control slaves.

This then is the general theory — of what predicts slavery in a country — that we can test with statistical estimates. Put into this form, the test of this theory or model of slavery requires that we find measures of each of the factors or variables posited to support slavery, and that we examine the statistical estimates of their ability to predict the incidence of slavery in a country. We must also include any other factors that might conceivably predict slavery. One point of interest here is that this test's only variable taken from my own estimates is the measure of slavery in a country. All the others come from official sources, though one, the measure of corruption, is more anecdotal and dubious. The information recorded for each country in the database comes from a number of sources, but primarily from the United Nations statistical handbook.[36]

Using multiple regression, I found the following individual variables to be statistically significant predictors of the estimated amount of slavery in a country;[37] the variables are given in descending order of their power to predict slavery:

- the country's infant mortality rate (.61)
- the proportion of the population below the age of fourteen (.49)
- the proportion of the workforce in agriculture (.34)
- governmental corruption (.30)
- the extent that a country has threatened or endangered species (.15)

The fractional numbers in parentheses are beta coefficients; these give the relative strength of each of the predictive factors. All the beta coefficients shown are statistically significant at the .01 level or better, with the exception of the variable measuring the number of threatened or endangered species (sig. = .05). For these data, the factors shown explain 61 percent (*r-squared*) of the variation in slavery between countries.[38]

In terms of explaining the nature of contemporary slavery, this test confirms many of the assumptions generally held about what predicts slavery, and it adds new information — *if* we accept that the dependent variable is in fact an acceptably valid measure. The expected predictive power of poverty and vulnerability, population pressure, and corruption are confirmed. What is shown for the first time is a significant relationship between environmental destruction and enslavement.

These findings parallel those of Robert B. Smith, who analyzed 138 countries using the United Nations' Human Development Index, which measures the capacity of a country to provide its citizens a decent life.[39] Smith put countries together in regional groupings to avoid unfair comparisons, such as Sweden with Senegal. He found that what best explained differences between countries in terms of their human development was the presence or absence of slavery and trafficking. At one level this seems obvious and the effect circular: people who are enslaved clearly have no hope of human development; and in a country where education and other resources are scarce, people are more vulnerable to enslavement. Both of these assertions are true, but the importance of Smith's finding has to do with emphasis. Put another way, in Smith's findings, trafficking and slavery were more important in explaining the differences in development between countries than cultural background, the extent of democracy, the level of national debt, the amount of civil conflict, and the level of governmental corruption.

Taken together, the analysis shown here and Smith's work point to factors that precede and follow on from enslavement — both causes and outcomes. Moreover, these findings underline basic assertions about what reduces enslavement: education, anticorruption measures, economic supports for the poor, and protection of the environment. This analysis also implies that government actions to reduce corruption could lead to improved *information* about trafficking and enslavement, as well as actual reductions in slavery. Human Rights Watch called for better information on corruption, too, in their critique of the State Department's *2002 Trafficking in Persons Report:* "Although many country chapters mention government corruption and complicity, they should be consistently clearer about exactly which type [border guards, police, immigration officials, etc.] of government officials are implicated."[40]

This little exercise simply demonstrates that there are many basic questions about slavery that might be answered at the macro level. For example, using the data set used above, I have analyzed the relationship between international debt loading and the incidence of enslavement, but this is just one small question among many.[41]

Conclusion and Recommendations

All of the foregoing raises the question of predictive validity. Following Jack Gibbs, I feel that the primary criterion for the assessment of social science should be predictive validity.[42] But how can predictions be made and tested when there is no way of being sure that the variables under consideration are valid? I have no clear answer to this question, except to point to the fact that all exploratory, newly opened fields of inquiry ("protosciences," in the words of the *Scientific American* editors) must face this problem. The small test of what predicts slavery, described above, shows that generally accepted notions of causation and relationship gathered from the field can be examined. Yet even in this test, the dependent variable is the most problematic, being constructed of hundreds of unrelated pieces of information.

To address the fundamental question of how to build greater validity in our work, at least six steps could be taken. These represent trends to coordinate and harmonize research. This, in turn, is part of a wider globalization process (see chapter 6). As Findlay puts it, "In its harmonious state, globalization tends to universalize crime problems and generalize control responses."[43] It would also be reasonable to say that this process generalizes detection responses — an example of this is the ongoing construction of an elaborate database, by the United Nations' Center for International Crime Prevention, that will measure human trafficking flows globally. Yes, the globalization of slavery and trafficking crime is a threat, but a key attribute of the globalization process is the increased mutual comprehension of information and its immediate and wide-ranging dissemination. My first recommendation is precisely concerned with increasing mutual comprehension.

1. Define variables.   One of the great achievements of the ratification of the United Nations' Convention on Transnational Organized Crime, and its Protocol to Prevent, Suppress and Punish Trafficking in Persons, Especially Women and Children, is that it established a uniform definition of "trafficking in persons." One worry concerning this definition is that it represents some political compromises rather than simply the search for precision in exploration. For slavery, no such generally agreed-upon definition exists. The same is true for debt bondage, which seems to be even more confusing to researchers and policy makers, since few realize that there are at least two types of debt bondage. Any real progress will require the careful construction of working definitions of key variables. The definitions given in ILO Conventions and Standards, like those in UN Conventions, require greater specificity for use in social science. The sooner a debate and a collective decision on key definitions can occur among researchers the better. My own working definition is offered to any researchers who might wish to use it as a jumping-off place, a stalking horse, or even a sacrificial straw man.

2. Bring in the economists and business analysts.   Slavery is, and always has been, an economic activity. The practice of business and the organization of the economy have changed dramatically in the past forty years. The economics of slavery have also altered, as has the nature of slave-based businesses. Much of my work on slavery to date has focused on the analysis of slave-based businesses. This was predicated, in part, on the assumption that one of the most potent means of intervention would be to make slavery unprofitable. We aim for a world where labor standards are respected; in the meantime the activities of criminal businessmen must be disrupted. The flows of people, drugs, and arms through illegal channels are the main sources of income for international criminal organizations. This is crime, but it is also business; and the analysis of business — at the local, regional, national, or global level — can help uncover ways to intervene, collect evidence, and prosecute. As one Interpol antitrafficking official told me, "The key is to follow the money; traffickers leave a trail of transactions, all of which can be used as evidence."[44]

3. Study the lived experience of slavery and forced labor. The rapidly expanding protoscience that examines slavery and forced labor is driven, in large part, by the demands of governments and international agencies who want numbers on which to build policy. This is proper: sound policy requires good estimates in order to determine the needed level of resources, the location of needed interventions, and the appropriate administrative mechanisms to be brought into play. The nature of a person's life in slavery, however, may not be captured in these aggregated numbers. The broad literature of slavery and forced labor is full of work that expresses outrage and concentrates on graphic depiction of the suffering of victims. Outrage is appropriate in the face of slavery, but it can dim our perception and insight. Demographic and economic change has brought changes in the nature of enslavement. The qualitative texture of slavery must be understood just as much as the aggregated reality of slave numbers.

4. Centralize information. Disciplines of inquiry rise and fall over time. We are witnessing not only the growth of human rights as a discipline and but also an increase in the consideration of such phenomena as contemporary slavery as a discipline or subdiscipline in its own right. In time, all disciplines develop centers of expertise and archives of information. At this moment there are few places collecting information crucial to answering questions about labor conditions. Building a collection of such information and organizing it will require significant resources. And doing so will also require a very catholic approach. The current tendency of international agencies to refer primarily to the work of national governments, other international agencies, and a handful of non-governmental organizations must be radically altered. I urge throwing the widest possible net and then using agreed-upon definitions to filter and order the information collected.

5. Survey victims. To my knowledge, there have been only three surveys that might be considered representative (albeit roughly so) of populations in slavery. They are Kielland's study of child labor in West Africa (a survey of villages and families); the State Department CIA study of human trafficking flows into the United States (the precise methods of this study are not clear but are assumed to be a canvas of law enforcement and social service agencies, as well as a review of news and other public sources); and the Indian study of debt bondage carried out by the National Academy of Administration (a combination of village surveys, case studies, and interviews with officials and informants).[45] None of these are representative in the same manner that victim surveys are as normally accomplished. If we are ever to achieve a broad understanding of the incidence of trafficking and enslavement, broad victim surveys must be carried out using representative population samples. The drawback is that such surveys are costly. They rely on a sufficiently large general sample of a population to illuminate those parts of the population that have been victimized. When the crime includes control and concealment of the victim, the methodological problems loom large. There are research agencies experienced in conducting victim surveys, and these might be supported to expand their terms of reference to include questions linked to forced labor.

In December of 2001, the heads of state of the countries of the Economic Community of West African States agreed to a joint plan of action to combat human trafficking in the region.[46] One key point of this action plan is: "States shall establish direct channels of communication between their border control agencies. They shall initiate or expand efforts to gather and analyze data on trafficking in persons, including on the means and methods used, on the situation, magnitude, nature, and economics of trafficking in persons, particularly of women and children. States shall share such information, as appropriate, within ECOWAS, and with law enforcement agencies and other agencies of countries of origin, transit and destination, as well as with the United Nations Center for International Crime Prevention and other relevant international organizations."

Such efforts will require supplying financial and technical assistance to developing nations to help them detect criminal slavery and trafficking activities. If the countries of the global North are committed to achieving useful measures of such extreme violations of human rights, and if non-governmental organizations such as Human Rights Watch are equally committed, both must do what they can to promote and develop a competent research infrastructure in all countries.

6. Build a protoscience.   Building a protoscience is not the same as conducting "normal" science. In my own work, I have found it necessary to step back, return to first principles, and consider how one goes about building from a very small foundation. My normal expectations of how to approach any research questions often have had to be shelved. In the current phrase, we "have to think outside the box." We must; we are building a new box.

CHAPTER 6

Globalization and Redemption

In this chapter I want to do two things. First, I want to explain how slavery mirrors other economic pursuits in becoming globalized. Second, I want to look at the traditional types of slavery practiced in Mauritania and Sudan in order to take up the thorny question of the "redemption" of slaves in Sudan and to shed a little light on this problem by contextualizing it historically and socially.

The Globalization of Slavery

Discussing *globalization* can itself be problematic because of the different meanings and interpretations given this word. In defining it, I follow the work of Martin Albrow, one of the originators of the term in its current usage.[1] As a result of his work, we can think of globalization as a dramatic shift from the stage of human history known as modernity. Whereas modernity was essentially defined by time, globality (the state generated by the process of globalization or from which the process of globalization arises) is essentially defined by space. Whereas modernity was embedded in the concept of the nation-state, globality transcends nation-state boundaries. In practical terms the process of globalization involves, in part, "the active dissemination of practices, values, technology and other human products throughout the globe,"[2] as well as the historical transformation that arises from this process.

This globalization process is especially clear in the economy. Whereas the nation-state promoted and organized trade and created and regulated money, globalized trade and money are rapidly freeing themselves of national controls and becoming supranational activities. In slavery there is a clear parallel: the nation-state is of diminishing significance in understanding or dealing with slavery, and slavery as an economic activity continues unabated. In the nineteenth century, slavery was, by definition, a social and economic relationship tied to, and determined by, nation-states. Slavery created a relationship, as did marriage or a business contract, that was given a precise legal status enforceable within the boundaries of a state. A slave in one place could be automatically free when moved to another jurisdiction. This conflating of slavery with its legal definition meant that the abolition of slavery came to be equated with the abolition of the laws that regulated slavery.

In fact the abolition of laws regulating slavery did not end slavery. While it was greatly diminished within certain jurisdictions, as an economic activity it has continued around the world. Within the shadow economy, it has grown whenever conditions permitted, and globalization has been important in fostering those conditions. As noted earlier, slavery emerges when economic vulnerability combines with sufficient population and a lack of regulation or control over the use of violence. The deregulation of world markets, seen as an opportunity by the Wall Street stockbroker and as a threat by the Indian farmer, adds significantly to the economic vulnerability of a large proportion of the world's poor. When this occurs in countries where corruption allows the illicit use of violence to capture and control vulnerable people, slavery emerges. But new forms of slavery are not just outcomes of the globalization of the economy: they are part of the globalization process itself.

Globalization, as opposed to internationalization, involves a functional integration of dispersed economic activities.[3] Consider how the transnational company must be aware of a potential advantage or threat arising in any part of the globe. This globalized trade also produces a challenge to national governments, which, as Albrow puts it, "is a loss of control, a control which governments hitherto thought the international system guaranteed."[4] Both the dispersal of economic enterprises based on slavery and the loss of government control are key attributes of slavery today. Meanwhile slavery has become globalized in other ways. Albrow asserts that globalization "now carries connotations of the commercialization of humanity."[5] In a very particular way, this commercialization indicates new forms of slavery. If the old forms of slavery were anything, they were the commodification of human beings. People as legal property was the basis of chattel slavery. Today slavery has moved away from slaves as capital investments to the use of slaves as inputs in an economic process. As is true of other key factors in the global economy, slaves are transformed from fixed assets into flexible resources.

This is clearly seen in the decreasing importance of time as an attribute of slavery. One of the drawbacks of old slavery was the cost of maintaining slaves who were too young or too old. Careful analysis of both American cotton plantations and the Brazilian coffee farms in the nineteenth century shows that the productivity of slaves was linked to their age.[6] Children did not bring in more than they cost until the age of ten or twelve, in spite of putting them to work as early as possible. Productivity and profits to be made from a slave peaked when the slave reached about age thirty and fell off sharply when a slave was fifty and older. Slavery was profitable, but the profitability was diminished by the cost of keeping infants, small children, and unproductive old people. In the past, slavery was legally mandated as a permanent, lifelong state. Altering the temporal nature of that state — for example, through manumission — required precise and strictly controlled legal acts. Today slavery is sometimes of short duration, and some people fall in and out of slavery and back in again. For the observer who still requires the existence of legal ownership to identify a slave, this might be seen as "virtual" slavery.[7] The contemporary slaveholder addresses questions of location, advantage, process, and flexibility, not concerns of fixed assets, inheritance, or the return on capital investment over time. The latter are the preoccupations of modernity, the former of globality.

What is important is that these attributes of the new form of slavery — this shift from ownership to control and appropriation — are present in virtually all contemporary slavery across national or cultural boundaries. Whether a slave cuts cane in the Caribbean, makes bricks in the Punjab, mines in Brazil, or is kept as a prostitute in Thailand, the basic relationship of slave and slaveholder takes on this form, becoming more reflective of global economic practice. In this respect we see the conflation of slavery in its culturally specific forms with an emerging globalized form.

In one final way, slavery has been transformed in the process of its globalization. One of the key debates about globalization is whether it is a process that is homogenizing the globe or increasing its diversity through hybridization, but this debate engenders a false dichotomy. Both processes are inherent in globalization, one often sparking off the other. The slaveholder in Pakistan or Brazil, for example, watches television just like everyone else. When he sees that industries in many countries are switching to a "just in time" system for the delivery of raw materials or necessary labor, he draws the same conclusions about profitability that captains of industry have drawn. As jobs for life disappear from the world economy, so does slavery for life. The economic advantages of short-term enslavement far outweigh the costs of buying new slaves when needed. Lifetime enslavement, like plowing behind a horse, may not be unprofitable, but what is the point when a much more lucrative method exists? One might see this as homogenization, but it takes place through the alteration of locally specific forms of slavery or debt bondage.

Through globalization, slavery is neither homogenizing nor becoming radically diversified. These are not useful categories in understanding contemporary slavery. Slavery existed in diverse forms long before the advent of modernity. What is happening now is both the proliferation and the elaboration of those forms. Proliferation happens when the right conditions occur and those people who have the power to do so choose to enslave others. The underlying and essential elements of slavery are then manifested — violence and its threat, absolute control, economic exploitation — but the form that these elements take reflects crosscutting currents of economic expediency and cultural influence. In this way new forms of slavery mimic the world economy by shifting away from ownership and fixed asset management, and by concentrating on control and use of resources or processes. These new forms are the elaboration of slavery into further iterations. The social and economic relationship is still one of slavery, but the expression of the relationship is constantly evolving. In these elaborated forms, slavery may be more or less temporary, more or less profitable, and more or less exploitative of children; and the bait that lures people into slavery may be money, food, work, the opportunity to migrate, or a color television. But whatever its form, it can still be identified as slavery. And while there are many ways into slavery, there are also many ways out. Some of the ways to freedom, such as redemption, are themselves controversial.

Reformation and Redemption

In southern Sudan a Western charity pays fifty dollars per person to free Dinka people. These people were enslaved after their villages were raided by militia linked to the Sudanese government. In northern India a group of women band together to form a small credit union. Over a period of months they save enough to repay the debt that holds one of their members in bondage; then they begin to save to buy another woman's freedom. In southern India a child is freed from slavery when a charity pays off the man who enslaved him to make *beedi* cigarettes. Today, with 27 million slaves in the world, redemption (making a payment to free a slave) can and does happen anywhere. But why is this happening? How can we understand the role of redemption in the global antislavery movement?

Whereas slavery has become globalized, much of our attention has been drawn by the media to the specific, but untypical, cases of slavery in Mauritania and especially Sudan. The existence of black chattel slavery in Mauritania resonates strongly with Americans.[8] The controversy surrounding the redemption, or buying back, of slaves in Sudan has gained even greater public interest. Thousands of U.S. schoolchildren have been involved in fund-raising to support redemption, yet UNICEF and other organizations have condemned it. For the average North American or European, slavery, as presented in the media, is a shocking remnant of the nineteenth-century form, caught up in modern geopolitics. The government of Mauritania actively promotes this perception.

In its ongoing public relations campaign to divert attention from the chattel slavery that continues in Mauritania, the government there established a National Committee for the Struggle against the Vestiges of Slavery in the late 1980s. This "independent" committee was cleverly named, defining the problem from the outset as one of "vestiges," mere pockets of an unfortunately surviving bad practice. The reality in Mauritania is rather different. Reliable information is chronically lacking, but estimates of the proportion of the population in slavery range as high as 20 percent.[9] In contrast, the government says there is no slavery at all, since, given the most recent abolition of slavery there in 1980, slavery was legally declared to have ceased to exist.

So where does this leave the slaves of Mauritania and Sudan? In fact, their situations are fundamentally different from one another in spite of having a number of common attributes. In both countries, Arabs (Berbers, or "white Moors"), tend to be the ones enslaving people, who are perceived to be "African," or non-Arab. But it is important to remember that slavery is both a process and a state of being. The use of slaves is very similar in these two countries, but the process of enslavement used in each is radically different. In Mauritania, generations of *abeed* (African slaves) have served white Moor families. The process of enslavement was accomplished long ago, and the concern of the elite is to maintain their own dominance. The stability of this institution in Mauritania means that it is marked by less tension and longer-term relationships. In Sudan, slavery had, in fact, all but disappeared by the time of World War II, only to start again with the civil war.[10] The issue today is one of increased and ongoing enslavement as a strategy within that war.

The civil war in Sudan between the Muslim North and the Christian and Animist South (particularly the Nuer and Dinka peoples) began in 1955, a year before the country gained its independence. A peace accord in the early 1970s led to a ten-year cessation in fighting but collapsed in 1983. In the current, second, round of the civil war, slavery emerged as a weapon used by northern militias against southern villages. It was a new factor in the war but also the revival of one of the most ancient processes of enslavement. In assaults on "enemy" villages, government-supported militias attack and kill people, destroy crops, take livestock, and capture and enslave some of the inhabitants. Like other civil conflicts, this one has degenerated into a war of terror and attrition against the civilian population; rape, torture, and random brutality are commonplace. Yet except for the automatic weapons, it is little different from the warfare practiced for much of human history: one group drives another from land while enslaving some of the enemy to help defray the costs of mounting an attack. The enslavement of captives helps to recoup the cost of the war effort. This is not the shadow economy: it is a war economy.

Nor is the process of ransoming slaves captured in battle anything new. It actually has a very long history. Long before there was slavery in the United States, slaves were being redeemed. In Greece, Rome, and other ancient societies, slaves were sometimes purchased from their owners and freed. During the Crusades, enslavement and ransom were central components of war finances and strategy. The first organizations that can be thought of as charities were set up in the Middle Ages to purchase the freedom of Europeans captured and enslaved by North African and Middle Eastern pirates and slave raiders. Indeed, a phrase in the U.S. "Marines' Hymn" — "to the shores of Tripoli" — refers to an early-nineteenth-century raid on these Barbary pirates to stop their slave raiding and ransoming of Europeans and Americans. Frederick Douglass, the famous nineteenth-century abolitionist and escaped slave, was himself redeemed after supporters of slavery mounted a series of attempts at kidnapping him. The redeeming or ransoming of slaves probably goes back to the very beginnings of human slavery, which is to say to the very beginnings of written human history.

Redemption, the simple economic exchange of money for the freedom of a slave, has to be seen within its cultural context. Before slavery was illegal in most countries, redemption was an act of charity and itself perfectly legal. Many cultures have a tradition of redemption, including northern African societies such as Sudan. Today, however, within the context of the general illegality of slavery, the buying of slaves, even in order to free them, is seen by many people as complicity in a crime. The complexity of the civil war and the preexisting role of slave trading in Sudanese society are often overlooked. Redemption is presented as a moral imperative by some, while others see it as fuel added to the fire of further enslavement.

What is new is the way the redemption drama is being played out on a global stage. While redemption can go on around the world wherever slavery exists, it came to the attention of most Americans when groups like Christian Solidarity International began to buy back slaves in Sudan. Slave raiding in Sudan was part of the government's strategy to destroy the resistance of the southern groups fighting for independence. Slavery existed for hundreds of years in Sudan, almost disappeared in the twentieth century, but was reestablished as an act of terror in the civil war there. Controversy arose when European and American groups began to buy back slaves in 1995. Some international agencies expressed the criticism that buying back slaves would create an expanding market for slaves, feed resources to the slaveholders, lead to fraud in the process, and ultimately not end slavery.

Not long after these criticisms emerged, I spoke with a man from southern Sudan who answered them in this way: "Of course we understand that the money paid to buy back our relatives may go to buy arms to be used against us in the future, but when it is your family, your children at stake, you pay." Likewise, a man involved in redemption pointed out to me that there may have been fraud (the "buying back" of people who had never been enslaved), but he asserted that "it is better to buy back some people who have never been slaves than to fail to rescue the many who are suffering in slavery."[11] On the question of whether redemption in Sudan has brought a greater risk of slave raids, there is insufficient evidence to make a clear judgment.

The process of redemption must also be seen in its cultural context. The civil war has been marked by recurrent truces between the Dinka and the Baggara tribesmen who make up the majority of the militia, truces that have provided the opportunity to recover, usually at a price, family members as well as livestock. Equally, the Nuer and Dinka tribes of southern Sudan, while now allied against the Muslim North, have long been in conflict that includes raiding between the two tribes. In early October 1999 their leaders met to discuss "the return of women, children, and cattle captured in raids or abducted during the years of hostility between the tribes."[12] The fact that tribes who were victims of raids have themselves raided other tribes has rarely been mentioned in the Western press.

If there is good news about the controversy over redemption in Sudan, it is that the civil war seems to have ended and public attention has transferred to the atrocities in the Darfur region. The U.S. government had become involved and exerted significant pressure on the northern government to end the raids and come to an agreement with the southern provisional government. However, the hoped-for end to the need for redemption in Sudan will not resolve the questions that surround redemption. But this change may allow us to enlarge the discussion to include how redemption fits into antislavery work around the world.

In India, for example, redemption is actually illegal. As described earlier, in that country the primary form of slavery is debt bondage, and the law that frees those in bondage forbids repaying their "debts" to bring about their freedom. The reason is that, since these debts were established and manipulated illegally in the first place, they have no standing. Further there is a resistance to "rewarding" any slaveholder. Since slavery itself is universally illegal, slaveholders should no more be recompensed for giving up slaves than burglars should be paid to return their stolen goods. That said, in India there are situations where, primarily because the police are slow to respond to the crime of slavery, redemption is the only immediate and effective way to remove a person from danger.

The lesson to be drawn from these examples is this: redeeming slaves has a role in the antislavery movement, but only when other actions have failed or are impossible. In one way, it is the lesser of several evils. The greatest evil is enslavement. Paying a slaveholder or a middleman to free a slave is regrettable, since freedom is a right and shouldn't have to be purchased. Yet when situations exist where the authorities will not take action, where the opportunity for freedom is available only through redemption, and where enslaved people are suffering and threatened, then redemption may be the only immediate answer. A good case can be made both for and against redemption; a key criterion has to be that it be used *only* when it won't make things worse. Redemption is a tactic in an overall effort against slavery, one to be used when other actions won't serve.

Meanwhile we have to expect the emergence of war slavery and redemption in other countries. Most Western observers have attempted to analyze the situation in Sudan as if it had a semblance of stability. It does not. War is highly dynamic, and a civil war that involves a large proportion of the noncombatant population — and that is acted out through guerrilla conflict in fluid, permeable, and rapidly changing areas of military control — is especially so. Any such war encourages clandestine economic trade across military lines. It is a straightforward way to make high profits, and as such may be both a military tactic and an example of private enterprise. The negotiation of the wilder fringes near the "front" — the crossing of no-man's-land and the delivery of scarce or valuable supplies to the other side — is dangerous but potentially enriching. Recently, it has served both combatants and freebooters in Bosnia and Kosovo, including those trafficking in people. It would be surprising if the traffic in people across the front lines in southern Sudan had not attracted economic mercenaries.

Layered over this typical war economy are other international economic interests. China, Malaysia, and Canada's Talisman Energy Corporation are major participants in Sudan's Greater Nile Oil Project controlling 12.5 million acres of land. The completion of a thousand-mile pipeline in June 1999 was a tremendous boost to the government's finances. At the same time that the first shipment of six hundred thousand barrels of oil left Port Sudan in September 1999, twenty Russian tanks were being unloaded there. The projected oil revenue approximately equals the $1 million per day the government is spending on the civil war.[13]

Other international players are drawn in by the fact that the trafficked commodity in Sudan is people. In September 1999, the U.S. secretary of state, Madeline Albright, toured the region and strongly supported the peace initiative based on self-determination for the south. From European and North American charity organizations come noncommercial kinds of foreign investment in this underdeveloped country. Some of these organizations invest in redeeming slaves. Acknowledging their genuine and heartfelt motivation, we can still note that their return on this investment is threefold: the good feeling generated by having freed slaves; the public relations and motivational power gained by reporting these redemptions; and, for some groups, reclamation of a set of pawns in the global chess game being played out between Christian and Muslim fundamentalists.[14] Additionally, some organizations concerned with freeing slaves but not with religious conflict are themselves attacked by the Nation of Islam (or Black Muslims) for being a tool of white Christian imperialists.

In many ways, both the strategy of taking slaves by the government-backed militias and the *strategy* of redemption practiced by Western organizations are wrong. War slavery will ultimately backfire on the

Sudanese government, bringing international attention and condemnation, which will increase pressure for the recognition of an independent southern ethnic homeland. For Western charities, redemption as a strategy is self-defeating as long as the unregulated war economy stays in place, for supply and demand are at their most fluid and uncontrolled in times of conflict. Buying back slaves does increase the possibility of fraud, of increased prices, and of dissension being sown among the international agencies who should be working together to resolve the conflict. But as a *tactic* in a struggle for power, and for ideological and religious supremacy, slavery and its redemption have alternately served all the combatants. Redemption may drive up the price of slaves, but it also frees some slaves and returns them to their families. For the southern Sudanese, this is the point that matters, and they have little patience with Western agencies that would leave people in slavery in the north when the funds for redemption are available.

The civil war in Sudan, like the ongoing civil war in Burma, has created a context in which slavery is an extension of military operations. In both cases breakaway ethnic groups are captured and used as forced labor. In both countries Western investors are allied with ruling regimes for mineral extraction. Unlike in Burma, in Sudan the Western aid agencies are able to operate in rebel-held territory and draw attention to government-supported slavery. For the southern Sudanese the cultural resonance of slavery in Western countries, especially of black slavery in the United States, is a powerful weapon in their fight for international recognition. It is a weapon they need in the face of international disinterest. The head of the United Nations' relief effort in southern Sudan, Dr. Sharad Sapra, bemoaned the lack of public interest in the region, but said, "It is not something exceptional to Sudan. . . . Look around you. It is the same story whether you are talking about the refugee problem, East Timor, or any type of emergency situation."[15]

Redemption will not end slavery in Sudan, nor will stopping the redemption movement. To end slavery you must stop the civil war and resolve at least some of the political issues that underpin it. That would be difficult even if the UN or the major Western powers were motivated to intervene. A peacekeeping force or significant international sanctions on weaponry would also help, but these also seem unlikely. In early 1999 a consortium of agencies, including Amnesty International, suggested that Sudan needs five things: a UN special representative; a UN Security Council embargo on arms; adequate humanitarian aid to end widespread starvation and suffering; a supported and continuous peace process; and, especially, "a monitored cease-fire covering all areas and including all parties — and for a long enough period to create confidence in peace negotiations," which is now in place.[16] Perhaps if the matter concerned only slave trading, Western countries might be willing to invest in its suppression. But the tangled affairs of Sudan defy attempts to simplify its war, its slavery, or its drama of redemption.

Within the global reality of slavery, the situation in Sudan accounts for only the tiniest fraction of today's slaves yet possibly garners the largest portion of the world's media interest in slavery. The slavery there does follow global trends: the slaves are relatively inexpensive when compared with other slaves around the world. Their enslavement is unlikely to be permanent; and given the reports of extreme brutality suffered by slaves in Sudan, we can assume their disposability. They do differ from other slaves around the world, in that their struggle has become emblematic of other struggles much wider than the Sudanese civil war. Physically, they are captured, enslaved, bought, and sold. Symbolically, they are pawns in two distinct but interrelated conflicts. One is the struggle between some Christian and Muslim fundamentalists who see a threat in each other. The second struggle is one that echoes the historical fight between the gradualists and the proponents of direct action in the abolitionist movement of the nineteenth century. While UNICEF supports the cautious, diplomatic approach normally used by the United Nations, other groups condemn any sort of hesitation when slaves might be freed. But the concentration on this controversy and the resultant media attention on Sudan indicate a faulty viewpoint on slavery. This view is best characterized as "not being able to see the forest for the trees." In spite of the fact that slavery is a pervasive social constant, our understanding of it is episodic and localized. While we must respond to the situation in Sudan, we must also expand our response to the global reality of slavery. Until we work to understand slavery as a global phenomenon with distinct characteristics, our response, both intellectually and practically, will be partial, ill formed, and ineffective.

Confronting Slavery

But how do we effectively address global slavery? Unfortunately the answer to that question is not clear. Governments, activists (with the exception of Free the Slaves and Anti-Slavery International), and academics have barely begun to take up the question of contemporary slavery, and little coherent policy has been developed. The following general and tentative viewpoints are based on my own research. First, globalization has both a positive and negative effect on slavery. The negative effect arises from the downward pressure on wage rates and prices engendered by increased competition and the portability of capital across borders. Everyone is aware of the relocation of jobs from the First World to the Third. What is less known is that the suppliers of raw materials (the economic area where enslavement is more likely) in the developing world feel the same pressure and sometimes use slavery as a way to reduce labor costs. This is true of some who supply raw materials such as grain, cotton, stone, and gravel or simple bricks. In addition, large-scale capital flows that go from foreign investors to countries lacking effective internal regulatory systems have also been known to increase corruption within political systems, one of the key factors that makes slavery possible. A third point relating to global trading patterns is that, on the whole, if businesses are able to seek the highest returns with little or no ethical restraints, slavery is a possible by-product.

On the other hand, one cultural by-product of globalization is the light thrown on exploitation. The most powerful prophylactic against slavery is education, and globalization is nothing if not a mass transfer of information. Further, within the past forty years there has emerged a global consciousness of, and a relative consensus on, human rights. While many states and individuals find some human rights to be debatable, the right not to be enslaved, along with prohibitions against murder and torture, achieves the highest level of general recognition. This consensus has been codified into several international instruments, such as the Universal Declaration of Human Rights. And while these instruments have few teeth, they are an important beginning.

More pragmatically, another outcome of this consensus is the move toward internationally recognized standards regulating trade. Here I am thinking of, for example, the social accountability standard that prohibits child labor (SA8000), established by the organization Social Accountability International. Independent auditing is required before a business is awarded SA8000 certification. Eight years after the establishment of the SA8000 standard, the European Union mandated that any company doing business within its borders must hold the certification. Obviously companies cannot be forced to submit to inspection and auditing, but the pressure becomes significant if access to markets depends on meeting standards. The application of standards concerning slave labor or child labor is in its infancy, but it represents an important regulatory and economic mechanism with global implications applied to the demand side of the equation.

This link between labor conditions and the regulation of trade is also apparent in the discussions begun within the World Trade Organization about a vision of a deregulated future that includes free workers as well as free trade. Any "social clause" to the overarching General Agreement on Tariffs and Trade (GATT) is controversial, since some developing economies consider such regulation to be prejudicial to their competitiveness. But the sign of hope is that the issue is now on the agenda, which was definitely not the case when GATT was first negotiated. The United Nations is also paying more attention to questions of enslavement. The recent International Labor Organization resolution, titled C182 Worst Forms of Child Labor Convention, 1999 (which includes child slavery), was the first ILO Convention to be passed unanimously, and for that reason it is moving toward rapid ratification.[17] Meanwhile the UN itself has convened meetings to develop a new Convention against trafficking in people (the modern slave trade), and the United Nations Institute of Criminological Research has launched a global study of human trafficking. All this movement is in the right direction, but concerns about contemporary slavery have yet to penetrate to the powerful center of the UN. For example, the Security Council mandated inspectors to search out biological and chemical weapons in Iraq, but it has yet to take up the question of slavery or to mandate inspection teams to search out slavery. There is no lack of UN Conventions and resolutions (some dating back to the League of Nations) calling on all member states to take all possible steps to end slavery, but consideration of the issue is sidelined to a working group whose work receives little notice.

The challenge for individual countries is to bring their legal systems up-to-date with reference to slavery. Some countries have yet to pass basic legislation banning forms of slavery that are not based on legal ownership of people. Nepal, for example, banned slavery as ownership of one person by another in 1926 but only moved to legislate against the debt bondage that has traditionally been part of that country's rural economy in 2000. In many countries the nineteenth-century laws against slavery define it in such a way that these laws are difficult to enforce against slavery's newly evolved forms. And even if the laws are updated, law enforcement personnel must be educated to recognize slavery. When the Comité Contre l'Esclavage Moderne began its work in Paris in the early 1990s, they were told by police officials that, as slavery no longer existed, the cases they were bringing would have to be charged under laws concerning unlawful detention or bad working conditions. Today this group and the police cooperate effectively, but activist groups around the world report similar confusion and lack of understanding. Given that human trafficking, in particular, is increasing and is a transnational crime, coordination of national law enforcement agencies would be an obvious response. The international task forces set up to address drug trafficking must be matched by well-funded slavery task forces.

This is only a partial list of what must be done to address global slavery, and one that must be augmented by an extensive public awareness campaign and the bolstering of those charitable and non-governmental organizations that address slavery. But even if all these suggestions were acted upon, there would still be the enormous task of rehabilitation to confront. The United States is still suffering from a failure to link social and economic rehabilitation to its mass emancipation of 1865. Around the world, liberation without rehabilitation has been shown to be ineffectual and often temporary. Surprisingly, this is an area of profound ignorance. With the exception of a handful of activists in the developing world, no one has fully studied the rehabilitative needs of freed slaves, nor has there been an international exchange of experience in this area. Academic disciplines and networks of activists focus on the rehabilitation of torture victims or children caught up in armed conflict, but no such discipline explores the psychological, medical, social, or training needs of ex-slaves. With something like 27 million slaves in the world, this is an area crying out for the attention of academics and cooperation between practitioners.

Overall the need is great, but the problem of slavery should not be as daunting as the numbers suggest. Within the world economy, the value of slave labor is actually very small. No one can argue today that stopping slavery would disrupt any economy, as was the case with the American South in the 1850s. Perhaps slavery has failed to generate a coordinated international response because its economic value (or threat to existing labor) is so small.

Of course, human beings may always find new ways to enslave others, but I believe there is reason for optimism in the fight against slavery. This is the first generation to have developed a general consensus against slavery, and the first generation that has the opportunity to develop global mechanisms to root out and eradicate slavery. It may be that slavery can never be permanently eradicated, but, like many infectious diseases, it might be generally suppressed and watchfully controlled as new forms emerge. Such mechanisms would be one of the best imaginable legacies of our generation.

CHAPTER 7

Human Trafficking

A Worldwide Concern

What Is Human Trafficking?

Human trafficking is the modern term for a phenomenon — that of forcing and transporting people into slavery — which has been a part of civilization since the beginning of human history. Slavery and the traffic in slaves have continued into the present day. Today, however, a narrow focus on trafficking for sexual exploitation has obscured the larger problem. Sometimes synonymous with the slave trade, at other times the word *trafficking* has been used only to describe transporting and forcing women into prostitution. At the end of the nineteenth century, there was significant official concern in Europe and North America over the white slave trade (again primarily concerned with the enslavement of white women for prostitution), and much less concern over the continuing enslavement and trafficking of other ethnic groups. One of the first international instruments concerning human trafficking grew out of this concern.[1]

After World War II, another Convention was adopted to confront this trafficking in persons that was linked to prostitution. In the 1949 United Nations Convention for the Suppression of the Traffic in Persons and of the Exploitation of the Prostitution of Others, it was agreed to "punish any person who, to gratify the passions of another: (1) Procures, entices or leads away, for the purposes of prostitution, another person, even with the consent of that person; (2) Exploits the prostitution of another person, even with the consent of that person." This Convention also set out ways for countries to cooperate in the suppression of trafficking and to protect immigrants and migrants in transit. To help prevent trafficking, the Convention called for countries "to arrange for appropriate publicity warning the public of the dangers of the . . . traffic [in persons]."[2]

These were important efforts, but they failed to confront the traffic in persons that was not linked to prostitution; at the same time, the social and legal response to prostitution in many countries was ambivalent. Historically, there has been a reluctance to deal with prostitution within the legal discourse on forced labor, the slave trade, or enslavement. As noted in chapter 3, the past willingness to define most prostitution as consensual, the stigmatization of prostitutes, and the ambivalence of male-directed law enforcement concerning prostitution meant that trafficking for prostitution was separated from "real" slavery and tolerated in many countries. Some international instruments — for example, the 1910 White Slavery Convention — attempted to separate unacceptable forms of forced prostitution (especially of white women) and forms of prostitution that lawmakers considered normal, acceptable, or inevitable. This separation, based on the differential and discriminatory treatment of women and certain ethnic groups, created distinctions that obscured the basic crime of trafficking in persons. In the same period that organizations like the League of Nations were concentrating on the sale of persons into prostitution, literally millions of people were being sold to do other forms of work. In Central Africa millions were forced into working in construction and the rubber trade. In the Americas, trafficked Chinese coolie labor was exploited in agriculture, construction, and a large variety of other economic activities. And the ancient trans-Saharan slave route across the Red Sea and Persian Gulf into Arabia remained active throughout the nineteenth and into the twentieth century.

In the second half of the twentieth century, slavery and trafficking in persons dramatically increased. As noted earlier, the population explosion following World War II raised the global population from 2 billion to 6 billion. Most of that growth has taken place in the developing world. At the same time, far-reaching changes in national economies and political systems are enriching some parts of the world population but impoverishing others. When large numbers of impoverished people come under the influence of corrupt government, particularly corrupt local law enforcement, they cannot protect themselves against enslavement and trafficking. Other factors also push the poor into being trafficked. Civil wars, ethnic violence, and invasion create millions of refugees whose precarious situations make them susceptible to being enslaved. Those whose poverty is desperate may find that the false promise of a better life draws them into the control of criminals, who then enslave and traffic them. At the same time, new technologies aid criminals involved in human trafficking. Better and more varied transport, increased methods of secure communications, the increased permeability of borders since the end of the cold war, and the confusion and turmoil in the wake of civil conflicts, all have helped fuel criminal involvement in trafficking. By the end of the twentieth century, it was clear that new and more encompassing international laws were needed to address trafficking in persons.

To clarify the crime of trafficking in persons and to better meet the significant increase in trafficking globally, the United Nations put forward the Convention on Transnational Organized Crime, along with its Protocol to Prevent, Suppress and Punish Trafficking in Persons, Especially Women and Children, also known as the Anti-Trafficking Protocol, in 2000.[3] It was recognized that a transnational crime, such as trafficking in persons, required a transnational solution, and that globalization and new technologies had created new opportunities for criminal organizations, just as they had for legitimate businesses (as discussed in chapter 6).

One of the key aims of the Convention and the Protocol to Prevent, Suppress and Punish Trafficking in Persons, Especially Women and Children is to standardize terminology, laws, and practices. This standardization aims to resolve many of the problems raised in chapter 3, the problems arising from the more than three hundred laws and agreements that have been written concerning, first, the slave trade, then trafficking, and which have defined the crime of human trafficking in different ways. For the first time the international community, in the Protocol, has an *agreed-upon standard definition* of trafficking in persons.

Defining Trafficking in Persons

The Protocol to Prevent, Suppress and Punish Trafficking in Persons, Especially Women and Children defines trafficking in persons in this way:

Trafficking in persons is

- the action of: recruitment, transportation, transfer, harboring, or receipt of persons
- by means of: the threat or use of force, coercion, abduction, fraud, deception, abuse of power or vulnerability, or giving payments or benefits to a person in control of the victim

- for the purposes of: exploitation, which includes exploiting the prostitution of others, sexual exploitation, forced labor, slavery or similar practices, and the removal of organs. (Protocol Art. 3.a)

Consent of the victim is irrelevant where illicit means are established, but criminal law defences are preserved. (Protocol Art. 3.b)

The definition is broken down into three lists of elements: criminal acts, the means used to commit those acts, and the forms of exploitation. This definition of trafficking is a key element of the Protocol. Representing the first clear definition at the international level, the definition should greatly assist in the fight against human trafficking. Adopting the Convention will help ensure that legislative and administrative measures are consistent from country to country, and it will help provide a common basis for investigation and prosecution.

While the new definition is crucial to an international response to trafficking in persons, it is important to remember that it is not an exhaustive definition, and that the Convention and Protocols are limited in scope. The Protocol is intended to "prevent and combat" trafficking in persons and facilitate international cooperation against such trafficking.[4] It applies to the "prevention, investigation and prosecution" of protocol offenses, but only where these are "transnational in nature" and involve an "organized criminal group," as those terms are defined by the Convention.[5] The Convention, the Protocol, and the definition of trafficking in persons that they put forward are essential to the fight against this crime, but they are not, and should not be, the only tools available. All countries must attack this problem from a criminological standpoint and be willing to address trafficking in any and every form it takes. Some trafficking in persons does not cross national borders; at other times, it is undertaken by individual criminals who are not part of an organized criminal group. National laws, law enforcement strategies, and services to victims must respond to all forms of this crime, from small-scale and local trafficking to large-scale transnational trafficking.

Trafficking is often only one of the crimes committed against trafficked persons. Often they are subjected to threats, to physical and sexual violence, or to being locked up; their passports are confiscated; they are forced to work without any payment; or they are forced to undergo abortions. Further, in a number of cases, corrupt state officials are involved in trafficking. These acts constitute criminal offenses in most countries, and this could be invoked to address certain elements of the full range of crimes. This could be useful in countries where trafficking does not yet constitute a distinct criminal offense. It could also be useful in countries where penalties for trafficking do not sufficiently reflect the nature of the crime and do not have any deterrent effect, or in cases where the existing evidence is not sufficient to prosecute the suspect for trafficking, but which may be sufficient to prosecute such cases as bodily injury or rape. It is important to stress, however, that prosecution for such offenses should not replace prosecution for trafficking.

For example, in a case before the Provincial Court of Vienna, a trafficker was sentenced to eight years imprisonment. The court found him guilty not only of trafficking but also of other criminal offenses, including bodily injury, rape, forced abortion, forgery of documents, and damage to property. The witness statements by the victims contributed to the result of the proceedings. The two trafficked women had been expelled first, but then had traveled back to Austria in order to testify at the main hearing. This was made possible by the cooperation of the court and the involved victim-support agencies in Austria and the country of origin.[6]

To ensure that the penalties applied reflect the gravity of the harm inflicted upon the trafficked person, countries should, in addition to prosecuting traffickers for the offense of trafficking in human beings, invoke other applicable provisions of criminal law. Such offenses include, but are not limited to, the following: slavery; slavery-like practices; involuntary servitude; forced or compulsory labor; debt bondage; forced marriage; forced abortion; forced pregnancy; torture; cruel, inhuman, or degrading treatment; rape; sexual assault; bodily injury; murder; kidnapping; unlawful confinement; labor exploitation; withholding of identity papers; and corruption.[7]

The Issue of Consent

One of the key issues in developing a response to trafficking has been the issue of whether the victim *consented* to being smuggled or trafficked. The language of the Anti-Trafficking Protocol on the question of consent represents a compromise. In many trafficking cases, there is initial consent or cooperation between victims and traffickers, followed later by more coercive, abusive, and exploitive circumstances. Some countries wanted to make any consent of the victim completely irrelevant to ensure that the victim's initial consent was not used by traffickers as a defense to charges arising from later exploitation not consented to by the victim. Other states felt that some element of consent was needed to limit the scope of the offense, to distinguish trafficking from legitimate activities, and for constitutional reasons. To resolve the issue, the definition clarifies that consent becomes irrelevant whenever any of the means of trafficking have been used. Consent of the victim could still be a defense in domestic law, but as soon as such things as threats, coercion, or the use of force are established, these would nullify any consent and overcome a defense based on victim consent.

The issue of consent is complex in that both consent and coercion take many forms. Drawing on just two cases uncovered in Italy, it is possible to see some of the variations.[8] Angela S. left her farming village in Moldova when she was promised a job as a waitress in Italy. Seeking a way to earn money to support her child and a way to escape an alcoholic husband, she agreed, when a relative referred her, to meet with a "recruiter," a woman who then arranged her transport to Istanbul. Once she was in Turkey, away from her family and friends, her documents were taken from her and she was sold to the first of a series of Albanian pimps. Over the next year she was resold several times, forced into prostitution, paid nothing, and brutally beaten. Ultimately she was smuggled into Italy, where she was picked up by the police and handed over to a non-governmental organization providing support. Angela's story is common in that she did consent to be taken to Italy for a job as a waitress. Normally such a false offer includes the promise of a valid work and residency permits. Sometimes the victim agrees to being smuggled into a country illegally in order to find work. What the victim clearly does not consent to is the brutal exploitation; nor is it possible under international law to consent to being tortured and abused in this way.

In a second example, a young woman from Nigeria was brought by a "recruiter" to Italy. This young woman understood that she would be a prostitute and had consented to being transported and to working as a prostitute. However, on arrival she found that she was required to repay an enormous sum. In addition, following Nigerian traditional "magical" practice, a sachet of her blood, hair, and nail clippings was assembled that gave traffickers extreme psychological power over her. Italian police report that freed Nigerian women often refuse to give statements until their "magical" sachets are recovered. While some Nigerian prostitutes are able to purchase their freedom, others fall into enslavement, are paid nothing, and are regularly brutalized.

It is not just the trafficking into prostitution that leads from consent to enslavement. Italy has also had a number of cases of men recruited from Romania to work in construction who consented to what they believed were legitimate temporary jobs, only to find themselves locked up at the work site, paid nothing, and physically abused.

Trafficking in Persons and Smuggling of Migrants

Many victims of trafficking begin their journey by consenting to be smuggled from one country to another. Because of this, the difference between smuggling and trafficking in persons has been an area of some confusion. Smuggling and trafficking both involve moving human beings for profit, but in smuggling the relationship between migrants and offenders (the smugglers) usually ends on arrival in the destination country. The criminal's profit is derived only from the process of smuggling the migrant. In cases of trafficking, some subsequent exploitation for profit, such as coerced labor or sexual exploitation, is also involved.

In order to deal with the smuggling of migrants, the United Nations Convention against Transnational Organized Crime also included the Protocol against the Smuggling of Migrants by Land, Sea and Air. The purpose of this Protocol is "to prevent and combat the smuggling of migrants as well as promote cooperation among States Parties, while protecting the rights of smuggled victims." The Protocol defines smuggling in this way: "procurement of illegal entry into a State of which the person is not a national or a permanent resident to obtain direct or indirect financial or other material benefit."[9] By this definition, many of the activities of traffickers in persons (such as the use of fraudulent travel documents) are also "smuggling," but trafficking goes beyond simply the "procurement of illegal entry into a State." Put another way, trafficking in persons is smuggling *plus* coercion or deception at the beginning of the process and exploitation at the end. Law enforcement officers encountering cases in progress often will not know whether smuggling or trafficking is occurring and will have to rely on measures against smuggling until the additional elements of trafficking are discovered. For that reason it is important for law enforcement personnel working in trafficking to be familiar with both instruments. That smuggling and trafficking in persons entail some of the same activities is demonstrated by the fact that some provisions of the two Protocols, concerning border controls and travel documents, are the same.

This definition, and the definition of trafficking in persons, also recognizes that, while victims of trafficking in persons should be treated as victims of criminal activity, migrants who are not exploited are not necessarily victims of crime. In the Protocol against the Smuggling of Migrants by Land, Sea and Air, some protection and support for migrants is provided, but these provisions are not as extensive as those for victims of trafficking in persons.

Crimes Linked to Trafficking in Persons

The borders between smuggling and trafficking are sometimes blurred.[10] Often both smuggled and trafficked individuals leave a country of origin willingly, though possibly under different pretenses. They may be exposed to similar cases of danger or discomfort during long journeys. However, upon arriving in the destination country, smuggled individuals are usually free to apply for asylum or look for work in the informal sector. Trafficked persons are, upon arrival, put in debt bondage or forced into slavery-like practices in the sex or labor markets. Exploitation usually occurs over a long period of time, during which interdependency may develop between the trafficked persons and the organized crime groups that traffic them. This interdependency often leads to further networking, extended exploitation, and possible recruitment for criminal purposes.

One can view the trafficking of human beings as a process rather than a single offense. It begins with the abduction or recruitment of a person and continues with the transportation and entry of the individual into another country.[11] This is followed by the exploitation phase, during which the victim is forced into sexual or labor servitude. A further phase may occur, which involves not the victim, but rather the offender. Depending upon the size and sophistication of the trafficking operation, the criminal or criminal organization may find it necessary to launder the criminal proceeds. Traffickers may commit other criminal offenses as well, such as the smuggling of weapons or drugs, in direct furtherance of the human trafficking activity. Examples of these crimes are victim procurement and violence associated with maintaining control over them. Other crimes, such as money laundering and tax evasion, are secondary and occur as a result of the trafficking activity.

A typology can be created to further explain the nature of these offenses related to the trafficking process. The perpetration of crimes can be characterized according to the victim (the individual victim or the country) or the phase of the trafficking process: recruitment, transportation of and illegal border-crossing by the trafficked person, the exploitation phase, or the subsequent phase of profit laundering. The numbers and types of offenses are often contingent upon the sophistication of the smuggling and trafficking operation and the criminal groups involved. These operations can be as simple as the smuggling and subsequent trafficking of an individual by another individual over a border without proper documentation — by transport vehicle or foot — or sophisticated operations moving large numbers of persons, using forged documents

TABLE 3. Crimes Related to Trafficking in Human Beings

Recruitment of Victim	Transportation of, or Entry with, Victim	Exploitation of Victim*	Disposition of Criminal Proceeds
Document forgery	Document forgery	*Unlawful coercion*	Money laundering
Fraudulent promises	Immigration law abuse	*Threat*	Tax evasion
Kidnapping	Corruption of officials	*Extortion*	Corruption of officials
	Damage to property	*False imprisonment*	
	Withholding of documents	*Kidnapping*	
		Procurement	
		Theft of documents	
		Sexual assault	
		Aggravated assault	
		Rape	
		Murder	
		Forced abortion	
		Torture	

Italics indicate that the offenses are perpetrated against the individual victim.

* In addition to violations of legal codes, Okawa has listed some of the symptoms experienced by victims of torture and of human trafficking: post-traumatic stress disorder, severe depression, overwhelming shame, a devastated sense of self, dissociation, loss of sense of safety, chronic fear, anxiety, phobias, and difficulty talking about rape. She points out that trafficked persons are subjected to many types of torture (physical, social, psychological, and sexual) and deprivation (hygienic, nutritional, health, sleep, and sensory). Judy Okawa, "Impact of Trafficking Offenses on the Individual," Program for Survivors of Torture and Severe Trauma, Center for Multicultural Human Services, January 2001 conference materials; noted in Ann Jordan, "Trafficking in Human Beings: The Slavery that Surrounds Us," International Human Rights Law Group, August 2001, http://uninfo.state.gov/journals/itgic/0801/ijge/gj05.htm.

and generating huge profits that must subsequently be laundered. Trafficking may involve offenses against the state, such as abuse of immigration laws, document forgery, corruption of government officials, money laundering, and tax evasion. Other violations are directed against the victims: unlawful coercion or threat, extortion, aggravated assault, sexual assault, rape, or even murder. Table 3 shows the various offenses perpetrated at different stages of the trafficking process and indicates whether the "victim" is the national government or the individual who has been trafficked.

Violence is seldom exercised during the recruitment phase, except in cases where victims have been kidnapped. During this stage, fraudulent promises are often made to secure the willingness of the victim to go with the kidnapper. It is during the transportation phase — and much more commonly during the exploitation phase in the destination country — that kidnappers are likely to use threats and violence against the victims. In cases of both labor and sexual exploitation, threats or actual violence are often used to maintain control and prevent the escape of the victim. Table 3 examines the offenses perpetrated by the traffickers to further the trafficking scheme. However, the networks that smuggle and traffic human beings, as well as the victims themselves, have been linked to other criminal activities.

Criminal groups have been known to make use of existing contacts, routes, corrupt government officials, and networks in order to expand their operations. A criminal organization may develop "horizontal interdependencies" by establishing connections among different activities.[12] The criminal organization is thus able to diversify and expand its markets. Intelligence sources at Interpol reveal that trafficking in human beings supplements more traditional criminal activities, such as drug trafficking, vehicle theft, trafficking in arms, and money laundering.[13] Traffickers have been linked to moneylending to repay debts, extortion for protection money, and physical violence. Furthermore, traffickers have been known to coerce their victims into prostitution (a criminal offense in some countries), drug selling, organized begging, and pocket picking.[14]

Trafficking in Persons: Understanding the Problem

THE DANGER OF POOR ESTIMATES

Accurate information about trafficking levels is difficult to obtain. Before the adoption of the Anti-Trafficking Protocol, there was no international definition to serve as the basis for research. The activity's covert nature makes gathering information from victims or offenders difficult — and even dangerous. Much of the hard information available is generated by specific cases. This information is useful for illustrating the nature of trafficking but may not be representative of trends or patterns. Even reliable estimates of worldwide trafficking are few. A global total of between seven hundred thousand and 4 million people trafficked each year has been suggested from a number of sources. There is little reason to think that this is an overestimate. The United States government estimates that up to fifty thousand women and children are illegally brought into the country and sold each year. The number of illegal migrants who entered the European Union in 2000 was estimated at five hundred thousand,

and a significant portion of the migrants were trafficked. The number of people illegally brought into and out of India and sold is also estimated in the tens of thousands. The International Organization for Migration suggests that, even in a small country like Kyrgyzstan, four thousand women may have been trafficked in 1999. Once again, what we do not know is much greater than what we do know, but the pattern is clear: trafficking in persons is extensive and growing.

Yet as with most crimes that affect public policy, there is a possibility that estimates will be emphasised or manipulated. Some non-governmental organizations may be tempted to inflate estimates when their aim is to push governments to take action. Because the definition of trafficking may vary, governments and organizations may be comparing different things when they discuss trafficking in persons. This fact underlines the importance of the common definition offered by the Protocol.

OBSTACLES TO RESEARCH ON TRAFFICKING IN PERSONS

As in the case of most criminal activities, conducting research on trafficking in persons is difficult. Effectively responding to trafficking requires a multistage process, yet at every stage of the process, we currently lack systematic research. However, there are opportunities for intervention at each stage, from the initial enticement by the recruiter in the source country, to the several stages of transporting a person through transit countries to a destination country, to the crossing of those borders, to the delivery of the trafficked person to an "employer," to their subsequent exploitation, and, possibly, to the point of contact with official agencies through investigation or outreach. Each step must be carefully understood if that intervention is to be effective.

The diversity of the offense of trafficking in persons means no single research strategy can always be appropriate. The research tools needed to gather data on trafficking women for sexual exploitation in Europe will not be the same as those needed to gather data on trafficking children for agricultural work in Africa. All forms of research on trafficking in persons are needed — from the broadest collection of information on crime trends and flows of trafficked people across borders, to the most highly focused research on the experiences of individuals who have been caught up in trafficking or who are involved in it in other ways. Around the world many research projects are beginning to address these needs, and although they explore many different examples of trafficking in persons, they confront similar obstacles to gathering meaningful information.

The following describes some of the most common obstacles.

- We lack a standard definition of trafficking in persons, one used within and between countries. This obstacle may be overcome through the ratification and implementation of the Anti-Trafficking Protocol. Working definitions for research can then be based upon the legal definition derived from the Protocol.

- The fact that trafficking in persons is a transnational crime means the data that must be collected and understood are spread across at least two, and often many more, countries. Likewise, the information needed to understand a single case of trafficking in persons might be in a number of languages. The nature of the information may also vary within a country, depending on whether that country serves as a point of origin, transit, or destination for a particular case of trafficking. The ultimate exploitative situations in which trafficked persons find themselves will also vary significantly and require different approaches in research. This obstacle points out the need for close cooperation and coordination between countries at several levels: in law enforcement, border control, victim services, and especially research.

- The covert nature of trafficking makes it difficult to get access to offenders and victims as information sources. Obviously criminals avoid any form of contact with officials or at least avoid sharing with them any information about their crime. To overcome this, researchers must establish good rapport with law enforcement personnel in order to discover what information they have compiled on the activities of offenders (without jeopardizing ongoing investigations). Victims of trafficking in persons are also often reluctant to give information to researchers. Commonly, in severe cases of trafficking and exploitation, offenders will attempt to convince victims that they have more to fear from police and other officials than they do from the trafficker. Once victims are liberated, researchers must convince them that their experiences and dignity will be respected before they will be likely to participate in research.

- For some victims of trafficking, the stigma of sexual exploitation or enslavement increases their reluctance to relate their experiences. Any incident of trafficking and enslavement can be a harrowing and

traumatizing experience, but the repeated sexual violation amounting to rape that characterizes forced prostitution causes tremendous psychological damage and requires intensive rebuilding of
self-esteem. For these victims, and for those who have been brutalized in other ways, special care is needed before they may be willing to share their experiences and participate in research. Indeed,
they may never reach a point of willingness.

- Intimidation of victims and witnesses is not uncommon in human
  trafficking. One form of control over trafficked persons is the
  threat to harm their family members in the country of origin. The
  often ambiguous legal and immigration status of victims increases
  their vulnerability to intimidation. The remedy to this situation is
  outside the control of researchers but is linked to a consistent and
  humane treatment of trafficking victims.

Each of these obstacles must be considered to be an element affecting
underreporting and, in terms of sampling, affecting both the researcher
and law enforcement. For example, the United States has estimated that,
of the up to fifty thousand women and children illegally transported into
and sold in the country each year, the cases of fewer than two hundred are
prosecuted. The disparity, the large "dark figure" between these two numbers, is a warning to any researcher who might base trafficking estimates
solely on the number of official cases.

Cultural sensitivity and gender sensitivity are also important when
dealing with cases of human trafficking. The stigmatization of prostitutes
and victims of sexual assault in most cultures probably leads to reluctance
to report and self-report and, hence, lowers the number of estimated
trafficking cases. In some countries this stigmatization may also affect one
cultural group (or one gender) to a different extent, suggesting false conclusions about the extent to which the various groups are trafficked.

CAUSES AND EFFECTS OF HUMAN TRAFFICKING

In any case of trafficking, there is a unique set of causes and effects. The
broad variation of trafficking in persons across regions and cultures
means that there can be no uniform answer to the question "What causes
trafficking?" That said, a number of commonalities exist. Root causes of
trafficking in persons include the greed of criminals, economic pressures,
political instability and transition, and social and cultural factors. Many

traffickers are involved in other transnational crimes as well. In part, criminal groups choose to traffic in persons because it is a high-profit and often low-risk venture; because people, unlike other "commodities," can be used repeatedly; and because trafficking in persons does not require a large capital investment.

Many trafficking victims fall prey because they seek a better life or enhanced economic opportunities. They are, therefore, vulnerable to false promises of good jobs and higher wages. Political instability, militarism, civil unrest, internal armed conflict, and natural disasters may result in an increase in trafficking. The destabilization and displacement of populations increase their vulnerability to exploitation and abuse through trafficking and forced labor. War and civil strife may lead to massive displacements of populations, leaving orphans and street children extremely vulnerable to trafficking.

In some countries, social or cultural practices contribute to trafficking: for example, the devaluation of women and girls in society, and the practice of entrusting poor children to more affluent friends or relatives. Some parents sell their children not just for the money but also in the hope that the children will be escaping a situation of poverty and will move to a place where they can have a better life and more opportunities. The fear of HIV and AIDS also influences those who sell victims into sexual exploitation, because children become more attractive to them and their customers due to the belief that the children are free from the disease.

At the macro level, I used statistical techniques to determine the factors that most strongly predict trafficking in persons from countries and to countries. This study concluded that the most significant factors predicting trafficking in persons in a country, given in descending order of their power to do so, are

- the level of a country's governmental corruption;
- the country's infant mortality rate;
- the proportion of the population below the age of fourteen;
- the level of the country's food production;
- the country's population density; and
- the amount of conflict and social unrest the country suffers.[15]

This statistical research confirms much of the common knowledge held by experts working on human trafficking around the world: this traffic is most likely to flow from poor countries suffering from instability and corruption. Each of these factors ("push" factors) exerts a powerful influence and can create the vulnerability in people that leads to being trafficked.

This statistical study also attempted to explain which factors influence people in their choice of destination country ("pull" factors) and to explain the relative permeability of a country's borders. Unfortunately, there is no way at this time to estimate the permeability of borders, though governmental corruption is one indicator of possible permeability, since corruption often plays a part in the opening of borders to traffickers. The opportunities perceived to exist in the destination country by trafficking victims while they are still being deceived in their home country can be linked to the availability of employment and to the demographic profile of the destination country. The demographic profile, for example, of the western European countries, is much older than that of the developing world, which can lead to a shortage of younger workers who might tend to take up low-skill jobs. A shortage of workers for low-skill jobs suggests a potential demand for immigrant workers willing to take such jobs.

However, the perception of such opportunity is often at variance with reality. Around the world, the stories told by recruiters to entice victims may have little relation to the actual situation in the destination country. Moreover, most of these factors, with the exception of governmental corruption, are negated when criminal involvement in trafficking leads to the coercion or enslavement of victims. When the potential, possibly smuggled, migrants lose their free will and become victims, their perception and pursuit of opportunity becomes moot. However, my statistical study found that pull factors were much weaker in predicting destination countries. Those that did emerge as significant were

- the proportion of the destination's country's male population over age sixty
- the level of governmental corruption
- the level of food production
- low infant mortality

For the most part, these are simply indicators of prosperity and stability, and they reflect the accepted knowledge that the traffic in persons flows from poorer to richer countries. From a trafficker's point of view, the perfect destination country would be a relatively rich country with just enough corruption to allow low-risk passage through its borders.

The Stages of Trafficking

Every case of trafficking is unique, but all share certain characteristics. At the most basic level are the common elements noted in the definition of trafficking given in the Anti-Trafficking Protocol: the action of transporting people by means of force or deception in order to control and exploit them. In can also be said that there are three underlying factors at work that foster trafficking: (1) within the origin countries, a large supply of victims is available for exploitation, (2) within the destination countries there seems to be an endless demand for the services of the victims, and (3) organized criminal networks have taken control of this economic supply-and-demand situation in order to traffic the victims and generate enormous profits for themselves.

What follows is an attempt to illuminate the stages of the trafficking process.

STAGE 1: THE CONTEXT OF VULNERABILITY

Those who have access to economic, social, and political power are not likely to be caught up as victims of human trafficking. Virtually all trafficked people have characteristics or circumstances that have made them particularly vulnerable to traffickers. Poverty and deprivation are important determinants. The desire for a better life, the need to escape conflict and oppression, the hope for a new start, all bring people into contact with traffickers. For some, relative powerlessness makes them vulnerable to immediate violence and kidnapping, but the person forcibly captured and trafficked is not the common victim. Traffickers understand that the cooperation of the victim improves the ease with which they can be trafficked.

In any event, it is not the most destitute and powerless that are trafficked. The ill, the elderly, the malnourished, the disabled, and the infirm are not sought out by traffickers. They are human commodities of insufficient value to bring high profits. Most usually, trafficking victims are young and healthy people from poor, but not necessarily the poorest, backgrounds. Often, trafficking victims have a level of education that seems incongruent with their enslavement. Research by Anne Kielland and Ibrahim Sanogo, discussed in chapter 1, has shown that children trafficked into domestic service in West Africa are more likely to come from families of average wealth in more affluent villages, rather than from the poorest families of the poorest villages.

Several factors might push a potential trafficking victim into contact with traffickers. Membership in an oppressed group, or a social category regularly discriminated against, may press a person to try their luck with a trafficking recruiter. Depending on the country and culture, being a member of a particular ethnic or tribal group, or being female, or both, can be a predictor of vulnerability to trafficking. It is important to keep in mind the essential humanity of victims of trafficking. Their motives in this case are often laudable: to escape oppression, to better provide for their children, to make a new start, or to gain new experiences and education. The crime of human trafficking is rare among types of crime, in that the people who become its victims often are simply trying to better themselves by being ambitious, by trying to make a safe life for their families.

Some factors operate to draw traffickers to certain victims. Vulnerability may be the first, and the key, variable, but, as a commodity, different human beings appeal to traffickers for different reasons. Traffickers will seek out those who most closely match the needs of their economic activity. Sometimes it will be question of language, sometimes of appearance. Certain ethnic groups prefer to include or avoid other ethnic groups as victims. Concepts of physical beauty differ from culture to culture, and this has an effect on what "type" of person is most likely to be victimized for sexual exploitation. Certain attributes of ethnicity and appearance are known to be worth more to traffickers, thus narrowing their choice of victims.

STAGE 2: RECRUITMENT

The process of recruitment also varies from case to case, but again there are many commonalities. Around the world, the role of family and community members in recruiting victims into trafficking is especially prevalent and discouraging. At the most personal level are those recruiters who visit individual homes in order to encourage emigration and to reassure other family members of the safety of the process. In West Africa, Thailand, and Central America, older women are known to recruit young people of the same ethnic and language group. They bring to local villages the consumer goods and nice clothes that they know will help entice the young. To older family members, the recruiters make promises about the money that can be earned abroad and remitted to the home village. They weave a picture of wealth, comfort, sophistication, and prestige that can be irresistible to the poor and isolated.

Kielland and Sanogo have discussed the "lottery" of recruitment into trafficking. Studying a large number of families in West Africa whose children had been sold to do domestic work, they found that the rare child who managed to return to his or her village often became an advertisement for being trafficked rather than a warning. According to Kielland and Sanogo, "They [the village children] are impressed by such wealth, and when the intermediaries return, new recruits will be eager to travel in order to get the same things."[16]

In eastern Europe and many other parts of the world, well-educated young people face an economy with no jobs. They may fall victim to a recruiter known in their community, or they may begin their descent into trafficking by contacting what appears to be a legitimate employment agency. The agency may advertise in the press or with posters offering good jobs overseas and help with obtaining visas. They will have plausible explanations ready for the reasonable questions asked by people about their services. For a fee, the agency ostensibly will facilitate migration.

Some victims know they going to work in prostitution but are deceived about the working and living conditions, the financial arrangements, and the level of personal freedom they can expect to experience. The stigma attached to those caught up in prostitution, when added to this implied consent, means that many trafficking victims are seen as having somehow contributed to or agreed to their own exploitation. This blaming of the victim, especially when it is done by governmental agencies or law enforcement, only worsens their situation.

STAGE 3: REMOVAL

At some point the potential victim places him- or herself into the hands of the recruiter. This is a crucial step and one that in itself has generated controversy in the understanding of trafficking. As noted earlier, in most cases this implies *consent* by the potential victim. In some cases the victim is consenting to take part in being smuggled and knows that this is an illegal activity. In other cases, as when recruited by a seemingly legitimate employment agency, the victim believes that he or she is consenting to take part in a legal migration and employment. For a minority of victims, the removal is violent — they are simply abducted by force, sometimes after having been drugged.

This stage is also crucial to the trafficker, for at this point the process of taking control of the victim begins. Having been forced or convinced to leave familiar surroundings, family, and community, the victim experiences a relative decrease in power; and the trafficker's power over the victim increases with every step. The protection and support of family and friends are left behind, and the victim enters a world controlled by the trafficker. In some cases the victim is moved to a collection point, a house where victims are brought together before being moved as a group.

STAGE 4: TRANSPORTATION

A. A. Aronowitz has looked closely at the organization of smuggling and trafficking operations, and the following draws heavily on her work.[17] She points out that the degree of organization within smuggling or trafficking chains can vary dramatically. Either smuggling or trafficking can be as simple as a single individual providing a single service — such as hiding migrants in the back of a truck and smuggling them across a border, only to abandon or exploit them once they reach the destination country. Smuggling or trafficking can be segmented, involving an interaction between a criminal network and a legitimate transportation company. Smuggling or trafficking can be sophisticated and complex, spanning long periods of time and large geographical distances and involving numerous people who provide the entire range of services.

Smuggling and trafficking operations constitute a process that, depending upon the complexity of the operation, can involve numerous players. Trafficking operations moving large numbers of persons through numerous countries over a longer period of time are, by nature, highly organized. A. Bajrektarevic has studied the horizontal design of smuggling and trafficking organizations and argues that they are divided into several subunits that specialize in a particular part or sequence of the operation.[18] These subunits provide various services, from recruitment to escort to logistical support. The management unit maintains a vertical structure and has knowledge of and controls the other subunits. All other subunits are organized horizontally and have very limited knowledge of one another. These include the following units:

- *management/supervising unit:* this unit drafts, plans, finances, manages, and supervises the whole operation and maintains a criminal structure that is both operable and profitable;
- *escort unit:* responsible for transport from the source countries through the transit countries to the country of origin;
- *corrupted public officials:* although they may not function as an integrated group, their behavior is instrumental in facilitating the smuggling and trafficking networks;
- *recruitment unit:* advertises the organization and recruits new clients through means ranging from the informal (word of mouth) to formal advertisements in the press or internet or the use of travel agencies;

- *guiding/navigating unit:* individuals who know and make arrangements in the local environment;

- *supporting/logistics unit:* this unit provides supporting services such as food and safe houses;

- *debt collecting unit:* responsible for collecting transportation fees and keeping smuggled and trafficked persons isolated in safe houses;

- *exploiting unit:* operates in the destination country and may consist of numerous subunits involved in various activities (exploitation in prostitution, pick-pocketing, car theft, drug smuggling or begging);

- *reescort unit:* these units are responsible for "escorting" or rotating trafficked persons (usually those forced into prostitution) between cities or countries.[19]

All but two of these units are common to both smuggling and trafficking rings. The exploiting unit and reescort units provide services only to networks dealing with trafficked persons. Not all of these personnel are involved only in transport, but they are mentioned here because transportation is a process rather than an event, and during that process other actions are taken and further controls are established over the victim.

The process of transportation is likely to involve several modes of travel. For example, one study of illegal migrants intercepted in Lithuania found that they had passed through an average of 3.6 transit countries, and that their journey had been multimodal, with an average of four modes of transport used. No migrant had covered the entire journey by the same means of transport.[20]

STAGE 5: ESTABLISHMENT OF CONTROL

Once transportation begins, victims are likely to have their travel and identity documents taken away. To be without documents while in transit is to be placed immediately in the control of the trafficker. Likewise, during the period of transportation, victims may be subjected to harsh, even brutal, treatment. They may be locked up in cramped, uncomfortable safe houses. The traffickers may use these periods between actual movements to introduce the victim to other victims, some of whom are already being exploited, to accustom them to what will come. The aim of the trafficker will be to disorient the victim, to increase his or her dependence, to establish fear and obedience, to gain control. This may be the work of a brutal, violent moment or a subtle process of degradation and subjugation. The victim may simply be sold to an exploiter who will then impose control. To return for a moment to the definition of trafficking provided in the Anti-Trafficking Protocol, this is the "threat or use of force, coercion, abduction, fraud, deception, abuse of power or vulnerability, or giving payments or benefits to a person in control of the victim." In this process of establishing control, the crime of smuggling becomes one of trafficking.

In the case of children being trafficked, the establishment of control occurs much more quickly. As soon as traffickers remove children from their normal environment, control is achieved. Since children are normally dependent on adults for their basic needs, and since they are often more trusting of the adults who supply these needs, they fall naturally into a situation of obedience.

STAGE 6: ARRIVAL

In many trafficking cases, the establishment of control over the victim occurs on or after arrival in the destination country. Often a victim's cooperation is needed to successfully navigate border crossings and immigration controls. It is when the victim has "safely" arrived at the destination that the full power of the exploitative control is exercised. Normally at this point in the process, the full nature of the fraud and deception becomes clear, when the victim's identification and travel documents are confiscated by the trafficker. The victim is told of the large (fraudulent) debts incurred, discovers the bad working conditions and lack of freedom he or she faces, and suffers the threat or violent control that is the hallmark of enslavement. Sometimes victims are also brainwashed: they are told repeatedly that the local police will kill them if they are found. For the exploiter, the slaveholder, the aim is to create fearful and obedient workers who do exactly as told; the establishment of control is complete.

STAGE 7: EXPLOITATION

Once under control, trafficking victims begin their period of enslavement and exploitation. To return again to the definition of trafficking given in the Anti-Trafficking Protocol, this is the "exploitation, which includes exploiting the prostitution of others, sexual exploitation, forced labor, slavery or similar practices, and the removal of organs." The types of work that trafficking victims are generally forced to do fall into several broad categories: prostitution, domestic service, agricultural work, work in small factories and workshops, mining, land clearance, selling in the market, and begging. That said, the creativity of criminals is such that almost any kind of job may be filled by a trafficked person. The period of exploitation is likely to last much longer than that of being trafficked. In many countries, trafficking victims have suffered exploitation for more than twenty years. In some cases, the victim has been sold several times to different exploiters and into different types of work.

Another commonality shared among trafficking victims exploited in different types of work is the psychological manipulation to which they are subjected. Despite the high level of violent control exercised over victims of trafficking, they are likely to know that their enslavement and exploitation is illegal. Force, violence, and psychological coercion are used to convince them to accept their situation. When victims of trafficking begin to accept their role and identify with their masters, their enslavement is mental; constant physical bondage then becomes unnecessary. This fact of psychological control is important when considering ways to best liberate and rehabilitate victims of trafficking. Cristina Tallens worked for several years to free and rehabilitate domestic slaves who had been trafficked and taken into France. She explains the paradox arising from psychological manipulation of victims:

> In spite of the violence, and the living and working conditions, people in slavery have their own mental integrity and their own mechanisms for surviving. Some may actually like different aspects of their life, perhaps the security, or their understanding of the order of things. When you disrupt this order, suddenly everything is confused. Some of the women who were freed have attempted suicide. It is easy to assume that this happened because of the abuse they had lived through. But for some of these women[,] slavery had been the major psychological building block in their lives. When that was destroyed, the meaning of their life was like a bit of paper crushed up and thrown away. They were told: "No, this is not the way it is supposed to be, start all over again." It was as though their life had no meaning.[21]

The period of exploitation leaves some victims terribly injured and others less so. One of the key areas needing further work concerns the best ways to help victims to recover from this experience.

STAGE 8: RESOLUTION

The experience of being trafficked can end in many ways. For far too many victims, the experience ends with death. Though there are no means to measure the mortality of trafficking victims, it is safe to assume that it is high. Trafficking victims are known to have died in many ways: when fire sweeps the house in which they are locked up; in accidents on building sites; of disease in rural work camps; and when murdered by their exploiters. Others are discarded when, through injury or illness, they become useless to their exploiters. Children, especially girls, trafficked into domestic service are often thrown out on the streets when they reach their teens. This can occur when they have been impregnated by one of the men of the family for whom they worked; both their sexuality and potential offspring are seen as disruptive. For women forced into prostitution, the onset of HIV infection can mean the end of their exploitation and the beginning of their physical collapse.

Some victims of trafficking manage to escape. When they do, their situation is often precarious. Without the necessary contacts or knowledge of the language, they are at the mercy of whomever they encounter. This can lead to reenslavement or to rough treatment at the hands of officials who should be protecting them, but who only see the escaped victim as an illegal immigrant. Sometimes they find their way to communities of people from their own country or culture. In such immigrant communities, they may find support and care, or they may be ostracized. If they are fortunate, they will find sympathetic individuals who recognize that they are crime victims and who will help them work toward their rehabilitation. Trafficking victims may also be rescued or apprehended by state agencies. Around the world, few are brought out of trafficking in this way, though the numbers are increasing. When this happens, their rights may be protected, or they may be ignored or violated.

Different Forms of Trafficking

One of the key facts about trafficking in persons is that it must be understood within its cultural and social context. Trafficking and slavery are truly ancient human activities, predating even written law. Any human activity with such a long history will have evolved to take many forms and will be deeply integrated in different cultures and societies. Today ancient forms of trafficking in persons are combined with new ways to traffic and exploit. The ease of international travel means that local, indigenous forms of trafficking may now be exported a great distance to very different countries and cultures. An agency or organization dealing with victims of trafficking in persons may find that the way one victim from one culture understands the process of being trafficked is very different from that of a victim from another culture. At times criminals will take advantage of existing social or cultural systems that allow for the transfer of people, often children, and subvert them into systems of trafficking. What follows is a brief review of different forms of trafficking, particularly those linked to existing cultural forms.

Child Placement.   The transfer of children between families, communities, or tribes is a human activity of very long standing. In European cultures the placement of children with other families, sometimes as apprentices intending to learn a craft, was normal for hundreds of years. As a social custom it faded only after the advent of compulsory universal education for children. In parts of the developing world, however, particularly in West Africa, this custom remains strong. The difficulty arises when unscrupulous people take advantage of this custom to exploit and abuse children. Distant relatives or nonfamily members may use the idea of placement to gain the trust of parents. Often an "advance" on the wages a child will supposedly earn is offered to parents as an inducement. Families suffering serious economic hardship may see the offer of employment and care for children as an attractive opportunity. The result, however, is that the parents may never see their children again. Once the traffickers have separated the children from their parents, they will exploit and abuse them as they choose.

Debt Bondage or Indentured Servitude.   Another custom with a long history is the practice of advancing money or services to people and then requiring them to repay the debt with their labor. In the past, many of the migrants to North and South America came as indentured servants — promising seven full years of labor in exchange for their transportation to the new world. Many forms of slavery that do not involve trafficking also rely on debt to initiate a victim into bondage. As noted earlier, there are, in fact, two forms of debt bondage.[22] For victims of trafficking, debts may be held over them as the reason they cannot be let free. The costs of smuggling the victim and of their food and shelter will be increased at will by traffickers, and increased again through high interest and false accounting. The result is a justification, though illegal, of the violent control exercised over the victim. In some situations there is the added pressure of threats to family members in the country of origin if the debt is not paid.

Removal of Organs.   The Anti-Trafficking Protocol specifically addresses the removal of organs from victims of trafficking. It is a clear indication of the power exercised over victims that their organs may be taken from them for sale. In this situation it may be only the organ that is trafficked, to be ultimately used by someone needing a replacement organ. Most states forbid the transfer of organs except to family members, or upon the death of the donor. Criminals, however, prey on the vulnerable and convince them to give up organs, such as kidneys, for a price or through trickery. Cases of this trade have been documented in India.

Mail-Order Brides.   The new technologies, and especially the Internet, have made possible new forms of fraudulent and criminal communications. Agencies that purport to make introductions between women (normally in poorer countries) and men (normally in richer countries) have expanded dramatically in the past ten years. Some of these agencies actually exploit the men of richer countries, soliciting and receiving payments for a number of services and then disappearing. Others are a front for the trafficking of vulnerable women. In many of these cases, what seems to be a legitimate opportunity for a poor woman turns out to be a fraudulent method of securing her entrance to a destination country and then her enslavement.

THE FUTURE OF TRAFFICKING IN PERSONS

It is important to remember that criminals are inventive and opportunistic. They operate in a context of extreme and violent competition. Their conditions of work are dynamic and prone to dramatic and abrupt change. For all these reasons, criminals are good at adapting to new situations and new technologies. As new forms of communication, new methods of transportation, and new ways of controlling and exploiting people emerge, traffickers will rapidly take them up and subvert them to criminal uses. The challenge to all who would address trafficking in persons is to be prepared for such adaptations, both through applicable law and creative enforcement.

What Is the Extent of Global Trafficking?

The truth is that we have no idea of the actual volume of human trafficking. Given the criminal and hidden nature of trafficking, mean-

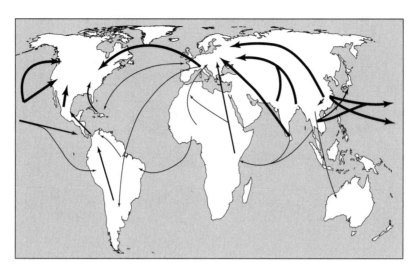

MAP 1. Estimated flows of global human trafficking. Thicker lines indicate greater flow. Source: International Organization for Migration, "Organized Crime Moves into Migrant Trafficking," *Trafficking in Migrants, Quarterly Bulletin,* no. 11 (June 1996): 2.

ingful measurement of its magnitude is difficult. According to a U.S. government estimate based on 1997 data, seven hundred thousand persons, mainly women and children, are trafficked across national borders worldwide each year. According to an International Organization for Migration estimate of the same year, the number of victims trafficked both internally and across national borders is 4 million. The economic value of human trafficking to criminals is estimated to be between 5 and 7 billion U.S. dollars.

While the precise number of trafficked persons is unknown, the pattern of trafficking flows is better understood. At the most basic level is the fact that trafficked persons flow from poorer countries and regions to richer countries and regions, as well as the fact that the economic and political contexts of both origin and destination countries help determine the supply of, and demand for, trafficked persons. Map 1 shows estimated flows worldwide. This map indicates flows but fails to capture the complexity of trafficking within regions and within countries.

Map 2, adapted from a map prepared by UNICEF, shows the trafficking flows of children for different forms of work exploitation in the West African region. Mapping the flows in this way, based on estimates

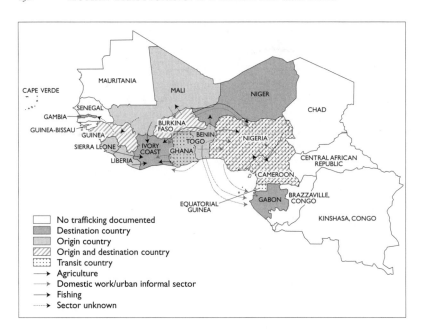

MAP 2. Estimated flows of trafficked children in West and Central Africa, including type of work for which they are exploited. Source: "Etude sous régionale sur le trafic des enfants en Afrique de l'Ouest et du Centre, 2000" [Study of child trafficking in West and Central Africa, 2000] (Bazzi-Veil: UNICEF West and Central Africa Regional Office, 2000).

built up from actual cases, gives the best indication of the extent of trafficking in persons in any country or region.

A great deal more must be learned and understood about trafficking in persons. Many basic issues and questions remain in need of examination. These include: Who are the victims of trafficking in persons, and what makes them vulnerable? Who are the offenders, and why have they chosen human trafficking as their criminal business? What are the precise internal, regional, and global patterns of the flow of trafficked persons? How do these patterns differ when they are broken down by the different types of exploitation that the trafficked person will suffer? For example, how does trafficking related to sexual exploitation differ from trafficking related to agricultural or construction work? How does trafficking relate to other forms of criminality, such as the trade in drugs, the trade in weapons, corruption, and terrorism? We know that some trafficked persons are forced to do work that is highly destructive to the environment, such as the clearing of Amazonian forests or open-pit mining. We also know that environmental destruction can itself be a force that creates the vulnerability that increases people's chance of being trafficked. Yet this link between the destruction of the natural environment and the destruction of the rights and lives of trafficked persons is not understood. How does it work? How extensive is it? At a more general level, we need to understand how recent developments in trafficking relate to the bigger social, political, and economic factors operating in the countries involved and to the global economic and political system. More research at all levels is needed.

CHAPTER 8

Understanding the Demand behind Human Trafficking

Our understanding of human trafficking is piecemeal and often based on anecdotal information, as is true of many other criminal activities. Moreover, our understanding is complicated by the global reach of trafficking, and by social and cultural variation in the ways that the crime of trafficking unfolds. Compared to other criminal activities, human trafficking is especially difficult to bring into focus. In part, this is because the victims of trafficking are more likely to be hidden or unreachable than, for example, the victims of burglary or even murder. The result is a crime for which the technique of using representative sample-victim surveys cannot be applied as discussed in chapter 5. This invisibility affects our understanding of the demand for trafficked persons as well. Trafficking, enslavement, forced prostitution, and kidnapping share the distinction that they are crimes in which the victim is also the moneymaking "product" of the criminal enterprise. Like the bag of cocaine that a trafficker keeps hidden at all costs, the trafficking victim-product will ultimately be used and, possibly, exhausted and disposed of. This fact, that the victim is also the product, may help us think through the demand for trafficked people. Products are conceptualized in a number of ways, and analyzing the selling points of trafficked people as products should help us understand the context and reasoning behind the demand for trafficking victims.

This chapter aims to explore the trafficking demand by using some perspectives from the field of marketing. It may seem repellent to use such terms when referring to human beings, but today there is a large and vibrant market for trafficked persons in a number of economic activities.

Traffickers are regularly thinking of how to stimulate and meet the demand for their product. Victims of trafficking, noticeably those trafficked for sexual exploitation, must somehow be presented and marketed to "consumers." If we are to begin to understand demand, we must put ourselves in the shoes of those who stand on both sides of the supply-and-demand equation. Before doing so, however, it is necessary to review some of the broad themes in trafficking and to examine any already existing information on demand for trafficked people.

Every case of trafficking is unique, but all share certain characteristics. At the most basic level are the commonalities specified in the definition of trafficking given in the United Nations Protocol to Prevent, Suppress and Punish Trafficking in Persons, Especially Women and Children: trafficking is the action of transporting people by means of force or deception in order to control and exploit them. It can also be said that there are three underlying factors at work that foster trafficking: (1) within the origin countries, a seemingly endless supply of victims remains available for exploitation, (2) within the destination countries, a seemingly endless demand exists for the services of the victims, and (3) organized criminal networks, some large and some small, have taken control of this economic supply-and-demand situation to traffic and exploit trafficked persons in order to generate enormous profits for themselves.

In chapter 7, I reported a small statistical study to determine the factors that most strongly predict trafficking in persons from countries and to countries. While most of this work concentrated on exploring the "push" factors that moved people to place themselves in situations in which they might be trafficked, I also sought to understand what best predicted the "pull" factors that influence people in their choice of destination country, as well as what predicted the relative permeability of a destination country's borders. One key factor exercising "pull" is the demand for workers in the destination country.

Globally, there is clearly an extensive demand. In attempting to conservatively estimate the productive capacity of enslaved workers worldwide — obviously a tentative exercise — I arrived at an estimate of $13 billion per year. This is the value generated by workers enslaved around the world, from the relatively low amounts of profit generated by rural bonded labor in India, to the extremely high profits generated by enslaved prostitutes in North America and western Europe. Within the global economy, $13 billion is a pittance, about the same amount that Americans spend on blue jeans each year. But within the criminal economy, and added to other trafficking profits from drugs and weapons, it is significant. That said, the traffickers cannot generate demand by themselves. Indeed, were there no demand whatsoever, criminals would be unlikely to attempt to generate it, because criminal businesses tend to be opportunistic rather than developmental. For trafficking to occur, there must exist in destination countries an economic context in which enslaved workers can be exploited and a social context that allows treating human beings in this way. Examining the worldview of the consumers will help us to understand demand for trafficked people.

Marketing People

It is not enough simply to say that the consumers of trafficked people want them for exploitation and profit. Within our thinking about slavery is the temptation to treat it as an issue that is black and white, good versus evil, a scenario of vicious perpetrators and innocent victims. In fact, trafficking and enslavement are much more complex. Slavery is a social and economic relationship. It is a relationship marked by extreme differentials of power, by violence, and by exploitation, but it is still a relationship between two or more people. As a relationship it exists within a context of social, economic, and moral expectations. What can we say about that context that helps explain the market for trafficked people?

First, it is important to recognize that the consumers of trafficked people operate within a moral economy that allows them to rationalize this activity. This moral economy will not normally be the dominant cultural or legal context, but a subculture that defines trafficked people in a way that allows their exploitation. Recall the slaveholder in chapter 2, who sees his control over his bonded laborers as benignly paternal: "I am like a father to these workers. . . . I protect them and guide them. . . . Of course, sometimes I have to discipline them as well, just as a father would."

Other slaveholders have also told me their slaves are like their children, that they need the close control and care of enslavement. Then there is the argument of tradition: since bondage has been going on for so long, it must be the natural order of things. For other slaveholders it is a simple question of priorities: enslaving others is unfortunate, they say, but their own family's welfare depends on it. Most disturbing are the slaveholders who have convinced themselves that their slaves are less than human, that they are replaceable and disposable inputs in their business.

In addressing this moral economy, we must remember that human rights are based on the privileging and then codification of the *victim's* definitions of an action, normally an action that harms them. Virtually every action that we now think of as a violation of human rights was once defined as acceptable. Trafficking and enslavement were once legitimate and legal activities, accepted economic pursuits in which the well-being of the slave was of concern only in the way that the well-being of cattle is the concern of beef farmers today. The public viewed the activity of enslavement from the perspective of the slaveholder. This was a business, and one that supported an extensive economy. While it was sometimes criticized on economic grounds, such arguments had little effect on reducing slavery. To bring an end to slavery required a public redefinition of the action of enslavement, a definition incorporating the point of view of the slave. When the experience and views of the victim of any harmful action are socially privileged, this is the beginning of the process that leads to the codification of a human right. Over time, the history of human rights is the extension of more and more rights to broader and broader populations. By more rights I mean the extension of rights beyond the original protections against murder and slavery — to free speech, to education, to religious expression (to name just a few). By broader populations I mean that rights historically were assigned to men, usually of a certain ethnicity, and over time were extended to women, to other ethnicities, and to children.

This digression into the origin of human rights is relevant because the consumer of trafficked people is operating within a moral economy in which this extension of rights to trafficking victims has not occurred. Demand for trafficked persons is based, in part, in an acceptance, at a personal level by the consumer, of trafficked persons' status as people without rights. Defining the victims in this way might be based on any number of justifications, which might be racist or sexist in character. The behavior of the traffickers and the consumer will be more or less hidden, depending on the extent to which the surrounding public also holds these views or is simply apathetic.

One key path to lessening demand is a general and pervasive public redefinition of the activity. When public awareness is keen and public attitudes toward trafficking and enslavement are very strongly negative, there may still be those who consider it an acceptable activity. But accomplishing the exploitation of trafficked persons will then be another matter. When a society's moral economy vigorously condemns trafficking and is willing to support that condemnation with resources, the number of prosecutions will be high and the costs of trafficking and enslavement will be prohibitive.

Wholesalers, Retailers, and the Unique Selling Point

Given that we have achieved neither a general public awareness of trafficking nor a broad political will and allocation of resources to its eradication, we must look to the process of trafficking to throw light on questions of demand. It is important to understand that, within a moral economy in which trafficking occurs, traffickers and the consumers of trafficked people are not necessarily the same individuals. Some are "wholesalers," the recruiters, transporters, and traffickers who harvest and move people into the trafficking streams. They convert free people into trafficking victims by taking control of their lives, brutalizing them, taking their passports and documents, and restricting their movement. There are certain attributes they seek in their potential "product"— gullibility, good physical health, and the most important attribute, profitability. Profitability, in turn, is determined by the demand by the "retail consumer" for certain attributes in the people that the traffickers wish to exploit. These attributes vary according to the jobs or economic sectors in which the retail consumer intends to use the trafficked person. Different attributes are needed for prostitution or agricultural work or domestic service, though there will be overlap as well.

One way to think about demand for any product is to consider its unique selling point(s) (USP). When marketing executives are presented with new products, their job is to find the products' USP, the attribute or attributes that differentiate these new products from all others and that feed into an existing or cultivated demand on the part of consumers. The notion of "cultivated demand" should not be alien to anyone who has been exposed to advertising; it can apply to the demand for trafficking victims as well. Demand is not simple; it is normally brought into being by a complex array of social, political, and economic forces. For our part, it is worth asking: what is the USP of trafficked people? What attributes make them attractive to the consumers of trafficked people?

Bridget Anderson and Julia O'Connell Davidson discuss this in their report on demand for trafficking victims:

> When employers and consumers pay for services/labour, they do not always simply wish to purchase a "thing" (the worker's disembodied

power to labour or serve) but also often wish to consume what has been termed "embodied labour." This is to say that they may wish to make use of the labour/services of persons of a specific age, sex, race, nationality, caste, or class. Consumers of commercial sexual service provide a clear example here, since few clients would be equally happy to buy sex from an elderly man or a young woman. They may also have specific preferences regarding the racial or national identity of the sex workers they use. The same point applies to those who wish to consume the labour of domestic workers, wives, adopted children or *au pairs* within the private household. Equally, those who make money by organising and taking a cut from street beggars are not necessarily indiscriminate about the kind of people they "employ" (a healthy muscular adult male is unlikely to earn as much from begging as a frail elderly woman or a small child). Similarly, a person's age and sex has a bearing on how effective a drug mule or pickpocket they are likely to make.[1]

The work of Anderson and Davidson, and other research, suggests that there are parallels in the attributes that consumers of trafficked people demand in prostitution and domestic work.[2] These attributes constitute the USP of trafficked people. The following sections look at each of these desirable characteristics in turn.

SLAVES COST LITTLE

Slaves across all of human history have shared a common situation, centered on violent control, loss of free will, and economic exploitation. The way this core situation is played out has varied tremendously according to local cultural, economic, political, legal, social, and religious conditions. Slaves today experience the same basic situation of total control and exploitation, but for the first time in human history there is a dramatic alteration in the economic conditions of enslavement. For a number of reasons linked to the population explosion, and to the ongoing impoverishment of much of the population of the developing world, slaves today are cheaper than at any time in history. This dramatic fall in the price of potentially enslavable people has had a profound effect on the use and treatment of trafficked persons.[3] Young men taken from Mali and sold in the Ivory Coast for agricultural work clearly demonstrate this trend. A nineteen-year-old, healthy male accustomed to agricultural labor can be acquired for around $50 in the Ivory Coast. The young man normally does not have any idea that he is being sold into slavery at the time, only that a fee is being taken to place him into work with a farmer. Once the young man is removed to the farm and placed under physical control, the farmer gets the entire productive capacity, the embodied labor, of this young man for as long as the farmer can control and exploit him. Compare that sum to the $1,000 that would have been the price in 1850 in the American Deep South for an equivalent young male accustomed to agricultural work. Note, especially, that $1,000 in 1850 is the equivalent of $38,500 in 2003. This fall in the price of slaves is in line with a handful of similar precipitous falls in history — computers being a good modern example (their cost having fallen from hundreds of thousands of dollars to hundreds of dollars for the same computing capacity in about thirty years). The point of this comparison is to emphasize how the plummeting price of trafficked people has opened up new areas of demand. When people cost so little, they can be used profitably in ways not previously economic.

SLAVES CAN BE MADE MALLEABLE

To be useful and profitable, a trafficked person must be malleable. Consumers of trafficked people must be able to get from the product the behaviors, services, and work that they want, and must do so at a sufficiently low cost in upkeep and control. For the most part, malleability is assured through violent intimidation, but this can be combined with psychological control and threats against victims' families. The power of the consumer to command anything he or she wants from, or do anything he or she wants to, the trafficked person is the mirror image of the victim's vulnerability. Members of the public who confront the realities of contemporary trafficking and enslavement for the first time often ask why trafficked people, finding themselves enslaved, do not simply resist or flee. The answer becomes clear when the array of tools used to ensure malleability is examined. At the most basic level, physical attack and sexual assault induce a state of shock in a trafficked person. In shock, he or she is, at least temporarily, unable to resist. When such physical coercion is combined with sleep deprivation, malnutrition, isolation, psychological intimidation, threats to other family members, and the withholding of documents, control becomes complete. Such control can be further assured when this occurs in a context in which the trafficked person does not speak the local language or have any familiarity with local culture. When the work required of the trafficked person is itself painful, demeaning, psychologically damaging, and exhausting, the initial state of shock can be extended into a state of disassociation from reality and even an identification with the consumer (abuser), sometimes known as the

Stockholm syndrome, such as that found in some torture victims. For the consumer the question is how to maintain control and ensure malleability at the lowest cost. For example, locks are cheap, but armed guards can be expensive. The cost of maintaining the malleable enslaved worker is also a function of the social and legal context. If the chances of apprehension for trafficking are high and the penalties severe, this increases the potential cost. This question of context is explored in more detail below.

SLAVES CAN BE LIKE THE "REAL THING"

A product's USP can easily be one that is more perceived than real. Were this not true, there would be no demand for clothing with certain designer labels. In trafficked people, in both domestic service and prostitution, there is a demand for enslaved workers that most approximate the "real thing." Defining what constitutes the "real thing" is problematic, but it would be reasonable to say that a "real" domestic worker is efficient in household tasks, can understand the instructions and wishes of the consumer, and is obedient, quiet, and deferential. Defining the characteristics of a real provider of sexual interaction within the context of prostitution is even more problematic, but some suppositions might be made. These characteristics might include a sexual partner of the preferred gender, age range, and appearance. The last, while subjective, also follows known broad cultural patterns of attractiveness. Additionally, in prostitution the real thing would, like the domestic worker, be compliant or at least minimally cooperative. Being able to understand the instructions and wishes of the consumer could also be important in approximating the real thing in prostitution. The demand for trafficked people who are close to being the real thing acts to reduce the pool of potential victims, since it entails both physical attributes — gender, age, and appearance — and the need for the enslaved worker to understand the tasks required. As noted, trafficking flows move from poorer countries to richer countries, but one of the reasons that trafficked people are rarely moved from the very poorest countries directly to the richest countries is that they are unfamiliar with, or unable to communicate about, their required tasks. In the example of the poor and usually illiterate young agricultural workers of Mali, they are taken to the relatively richer Ivory Coast and sold. They rarely speak the local language, but they are familiar with the agricultural tasks they will be required to do. Were they to be trafficked directly into suburban homes in one of the richest countries, they would be completely unfamiliar with the language, tasks, tools, and so forth. Sexual exploitation within prostitution avoids some of this difficulty by concentrating on a fundamental biological act, but the prostitute still carries out that act within a complex context specific to the local culture.

SLAVES CAN BE EXOTIC

In prostitution, especially, there is a demand for the exotic. I quote again from the study on demand carried out by Anderson and O'Connell Davidson for the Global Alliance against Trafficking in Women:

> There are many studies that have explored the attitudes and practices of clients who *do* have a particular and focused interest in sex workers of a different racial, ethnic or national identity to themselves. Interview research with white Western men who practice sex tourism to Southeast Asian, Latin American and Caribbean countries reveal a constellation of attitudes towards gender, race and sexuality that simultaneously sexualise racially "othered" persons, and de-sexualize white women. Western women who practice sex tourism voice similar forms of sexualized racism.[4]

It is clear that such attitudes are based within racist and nationalist notions of the superiority and inferiority of different groups. Exoticism may also be a desired characteristic in the trafficked domestic worker or other trafficked persons, but this has not been studied to the same extent.

SLAVES ALLOW THEIR CONSUMERS THE ENJOYMENT OF POWER

The basic relationship of exploitation is an expression of power. For some, this expression is in itself a benefit, a USP of the trafficked person. The exercise and enjoyment of power in this relationship can take several forms. At the simple economic level, it involves being able to exert complete control over a worker and reducing drastically the cost of the worker — through nonpayment of wages, through substandard and inadequate subsistence, through forcing the slave to work extremely long hours. But for many who exploit trafficked people, this exercise of power also carries a violent and sexualized meaning. The trafficked worker, under complete control, can be regularly brutalized or raped. In the case reports on trafficked domestic workers, examples of this are far too numerous to list. In some cases, such as the Lakireddy Bali Reddy case in San Francisco,[5] the opportunity to enjoy the exercise of physical and sexual power seems to have been the primary determinant of the exploitation — given that the perpetrator was already rich and not in need of the profit he made from the young women he brought into the United States as slaves.

All these attributes also must be considered along with what at first seems to be a contradictory "selling point": *sameness*. Exploiters of trafficked people may want their victims to be exotic, but they want to them be so within certain limits. Many products are sold to consumers with a balance of exoticism and sameness. A soft drink may be billed as "wild," "unknown," or "exotic," but it will not be placed in a container that the consumer would fail to recognize as holding a soft drink. Nor would it violate the usually unstated dietary rules of the consumer's culture in, for example, Western countries, by using blood as a key ingredient, no matter how nutritious or tasty that might be. The consumer of trafficked people wants a victim who can understand sufficiently what is expected, and for whom there is a basic understanding of the most fundamental of the physical artifacts of the culture in which he or she is exploited.

It is also worth considering the idea of "sameness" alongside the assembling of trafficked people's unique selling points into "skill bundles" including their other human skills. Demand for slaves tends to focus on people whose skills place them on the next lower rung of the economic ladder, not on those occupying rungs at a great distance. The consumer wants the trafficked person to have just enough skill and education to be really useful, but not so much as to be uncontrollable.

In understanding consumption, however, it is not enough to understand the attributes of the "product." One must also come to grips with the context in which consumption occurs.

A Location of Control

In most developed countries, the exercise and enjoyment of power over the trafficked person cannot be accomplished in public. Since violence is a key, ever-present ingredient in the relationship of exploitation, the consumer of trafficked people needs a location where violence can be used with impunity. In the developed North, this usually means a private home or a brothel — private spaces where total control over the trafficked person can be established and the movements of the victim can be restricted. For those economic sectors in which the trafficked person is exploited outdoors, this normally occurs in secluded areas, such as the more remote farms where trafficked agricultural workers have been used. It is interesting to note that one of the most public uses of trafficked people, the "deaf Mexican" cases of New York, employed the disability of the victims as an isolating barrier. In spite of being in public places in a densely populated city, the trafficked persons were cut off by virtue of their deafness and their inability to use North American sign language. For a significant period, this inability to communicate added to the violent control exercised over them, preventing them from escaping or gaining help in spite of the fact that they were literally standing in a crowd. When some of the trafficked people did begin to initiate communication outside their group, it led to their rescue.

Sweatshops also provide a locked-down context of control. Trafficked people forced to work in sweatshops exhibit some but not all of the USP attributes noted above. Those exploiting trafficked people in sweatshops are not interested in the exotic nature of their workers, but they are keenly interested in low cost, malleability, and the ability to exercise power over them. The result is high profits and the potential for profit in products that would not be feasible with any but the most negligible labor costs. The most telling example of this in my own experience is the use of families brought from the state of Bihar in India to the state of Uttar Pradesh, and used there to make sand by pounding rocks with hammers.[6] Sand is such a ubiquitous substance, the manufacture of which is so simply accomplished with basic machines, that it is difficult to imagine that handmade sand could ever be economically viable without a virtual absence of labor costs.

Across the world there are a great many trafficked people laboring at work sites where a context of control can be established and the victim isolated: quarries, mines, remote farms, offshore fishing platforms, and locked workrooms. The total number of these people easily must be in the hundreds of thousands, making slavery much more than a "niche" market, and an area that deserves some of the illumination currently concentrated on trafficking of people for sale into prostitution and domestic service.

Extinguishing Demand

The point of examining the demand for trafficking, of trying to think here like marketing executives, is obviously that we must find ways to reduce the demand for trafficked people. Criminals will always look for ways to exploit people; the unscrupulous will always be willing to reap a profit even when it involves the suffering of others. Yet if the attributes demanded by those who exploit trafficked people can be understood and countered, then demand might be lessened.

Several points about countering demand arise from this discussion. First, at a basic level, is the need to counter the moral economy that allows those who exploit trafficked people to rationalize this activity. In part, this means raising public awareness of the crime of trafficking, and especially awareness of the realities of the lived experience of trafficked people. As noted above, human rights are based on the privileging and then codification of the *victim's* definitions of an activity. Virtually every action that we now think of as a violation of human rights was once defined as acceptable. This process of recognizing the rights of the victims of trafficking is still under way. That the rights of trafficking victims are not fully accepted is evident in the fact that the crime itself is not yet codified in many countries. It also indicates that the public tends not to have a clear understanding of the crime, even where it has entered the criminal code. The U.S. Trafficking Victims Protection Act (2000) has been hailed as breakthrough legislation precisely because it specifically recognizes that trafficked people are victims of a crime, and because it sets their status as victims at a higher priority than other factors — such as their status as illegal aliens. Criminals using trafficked people may themselves decide not to recognize their victims' rights, but when the society in which they operate becomes aware of the crime and able to identify a trafficking victim as such, this increases the likelihood that crime will be reported and the victim freed. This in turn increases the risk to the perpetrator and acts to reduce demand.

The Trafficking Victims Protection Act also dramatically increased the penalties for trafficking offenses. This can be important in reducing demand, since demand is based on decisions that reflect the costs of acquiring a trafficked person. Many crimes defy an economic analysis: crimes of passion, in particular, are rarely the result of the calculation of cost and benefit. Trafficking, however, is primarily an economic crime, and as such it responds to changes in its cost-benefit structure. If the cost includes the potential of a high penalty in both economic and legal terms, demand will at least seek new lower-risk "products." High penalties and a high likelihood of apprehension might be the most effective way to reduce demand, if they are applied to all forms of trafficking and the exploitation of trafficked people.

The fact that there is both a wholesale and retail market for trafficked people also suggests counteractions. The wholesalers are the recruiters, transporters, and traffickers who harvest and move people into the trafficking streams. Disruption of the wholesale chain also increases costs to the consumer. Effecting this disruption, however, requires international cooperation and resources. It also requires addressing the attributes the wholesaler looks for in the trafficked person. While reducing the physical health (an attribute sought by wholesalers) of trafficked people would be not be acceptable, reducing their gullibility would (though this is a preventative against trafficking, rather than a measure that reduces demand). This is the aim of public education and awareness campaigns in origin countries.[7] A much greater challenge would be to reduce the malleability that follows from economic deprivation and the lack of opportunity. Throughout the developing world, economic change has pushed large numbers of people into extreme social and economic vulnerability. In the developed world, there is a continuing demand for low-paid workers. At a very basic level, the barriers that exist between the locations of the supply of workers and the demand for workers tend to reward those who find ways to overcome those barriers. This is simplistic, of course, and does not touch the deeper underlying themes of the extreme inequalities in wealth between countries. Addressing those inequalities is not yet an aim that has received any significant allocation of resources in the northern destination countries.

In addition, a number of structural and legal measures can be taken to reduce demand. One is to increase the availability of *legal* possibilities for people to emigrate for work. Such legal opportunities would mean that potential trafficking victims would be less likely to rely on traffickers who would provide false documents, arrange travel, and find them work abroad. This would lessen demand in the destination country for illegally supplied labor by forcing it to compete with legally supplied labor. Such legal arrangements are possible. For example, a bilateral agreement between Italy and the International Organization for Migration (IOM) office in Tirana, Albania, provides for the management of labor migration flows from Albania, smoothing the integration of migrant workers into Italy. The agreement allows five thousand Albanians to work in Italy for one year. The IOM office in Tirana interviews applicants, who undergo job-skills testing. The profiles of would-be migrants are entered in an IOM database available to Italian employers on the Internet. The database also posts offers for jobs in Italy, mainly in six regions where the need for workers is high. By matching their skills to existing vacancies, the database allows applicants to leave Albania with a labor contract, enabling them to start work upon arrival in Italy. When the workers arrive in Italy, the IOM in Rome provides orientation and vocational training courses to some of the newcomers. Since most applicants are men, men have benefited most from this agreement. Clearly, such an agreement reduces demand for illegal labor in some sectors, though not all. The involvement of criminal organizations in prostitution means that exploitation for sexual purposes continues outside any such monitoring of labor flows.

Reducing Demand for Prostitution: Legal Approaches

Since a large number of trafficked people are used as prostitutes, it is important to attempt to reduce the demand for prostitution. We might look for clues to the demand by noting the ambiguity in the official responses to this particular market for trafficked people. Trafficking leads to enslavement, and this prompts the question of why enslavement into prostitution has been consistently treated differently in laws concerning trafficking. This differentiation has occurred for two reasons, one historical and negative, one contemporary and positive. Historically, there has been a reluctance to deal with prostitution within the legal discourse on slavery. The willingness to define most prostitution as consensual, the stigmatization of prostitutes, and the marked ambivalence of (primarily male-directed) law enforcement concerning prostitution led to its separation from "real" slavery and its toleration in many countries. Past instruments — the 1910 White Slavery Convention being a good example — resulted from attempts to establish a line between unacceptable forms of forced prostitution (especially of white women), and forms of prostitution that the framers of these laws and Conventions considered normal, acceptable, or inevitable. This, in turn, speaks to a more generalized moral economy that, since it does not allow prostitution, turns a blind eye to the trafficking activities supplying the prostitutes and, thus, erects no barrier against demand.

More recently and more positively, Swedish lawmakers took an opposite tack. In 1999 Sweden passed a law that criminalized the purchase of sex. According to the Swedish law, the economic and social relationship between a woman selling sex and a man buying sex is not a relationship that even approaches equality. The rationale behind the law is that, as long as society remains male dominated, women selling sex will be in a more vulnerable position than men buying sex. Men's right to buy women's bodies is seen as a form of male dominance to be resisted and controlled.

This law lets the *sale* of sex remain legal — it is only the *purchase* that is made illegal — and thus attempts to redress the imbalance of power between men and women. An official report by the government concerning the law explains: "The proposal by the Prostitution Report to criminalise both buyer and seller has been subjected to extensive criticism by almost all referral bodies. The government also deems that, even if prostitution in itself is not a desirable social activity, it is not reasonable to prosecute the party that, at least in most cases, is the weaker party, exploited by others to satisfy their sexual drive. This is also important if prostitutes are to be encouraged to get help to leave prostitution and can feel they will not have to worry about the consequences of having been prostitutes."[8]

This approach is unique, and it runs counter to recent laws in Germany and Holland that attempt to reduce demand for women trafficked into prostitution by legalizing and controlling brothels. Sweden is trying to extinguish demand for prostitution (and trafficked people) at the point of consumption; Germany and Holland are attempting to break the supply chain by arresting traffickers. Do either of these approaches work? At this point, no one knows for certain. Criticism leveled at the Swedish law states that it has simply pushed prostitution underground and toward trafficking, but no evidence has been forthcoming. Likewise, the government has stated that the law is reducing the number of women exploited in prostitution, but again little evidence is available. By the same token, the legalizing of brothels in one state in Australia has been interpreted both as decreasing trafficking, according to some commentators, and as increasing it, according others. Given that demand for prostitution is often met with women (and children) who have been trafficked, it is critical that detailed and unbiased research be carried out as quickly as possible.

One other demand-reduction strategy exists in educating the men, especially the young men, who may seek out prostitutes. We know little about how young men are first brought to purchase sex. This is significant because there is great variation — among locations, societies, and historical periods — in the use of prostitutes. Demand seems to have been reduced in some locations, and it is necessary to explore ways to re-create the conditions that led to such reduction. Clearly, improvements in the power and status of women are defining factors. One hypothesis suggests that young men in the military are especially likely to be introduced to prostitution. One suggestion to reduce demand is to target young men in the military with messages that help them to understand that the women they use may well be trafficked and, at the least, are almost certainly under the violent control of pimps. The rationale behind this is that these young men will have to consider what effect their sexual use of prostituted women will have on the lives of those women. To my knowledge, no such awareness-raising program has been tried.

The exploration of demand for trafficked people presented in this chapter is based on very little hard evidence and on only a working knowledge of marketing. We have a profound need for better research on the entire product chain of human trafficking and, especially, on consumers of trafficking victims. The hypothetical marketing manager charged with increasing the number of people trafficked and exploited would likely concentrate first on the most promising sectors. Which of these two efforts would maximize profits: generating the greatest volume of trafficking or trafficking a high-value "product"? The profitability of the former depends on permeable borders and a significant demand for labor, while the profitability of the latter depends on the demand for a high-value product. In either case it would be necessary to determine how vertically integrated the enterprise is. If the trafficking enterprise can control the process across borders and from top to bottom (origin to destination), then, in effect, the trafficker is faced with a need for consumer marketing. In that case, the trafficker would aim to increase business in the origin country by using consumer marketing tools to increase demand at the destination.[9]

The foregoing represents a general view, but the reality is (always) more complex. Borders are more or less permeable, and vertical integration varies from trafficking group to trafficking group. In some countries there is a demand for volume, in others a demand for a high-value product, and in some countries both. The point is that these variations must be studied before we can arrive at an understanding of demand for trafficked people.

One other variation must be understood in each context of trafficking. Earlier I referred to wholesalers, retailers, and consumers of trafficked persons. These are important in understanding demand because much of the marketing required to move trafficked people across borders and to consumers is what the marketing manager would call business-to-business, rather than business-to-consumer, marketing. Many traffickers are dealing with "employers" rather than consumers of trafficked people. Marketing theory and practice could still help with the analysis of this situation, but it would create a rather more complicated scenario. This would require a form of broad-spectrum diversification, or "channel marketing" to wholesalers and retailers, within which there is perhaps room for some system integration to create a value-added product (trafficked people that speak English perhaps, or who know how to operate certain machinery). Linked to understanding the "channel" is the task of determining how the buyers and sellers of trafficked people find each other. Theirs is not an open marketplace or one that uses the usual forms of advertising (though they do use the Internet and some other methods). Locating the point at which contact is made and the sale takes place would also be important to those who wish to disrupt the trafficking flow.

That said, price is a key marketing variable, and in this context it is the one that matters. If trafficked and enslaved labor weren't cheap, trafficking wouldn't endure. For that reason, it is worth concluding with a quick review of questions concerning the elasticity of demand for trafficking victims. *Elasticity* is the term that economists use to describe the potential rise and fall in demand for any product. Some products have a great deal of elasticity, others very little. The demand for solid gold designer watches, for example, is highly elastic: if there is a cheaper acceptable alternative, and if consumers have limited resources (for example, during a recession), demand for luxury goods shrinks. Basic foodstuffs, on the other hand, have low elasticity: even if the cost of bread doubles, people still need to eat and will continue to buy it. In describing elasticity, economists point to addictive drugs, like heroin, as products with virtually no elasticity of demand, since the force of addiction drives the demand no matter what the cost of the product.

The most important determinant of the elasticity of demand is the availability of substitutes. The elasticity of demand tends to be greater for products that have more close substitutes available. This general rule of economics suggests some responses to human trafficking. First, it supports the idea that alternative, legal, and controlled forms of labor migration would help reduce demand for trafficked people. If the demand for cheap labor can be met with a competitive alternative that does not involve illegal and abusive trafficking, consumers will shift to the legal labor. Second, if the cost of using trafficked labor is increased, through more law enforcement and prosecution, legal alternatives become more attractive.

The role of the cost of labor is also reflected in a second known determinant of demand elasticity, the proportion of the consumer's budget devoted to the product. Put simply, the more expensive a product is (the greater the proportion of the consumer's budget it demands), the more elastic will be the demand for the product. A sandwich may double or triple in price without significantly reducing demand; a house (which takes up a sizeable portion of most budgets) that doubles or triples in price will dramatically reduce demand. The unfortunate reality of human trafficking, and one of the key reasons for its explosive growth in the past decade, is that the relatively low cost of trafficked people means that their consumers are not sensitive to the cost of trafficked labor. Again, this rule of economics supports the idea that policies must work to dramatically increase the costs of using (or consuming) trafficked labor.

This brief discussion of elasticity of demand is also aimed at highlighting the fact that different forms of trafficked labor have different levels of elasticity of demand. None of these different levels have been estimated, and so they represent another area of needed research. That said, we might nonetheless surmise that the demand for trafficked people to be used in domestic service is more elastic than the demand for trafficked people to be exploited in prostitution. Individuals seeking the former have a potentially greater number of alternatives; those seeking the latter have limited alternatives, since prostitution exists within an illicit market and is driven by what some might describe as biologically driven need. This demand is also linked to one of the USP attributes described above: some men express low elasticity in their demand for "the real thing." Whatever the case, the different levels of and elasticity of demand, the different levels of integration, and the question of high volume versus high value, all require exploration for each subtype of human trafficking. Undertaking this exploration would in itself be a step toward demand reduction.

Three Steps to Stopping Slavery

(And Four Things You Can Do Right Away)

This book shows that slavery may be widespread, but that it can be stopped. The national laws are in place, and international agencies like the UN are ready to act, but nothing will happen until the public demands action and antislavery work is funded. When every person who doesn't want to live in a world with slavery takes the following three steps, it will be the beginning of the end for slavery.

STEP 1. LEARN

If you have just read this book, you've already taken this step. Now share this book with a friend, your church, or your class and order one for your local library. Every penny of the author's royalties from this book goes to antislavery work. Keep educating yourself about how slavery infiltrates our world and our lives. There is a constantly updated flow of information at www.freetheslaves.net and www.antislavery.org.

STEP 2. JOIN WITH OTHERS WHO WANT TO END SLAVERY

Around the world Free the Slaves and Anti-Slavery International are working to end slavery. They do this by supporting local organizations that liberate people who've been enslaved; by helping businesses and consumers stop buying slave-made goods; and by persuading national governments to enforce antislavery laws. There are millions of people just like you who want slavery to end today. To make your voice heard, join with Free the Slaves in the United States or its sister organization, Anti-Slavery International, in Europe. To do so, simply contact them at www.freetheslaves.net and www.antislavery.org. Or you can write or call them.

Free the Slaves	Anti-Slavery International
1012 - 14th Street NW	Thomas Clarkson House
Washington, DC, 20005, USA	Broomgrove Road
Phone: 202–638–1865	London, SW9 9TL, England
	Phone: 020–7501–8920

STEP 3. ACT!

When you have joined with Free the Slaves, two things will happen: First, you'll be alerted to effective and timely actions you can take against slavery. Second, you'll be able to add your thoughts, energies, and commitment to ending slavery. Young or old, skilled or not — every mind and every heart is needed.

You may also be asked to make a donation. It is truly needed. If you add up all the money spent in the world to fight slavery every year, it wouldn't equal the cost of one new B-1 bomber. When you consider that the cost of freeing most slaves, through activism and law enforcement, may be as little as thirty-five dollars, this disparity is obscene. As the (unpaid) president of Free the Slaves, I've met dozens of ex-slaves who are starting new lives because local activists were funded to rescue and support them. As you know from reading this book, I've also met hundreds of slaves around the world who haven't been reached by the underfunded local organizations struggling against slavery. I will never accept that slavery should continue to be their fate.

And while you're at it, here are four more things you can do right away:

Don't put this book on the shelf.   Give it to someone else to read. Ignorance about slavery is one of the main reasons why it still grows. Take this book to your school, book club, or other groups where books are borrowed and discussed. Give a copy to your local or school library.

Ask hard questions of charities.   If you currently support any charity that works in the developing world, be it child sponsorship, missionary work, or medical relief, ask them: What are you doing to stop slavery or to prevent people from being vulnerable to slavery and human trafficking? And if they're not doing anything, tell them what you know about slavery and help lead them to action.

Ask hard questions of politicians.   Some of the most powerful weapons against slavery are the "sticks and carrots" of economic sanctions, trade, and support of developed countries. A law passed by the U.S. Congress all but stopped child slavery in the Dominican sugar fields overnight. When politicians want your vote, ask them what they are doing to stop slavery. We all want our taxes to be spent effectively, and stopping slavery isn't expensive. The $945 million estimated to bring slavery to an end is just .000043 percent of the U.S. government's budget. The space program costs fifteen times that amount.

Ask hard questions of businesses, pension funds, and investments.   What is the supply chain that leads to your company's products? Can the managers of your pension fund or mutual fund assure you that they are investing your money in companies working to take slavery out of their supply chain? What criteria besides profit guide their choice of investment? If they can't or won't give you a straight answer, move your money. There are ethical funds that avoid investing in companies that might be linked to slavery. While boycotting products isn't normally effective, getting companies to take responsibility for their product chain is one of the best ways to stop slavery at its source. Companies that do so should be supported.

Slavery Research Questions Used in Case Studies

Demographics

For each unit (that is, a farm, a brothel, a brickyard, and so on — the local and specific unit of production) the following questions were asked.

1. SIZE

How many slaves/unfree laborers are held in the unit (kiln/factory/brothel/farm, and so on)?

How does this unit compare with others of its type (same business) in the same geographical area in terms of total number of employees and the amount of business/production?

Is it big, small, or average when compared to other such units?

What is the range of sizes of such units within the same geographical area?

Are such units known to be different in size in other geographical areas?

2. SCALE OF ENSLAVEMENT

What proportion of the local workforce in that sector are enslaved/unfree?

What proportion overall in the workforce in that particular village/region?

What is the population of the nearest geographical unit (village/town/district)?

What is the best estimate of the number of enslaved/unfree laborers within that geographical unit?

3. GENDER AND AGE BREAKDOWN

What proportion of the enslaved/unfree laborers in each unit are male/female?

What proportion are children; what is the age breakdown?

Is the work they are doing specifically categorized for men or women?

Is there segregation of tasks (that is, if the ultimate product requires several steps of stages in its production, are these jobs segregated to different groups — men, women, or children)?

Are the slaves/unfree laborers held as individuals or as families?

4. ETHNIC DIFFERENCES

What ethnic backgrounds are the slaves?

Are the slaves from a different ethnic group than slaveholders?

Are there ethnic differences between others involved in slavery, for example, the community around the unit, or users of products of slavery — for example, brothel users?

Is there a history of domination by one of these groups over another?

5. RELIGIOUS DIFFERENCES

Are there religious differences between slave and slaveholder and/or the consumer of slave products?

What is the nature of the religiosity of all the people in the context? That is, what is the religious context within the village/city/country — a predominate religion? regular practice? institution of religious law?

6. LOCATION OF SLAVERY

Are the units using slave labor mainly in rural or urban settings or both?

Are they geographically or otherwise isolated?

Do they tend to exist in places where "modern" norms and ideas do not prevail?

Do local people know of the existence of slavery in their area?

Does the local/national government know?

7. EFFECT OF THE WORK ON SLAVES

How does enslavement affect their life expectancy?

Does the production process bring any specific health dangers?

At what age are slaves normally not able to continue the work, and what happens to them then?

8. THE SLAVEHOLDERS

Who are they: ages, sex, education level, class/caste background?

How do they fit into the society/community? What is their role?

How are they perceived by other members of the community?

How long have they lived in this community?

Do they have other jobs/enterprises?

Is slaveholding an inherited occupation?

Why are they slaveholders compared to others of similar background who are not?

If they were not slaveholders, what would they be likely to be doing?

How do they/would they explain their holding of these laborers?

Forms and Processes

I. ECONOMICS OF SLAVERY

How much capital is needed to establish this form of production?

Details on overhead:

What is the cost of a slave?

What costs are there in addition to the purchase price/loan?

What is the subsistence cost of a slave?

What rents are paid by the slaveholders?

What other expenses do they have connected to labor?

What is the cost of any necessary raw materials?

What is the cost of the legitimating mechanism that conceals the illegality?

What kinds of permits, bribes, and so on are needed to start and maintain production/operation?

What other workers are needed, and how much are they paid?

What is the cost of free labor[ers] if hired to do the same work?

What is their [slaveholders] estimated total turnover?

What profit does the owner make?

What is the competition?

Is the market for the product or service increasing or decreasing?

Do they [slaveholders] pay any taxes and/or bribes?

What is the potential for mechanization to replace slaves?

Is the production unit part of the formal or informal economy?

If the item is also produced through mechanized rather than slave production, does the mechanized production serve a different market?

Is mechanized production becoming more economic?

What are the obstacles to mechanization?

2. PROFIT ON INVESTMENT

How does the profit from slave production compare with profit from paid labor production? Are there other ways that the slaveholder could invest their capital?

If so, would they invest their capital elsewhere if given the choice?

Do they have the choice?

How committed are the slaveholders to enterprise using slave labor?

Could they easily and profitably shift to other forms of investment — or is their stake in slaveholding too high?

3. ECONOMIC INDICATORS FOR THE LOCAL AREA, REGION, NATION

What are local wage rates, and what is the local cost of living?

What are the absolute and relative poverty levels?

What does it cost to keep a person alive?

What is the rate of inflation?

How has the local economy been changing?

What is the unemployment rate?

4. WORK AND PRODUCTION PROCESSES

What is a full description of the work being done?

Within this area of production, which element of the work is done by slave labor?

Is the work seasonal?

Is it the top end of the product range or the lower end? (That is, is it a "high quality/high cost" product or a "low quality/low cost" product when compared to the same product as produced by others in the same context?)

Is the slave-produced item part of a bigger product? (That is, is the product a "finished" product ready for sale/use, or will it require further processing before sale/use; if a service rather than a product, is it a "final" service or part of a larger/longer service?)

Is the market for the product local, national, or international?

How many processes/stops does the item go through before reaching its end use?

5. CONSUMER CHOICES

Who is the end consumer of the product?

How does the slave-produced item compare with the product from other sources?

If the consumer chose not to use slave-produced items, where could they get the item from, and what would be the price difference?

6. PROCESS OF ENSLAVEMENT

Is it debt, trickery, use of contracts, violence? Or a combination?

What would be a typical story of enslavement in this situation?

Is there a legitimating social, cultural, or legal mechanism? If so, what is it?

Is it possible to copy/transcribe any "contract" or debt bond?

What is the first point of contact between potential slave and slaver?

How is the potential slave approached?

What are the factors that might push or pull a person into enslave-ment — social, family, economic, cultural? (What is the slaver offering that draws the person into the relationship?)

What are the aspects of the potential slave's life that are pushing them toward enslavement?

What makes them vulnerable to enslavement?

What alternatives exist to enslavement for the slave?

How would they survive if not enslaved?

How do they seal the bargain?

At what point is it irrevocable?

Is it really irrevocable, or is that just the perception on the slave?

Once enslaved, are they likely to be retained by the person who enslaved them, or will they be sold?

Is the slaver a procurer, a middleperson, or the person who uses the slaves?

What is the process until they end up in the place they're likely to stay?

Once they're there, are they likely to be later sold or traded to others?

What makes them attractive slaves — what attributes do they need to have?

Are they enslaved with a view to filling a particular job?

Might they be moved to other work at some stage?

7. THE RELATIONSHIP

How does the enslaved person see the situation they're in?

Does their perspective change at different points in the relationship?

What is the social relationship between the slave and the slaveholder? (That is, how is it perceived by each of them, and how is it perceived by the people around them?)

Does the person who enslaves try to justify enslavement — to themselves, the community, the government? If so, how?

What is the nature of control over the slave; how is violence used or threatened?

What social or psychological violence might be used to control the slave?

What social norms, beyond the threat of violence, bind the slave and the slaveholder?

What is the role of government or official acquiescence or participation in enslavement?

Is the slave/slaveholder relationship "enforced" by local "law enforcement"?

Is there any possibility of manumission? If so, how can that process take place?

If you've been a slave, does it affect what you can do afterward?

If you stop being a slave, are you socially marked or otherwise affected?

8. CHILDREN OF SLAVES

What happens to any children of slaves?

What control do slaves have over their offspring?

Are children a help or hindrance to the slave?

Do they increase or decrease the value of the slave to the slaveholder?

Do slaves control their [own] reproduction at all?

9. NECESSARY PRECONDITIONS

Can it be said that violence and its threat are not the monopoly of the state in this local area/region/country? (That is, are people with power or weapons able to use them without a high chance of state intervention, and specifically to use them to capture and/or hold slaves?)

Are there social norms that validate or allow enslavement (at least for the slaver and those with whom immediate trading of slave-produced goods or services takes place)?

What is the legitimating mechanism that allows the legal concealment of slavery, since slavery is tacitly illegal?

Rankings of Countries on Ordinal Scales for Slavery and Trafficking

Including Ranges of Estimated Number of Slaves

Slavery: 1 = low, 4 = high; trafficking variables: 1 = low, 4 = high

Country	Incidence of Slavery	Flow of Human Traffic To	Flow of Human Traffic From	Number of Slaves, Low Estimate	Number of Slaves, High Estimate
Afghanistan	3	2	3	20,000	50,000
Albania	2	1	3	5,000	10,000
Algeria	2	2	2	1,000	2,000
Argentina	2	2	2	1,000	2,000
Armenia	2	1	2	2,000	4,000
Australia	1	3	1	4,000	6,000
Austria	1	2	0	1,000	2,000
Azerbaijan	2	1	2	1,000	2,000
Bahrain	2	2	2	1,000	2,000
Bangladesh	2	1	4	10,000	20,000
Barbados	1	1	1	0	100
Belarus	1	1	3	2,000	3,000
Belgium	1	2	1	5,000	7,000
Benin	3	4	4	20,000	40,000
Bosnia and Herzegovina	1	2	2	3,000	4,000
Brazil	4	4	4	100,000	200,000
Bulgaria	1	2	4	2,000	4,000

(continued)

Rankings of Countries *(continued)*

Country	Incidence of Slavery	Flow of Human Traffic To	Flow of Human Traffic From	Number of Slaves, Low Estimate	Number of Slaves, High Estimate
Burkina Faso	3	3	3	2,000	4,000
Burma	4	1	4	50,000	100,000
Cambodia	2	2	3	3,000	6,000
Cameroon	3	3	3	6,000	12,000
Canada	1	2	1	10,000	20,000
China	3	3	3	250,000	300,000
Colombia	1	2	3	5,000	10,000
Congo (Kinshasa)	2	2	3	1,000	1,500
Costa Rica	1	1	2	0	100
Croatia	2	2	3	1,000	2,000
Czech Republic	2	4	4	2,000	5,000
Denmark	1	1	1	1,000	2,000
Dominica	1	1	1	0	100
Dominican Republic	1	1	2	5,000	6,000
Egypt	1	2	2	1,000	2,000
Equatorial Guinea	3	3	4	1,000	2,000
Estonia	1	2	2	1,000	2,000
France	2	3	1	10,000	20,000
Gabon	3	2	3	5,000	10,000
Gambia	3	4	4	3,000	6,000
Georgia	2	2	4	1,000	2,000
Germany	1	3	1	5,000	9,000
Ghana	2	3	3	10,000	20,000
Greece	1	2	1	5,000	9,000
Guinea-Bissau	3	2	3	1,000	2,000
Haiti	4	2	4	75,000	150,000
Hong Kong	1	3	2	1,000	2,000
Hungary	1	3	3	1,000	2,000
India	4	3	4	18,000,000	22,000,000
Indonesia	3	2	3	4,000	8,000
Israel	1	4	1	4,000	6,000
Italy	1	4	2	30,000	40,000
Ivory Coast	4	4	4	30,000	80,000
Jamaica	1	2	2	0	500
Japan	2	4	2	5,000	10,000
Kazakhstan	2	1	2	1,000	2,000
Kenya	2	1	2	3,000	5,000

Country	Incidence of Slavery	Flow of Human Traffic To	Flow of Human Traffic From	Number of Slaves, Low Estimate	Number of Slaves, High Estimate
South Korea	1	2	2	10,000	15,000
Kuwait	3	2	1	1,000	2,000
Kyrgyzstan	1	1	1	1,000	1,500
Laos	2	1	3	5,000	10,000
Lebanon	1	2	2	1,000	1,500
Liberia	3	2	2	3,000	6,000
Luxembourg	1	2	1	2,000	3,000
Macedonia	1	2	3	1,000	1,500
Malaysia	2	3	3	3,000	6,000
Mali	4	4	4	10,000	20,000
Mauritania	4	2	3	250,000	300,000
Mexico	2	3	3	3,000	6,000
Moldova	1	3	3	1,000	1,500
Morocco	2	4	4	1,000	2,000
Nepal	4	2	4	250,000	300,000
Netherlands	1	3	1	3,000	5,000
Niger	4	4	4	3,000	5,000
Nigeria	3	2	4	20,000	40,000
Oman	3	3	2	1,000	2,000
Pakistan	4	3	4	2,500,000	3,500,000
Panama	1	1	1	0	100
Peru	2	2	2	3,000	5,000
Philippines	4	2	4	3,000	10,000
Poland	2	4	4	2,000	4,000
Portugal	2	3	2	5,000	6,000
Puerto Rico	1	1	1	0	100
Qatar	3	3	2	1,000	2,000
Romania	2	3	4	5,000	6,000
Russia	2	4	4	8,000	10,000
São Tomé and Príncipe	4	4	4	1,000	2,000
Saudi Arabia	4	4	4	2,000	5,000
Senegal	4	4	4	6,000	12,000
Sierra Leone	4	4	4	3,000	6,000
Singapore	1	3	3	1,000	1,500
Slovakia	1	3	3	2,000	3,000
South Africa	2	3	3	5,000	6,000

(continued)

Rankings of Countries *(continued)*

Country	Incidence of Slavery	Flow of Human Traffic To	Flow of Human Traffic From	Number of Slaves, Low Estimate	Number of Slaves, High Estimate
Spain	1	2	2	10,000	15,000
Sri Lanka	2	2	4	5,000	10,000
Sudan	4	4	4	20,000	50,000
Sweden	1	1	0	2,000	3,000
Switzerland	1	1	1	1,000	1,500
Tajikistan	2	2	2	2,000	4,000
Tanzania	2	2	2	2,000	4,000
Thailand	4	4	4	30,000	60,000
Togo	2	2	3	6,000	8,000
Trinidad and Tobago	1	1	1	0	100
Turkey	2	4	4	20,000	30,000
Turkmenistan	2	3	3	1,000	2,000
Uganda	2	2	3	5,000	8,000
Ukraine	2	2	4	3,000	5,000
United Arab Emirates	3	4	2	1,000	2,000
United Kingdom	1	1	1	4,000	5,000
United States	1	1	1	100,000	150,000
Uzbekistan	2	2	2	1,000	2,000
Vietnam	2	2	3	5,000	7,000
Yemen	3	3	2	1,000	2,000
Yugoslavia	2	3	4	8,000	10,000

Notes

Chapter 1. Understanding Slavery Today

1. Sankalp is an Indian social movement that was set up 1994, and that has worked in partnership since 2001 with the American antislavery organization Free the Slaves. Based in a poor, remote region of Uttar Pradesh in North India, Sankalp enables members of communities who have been enslaved as stone quarry workers, often for several generations, to leave the slaveholders and work for themselves. In the past few years, over four thousand adults, and many more children, have been able to walk away from slavery and begin sustainable livelihoods with Sankalp's assistance.

In slavery, families receive less than half the state-determined minimum wage and barely survive; children are forced to work carrying sand and rocks to waiting trucks, missing out on the education that might radically improve their future prospects. Tuberculosis, malaria, and silicosis have been endemic in the area, and forests have been reduced to barren deserts through indiscriminate felling of trees and mining by profiteering contractors.

With Sankalp's help, the laborers form self-help groups and gain control over the key economic resource from which they earn a living. They do this by saving tiny amounts together and using their savings to obtain loans from local banks. With these loans, they pay for legal quarrying leases. Having their own leases allows laborers to immediately triple their income.

Simply being organized into local groups and knowing their civil rights makes former slaves less vulnerable to violent reprisals by slaveholders. Group members in villages that have their own leases now provide sanctuary to people fleeing violence from villages still in slavery. Now, with the formation of a federation of two hundred of these self-help groups, the balance of power in the whole region — between laborers and slaveholding quarry contractors — is rapidly changing. Laborers are starting to think of other ways to earn a living — and hope to leave stone crushing behind forever.

The former slaves are pursuing their children's education with a passion: village education committees are mushrooming in areas where leases have been acquired. These committees monitor attendance of every child and ensure that teachers do not shirk their duties. Also from the villagers themselves has come a powerful demand to renew the forests and to introduce species yielding sustainable forest products, to help them survive. To know more about and support Sankalp's work, see www.freetheslaves.net.

2. General William T. Sherman issued Special Field Order Number 15 on January 16, 1865, setting aside land in South Carolina for the exclusive settlement of freed slaves. Each family was to receive forty acres of land and an army mule to work the land. Forty acres was commonly accepted as the amount of land one person could effectively cultivate with one mule. The Freedmen's Bureau also used this formula in awarding confiscated or abandoned land to former slaves. However, in late 1865, President Andrew Johnson issued pardons returning the property to former Confederates.

3. Desmond Tutu, *No Future without Forgiveness* (London: Rider, 1999), 31.

4. Kevin Bales, *Disposable People: New Slavery in the Global Economy* (Berkeley: University of California Press, 1999).

5. R. Ouensavi and A. Kielland, *Child Labour Migration from Benin: Magnitude and Determinants* (Washington, DC: World Bank, 2000).

6. Anne Kielland and Ibrahim Sanogo, *Burkina Faso: Child Labor Migration from Rural Areas. The Magnitude and the Determinants,* Terre des Hommes and World Bank, 2002, p. 5, http://home.online.no/~annekie/Africa_docs/BFEnglish .pdf.

7. See, for example, *Guns or Growth? Assessing the Impact of Arms Sales on Sustainable Development* (Oxford: Oxfam UK, 2004). Available from www.control arms.org/.

8. *Addressing the Challenges of International Bribery and Fair Competition* (U.S. Department of Commerce, International Trade Administration, Washington, DC, July 2002).

9. Bales, *Disposable People.*

10. Rainforest Action Network. See www.ran.org/info_center/.

11. Binka Le Breton, *Trapped: Modern Slavery in the Brazilian Amazon* (Bloomfield, CT.: Kumarian Press, 2003), p. xxii.

12. "Government Misleads Parliament on Narmada Issue," Narmada Bachao Andolan Press Release, November 20, 2002. Available at www.narmada .org/ nba-press-releases/.

13. C. M. Peters, A. H. Gentry, and R. O. Mendelsohn, "Valuation of an Amazonian Rainforest," *Nature* 339 (1989): 655–56.

Chapter 2. Slavery and the Human Right to Evil

An earlier version of this chapter appeared as "Slavery and the Human Right to Evil," *Journal of Human Rights* 3, no. 1 (March 2004): 53–63.

1. See especially Roy F. Baumeister, *Evil: Inside Human Cruelty and Violence* (New York: W. H. Freeman and Company, 1997).

2. What is not made clear by such a definition is the question of severity. Does an action have to reach a certain level of severity to be considered evil? Is the small snub that harms one's feelings, while uncomfortable, evil? This is a question I intend to dodge. Since this book considers evil and human rights, and since most codifications of human rights do not include actions whose outcomes are of very low severity (such as a social snub), for the purposes of this book I consider to be "evil" only those actions leading to severe harm.

3. Baumeister, *Evil*, p. 73.

4. Ibid., p. 75.

5. Milton Meltzer, *Slavery: A World History* (New York: DeCapo, 1971), p. 44.

6. Hugh Thomas, *The Slave Trade: The History of the Atlantic Slave Trade, 1440–1870* (New York: Simon and Schuster, 1997), p. 458.

7. Ibid., p. 468.

8. Ibid., p. 491.

9. Henry Mayer, *All on Fire: William Lloyd Garrison and the Abolition of Slavery* (New York: St. Martin's Press, 1998), p. 65.

10. Ibid., p. 469.

11. Corporate Watch UK, www.corporatewatch.org.uk/.

12. Martin Albrow, *The Global Age* (London: Polity Press, 1996), p. 88.

13. Baumeister, *Evil*, p. 6.

14. There are in fact two distinct forms of debt bondage, both of which meet this criterion but in different ways. In many cases of debt bondage, the labor power (and indeed the very life of the debtor) becomes collateral for the debt. This establishes the trap of bondage: since all the labor power of the debtor is the collateral property of the lender until the debt is repaid, the debtor is unable to ever earn enough to repay the debt by his or her own labor. This arrangement is a hallmark of debt bondage on the Indian subcontinent. In other areas the work of the debtor ostensibly may be applied to the debt, but, through false accounting or extortionate interest, repayment remains forever out of reach. In the first form of debt bondage, the very nature of the agreement, which transforms labor power into collateral, practically disqualifies the debtor from ever repaying the debt. In the second form, a violation of the agreement traps the debtor — that is, this form occurs when "the value of those services as reasonably assessed is not applied towards the liquidation of the debt."

15. "Baldev," quoted in Kevin Bales, *Disposable People: New Slavery in the Global Economy* (Berkeley: University of California Press, 1999), p. 206.

16. Bales, *Disposable People*.

17. Baumeister, *Evil*, p. 101.

18. Julia Baker, Mobile, Alabama, August 1937, cited by Mary A. Poole in *Works Progress Administration Ex-Slave Narratives*, CD-ROM (Orem, UT: Myfamily.com, 2000).

19. Bales, *Disposable People*, p. 62.

20. Another example of psychological control, that of young women enslaved as domestic workers in Paris, is given in chapter 7.

21. Mayer, *All on Fire*, p. 537.

Chapter 3. No One Shall Be Held in Slavery or Servitude

Peter Robbins coauthored this chapter, a version of which first appeared in *Human Rights Review* 2, no. 2 (January 2001). This article draws upon a report made to the United Nations Working Group on Contemporary Forms of Slavery, prepared by Professor David Weissbrodt and Anti-Slavery International. (See *Report of the Working Group on Contemporary Forms of Slavery on Its Twenty-third Session*, UN Doc. E/CN.4/Sub.2/1998/14, para. 22 (1998), www.antislavery .org/homepage/resources/weissbrodt%20report%20final%20edition%202003 .pdf. Michael Dottridge, director of Anti-Slavery International, and Professor Weissbrodt were lead authors of that report; Norah Gallagher provided important research for it, as did Matthew Armbrecht, Marcela Kostihova, and Mary Thacker. Production of the report was supported, in part, by Kevin Bales and Roehampton University London. Caroline Tendall helped edit this article.

1. According to the *Oxford Encyclopedic English Dictionary*, an international law is "a body of rules established by custom or treaty and agreed as binding by nations in their relations with one another."

2. A declaration is a statement asserting or protecting a legal right; an instrument is a formal, especially a legal, document. See Declaration Relative to the Universal Abolition of the Slave Trade, February 8, 1815, Consolidated Treaty Series, Vol. 63, No. 473.

3. Margaret E. Burton, *The Assembly of the League of Nations* (Chicago: University of Chicago Press, 1941). See also Weissbrodt and Anti-Slavery International, *Report of the Working Group on Contemporary Forms of Slavery on Its Twenty-third Session*, p. 3. According to Article 22 of the League of Nations Covenant, "the Mandatory must be responsible for the administration of the territory under conditions which will guarantee . . . the prohibition of abuses such as the slave trade."

4. M. Cherif Bassiouni, "Enslavement as an International Crime," *New York University Journal of Law and Politics* 23 (1991): 445.

5. Statute of the International Court of Justice, June 26, 1945, Chapter 2, "Competence of the Court," Article 38, Part b, 59 Stat. 1055.

6. Mark W. Janis, "The Nature of Jus Cogens," *Connecticut Journal of International Law* 3 (Spring 1988): 359, www.law.uconn.edu/journals/cjil/.

7. *Report of the International Law Commission to the General Assembly*, UN Doc. A/CN.4/Ser.A/Add.1 (1963). See the International Law Commission's Website, www.un.org/law/ilc/index.htm.

8. Found in General Comment No. 24, UN Doc. CCPR/C/21/Rev.1/Add.6, 11 November 1994, para. 8.

9. Renee Colette Redman, "The League of Nations and the Right to Be Free from Enslavement: The First Human Right to Be Recognized as Custom-

ary International Law," *Chicago-Kent Law Review* 70 (1994): 759, 780. See also Weissbrodt and Anti-Slavery International, *Report of the Working Group on Contemporary Forms of Slavery on Its Twenty-third Session,* p. 3.

10. Bassiouni, "Enslavement as an International Crime," p. 445. Forced labor can be defined as paid or unpaid work that is compulsory, often taking place under harsh conditions.

11. Barcelona Traction, Light, and Power Company, Ltd. (New Application: 1962), Judgment February 5, 1970 (Reports 1970, p. 3) [3.32]. Weissbrodt and Anti-Slavery International, *Report of the Working Group on Contemporary Forms of Slavery on Its Twenty-third Session,* p. 3.

12. A convention is an agreement between states that is less formal than a treaty. The 1815 Declaration did not include a definition of slavery or the slave trade, as these were considered to be self-evident practices at the time. The 1890 Convention Relative to the Slave Trade and Importation into Africa of Firearms, Ammunition, and Spirituous Liquors (the "Brussels Convention"), although one of the longest and most comprehensive instruments dealing with the slave trade (primarily the export trade), did not include any definitions in its text.

13. Slavery Convention of 1926, League of Nations Treaty Series, Vol. 60, p. 253, Article 1(1).

14. Ibid., Article 1(2). A distinction can be made between the state of slavery and the process of enslavement. The state of slavery is the condition of being a slave; the process of enslavement concerns the way in which someone becomes enslaved, itself a large conceptual and substantive area. Although I acknowledge that the latter is an important part of slavery, in this book I focus on the state, rather than the process, of slavery, due to space limitations.

15. Ibid., Article 2(b). All of the nation-states that make themselves party to the Convention by ratification are known as "states parties."

16. Ibid., Article 5. In the Belgian Congo, for example, indigenous populations were forced to work in the production of cash crops such as rubber. Extreme cruelty, torture, cancellation of all personal freedom, and the use of violence to enforce work requirements were hallmarks of forced labor.

17. Many international agreements include references to serfdom as a form of slavery. I do not see serfdom as slavery, because it is based on a system of land tenure and does not have the element of absolute control present in the forms of slavery explored later in the chapter.

18. The *Oxford Encyclopedic English Dictionary* defines *servitude* as "1. slavery 2. subjection (especially involuntary); bondage." Of the main terms used in international agreements (*slavery, servitude,* and *forced labor*), *servitude* is least well defined. For practical purposes it can refer to a set of practices and institutions that include serfdom, debt bondage, unfree marriages, and unfree forms of child labor. The victims are identified as persons of servile status rather than as slaves.

19. *Report of the Temporary Slavery Commission to the Council of the League of Nations* (A.17.1924.VI.B), 1924, quoted in *The Suppression of Slavery (Memorandum Submitted by the Secretary-General to the Ad Hoc Committee on Slavery),* UN Doc. ST/SPA/4 (1951), para. 22.

20. Ibid.; Weissbrodt and Anti-Slavery International, *Report of the Working Group on Contemporary Forms of Slavery on Its Twenty-third Session*, p. 3. The *Report to the Sixth Committee of the League of Nations Assembly* in 1926 also clarified, in relation to Article 2(b) of the final text of the Slavery Convention, that the words "notably in the case of domestic slavery and similar conditions" were being omitted on the grounds that "such conditions come within the definition of slavery contained in the first article and that no further prohibition of them in express terms was necessary. This applies not only to domestic slavery but to all those conditions mentioned by the Temporary Slavery Commission . . . i.e., debt slavery, the enslaving of persons disguised as adoption of children and the acquisition of girls by purchase disguised as payment of dowry." Quoted in *The Suppression of Slavery (Memorandum Submitted by the Secretary-General to the Ad Hoc Committee on Slavery)*, p. 15.

21. Seventh Assembly of the League of Nations, Resolution of 25 September 1926, A.123.1926.VI, *League of Nations Official Journal*, LNOJ-1(E) (Geneva: League of Nations, 1926).

22. V. Nanda and C. Bassiouni, "Slavery and the Slave Trade: Steps toward Eradication," *Santa Clara Lawyer* 12 (1971): 424, 430. It should also be noted that Nepal denied that pressure by the league brought about abolition in that country, claiming instead that it was part of an ongoing modernization program. Burma was, of course, part of the British Empire and was administered through the colonial government of India. The British ransomed slaves in the Hu Kwang Valley but also created a reservation in the border area of the Naga Hills that was not withdrawn until 1936. I am grateful for Suzanne Miers for helping me come to grips with this period and region. See her *Slavery in the Twentieth Century* (Walnut Creek, CA: AltaMira Press, 2003).

23. See chapter 7 for a brief discussion of the White Slavery Convention.

24. Supplementary Convention on the Abolition of Slavery, the Slave Trade, and Institutions and Practices Similar to Slavery, United Nations Treaty Series, Vol. 226, p. 3, entered into force April 30, 1957, Section 1, Article 1.

25. Universal Declaration of Human Rights, 10 December 1948, UN Doc. A/810 at 71, Article 4.

26. UN Doc. E/1988, par 11.

27. *Report of the Ad Hoc Committee of Experts on Slavery*, UN Doc. E/AC.33/13 (1951), p. 13.

28. *Servile* can be defined as "of or being like a slave or slaves," according to the *Oxford Encyclopedic English Dictionary*. The term *servitude* is not used in the Supplementary Convention, which refers instead to "institutions and practices similar to slavery" and "persons of servile status."

29. Supplementary Convention, Section 1, Article 1.

30. *Report of the Sub-Commission on Prevention of Discrimination and Protection of Minorities*, UN Doc. E/CN.4 Sub.2/1982/20, para. 9 (1982).

31. According to *The Oxford Encyclopedic English Dictionary*, a covenant is "a contract drawn up under a seal."

32. *The Oxford Encyclopedic English Dictionary* defines *protocol* as "the original

draft of a diplomatic document, especially of the terms of a treaty agreed to in conference and signed by the parties." Ninety-five of the states that have ratified the Civil and Political Covenant have also ratified the Optional Protocol. It appears that, to date, no such claim has been made directly to the Human Rights Committee by an individual alleging that a violation of his rights has occurred in contravention to Article 8 of the Civil and Political Covenant.

33. International Covenant on Economic, Social, and Cultural Rights, December 19, 1966, United Nations Treaty Series, Vol. 993, p. 3, Article 6(1).

34. "No one shall be held in servitude": International Covenant on Civil and Political Rights, United Nations Treaty Series, Vol. 999, p. 171, Article 8(2).

35. Article 8 (3) of the International Covenant on Civil and Political Rights.

36. *The Oxford Encyclopedic English Dictionary* defines an act as "a written ordinance of a parliament or some other legislative body."

37. Rome Statute of the International Criminal Court (A/CONF.183/9) (1988), Article 7(2)c.

38. Protocol Art. 3.b, Protocol to Prevent, Suppress and Punish Trafficking in Persons, Especially Women and Children, Supplementing the United Nations Convention against Transnational Organized Crime, G.A. Res. 25, annex II, UN GAOR, 55th sess., Supp. No. 49, at 60, UN Doc. A/45/49 (Vol. 1) (2001). See chapter 7 for a further discussion of the Anti-Trafficking Protocol.

39. In this context, slavery-like practices are synonymous with those designated as "servitude" — i.e., debt bondage, serfdom, unfree marriages, and exploitation of young people for their labor.

40. Slavery Convention of 1926, League of Nations Treaty Series, Vol. 60, p. 253, Article 2.

41. Vienna Convention on the Law of Treaties, United Nations Treaty Series, Vol. 1155, p. 331, Article 31.

42. Tom Brass, *The Political Economy of Unfree Labor* (Cambridge: Cambridge University Press, 1999), p. 10.

43. Ibid.

44. Orlando Patterson, *Slavery and Social Death: A Comparative Study* (Cambridge: Harvard University Press, 1982), p. 7.

45. Kevin Bales, *Disposable People* (Berkeley: University of California Press, 1999), p. 84.

46. Jose de Souza Martins, "Escravidao Hoje no Brasil" *Folha de Sao Paulo,* 13 (May 1986): 7; quoted in Bales, *Disposable People,* p. 128.

47. Elie Wiesel, *Night* (New York: Bantam Books, 1982).

48. Eugene Genovese, *Roll, Jordan, Roll: The World the Slaves Made* (New York: Vintage, 1976).

49. David Hecht, "Where African Slavery Still Exists in the Eyes of Many," *Christian Science Monitor,* February 13, 1997, p. 6.

50. Cases where migrant workers and prostitutes become enslaved are examined in detail later in the chapter.

51. Supplementary Convention, Section 1, Article 1(a).

52. Ibid., Article 7(b).

53. *Report of the Temporary Slavery Commission to the Council of the League of Nations,* p. 9.

54. Benjamin Whittaker, *Updating of the Report on Slavery Submitted to the Commission in 1966,* UN Doc. E/CN.4/Sub.2/1982/20 (July 5, 1982).

55. *Report of the Working Group on Contemporary Forms of Slavery at the Ninth Session,* UN Doc. E/CN.4/Sub.2/Ac.2/1983/9 (1983), Annex II, p. 2.

56. Whitaker, *Updating of the Report on Slavery Submitted to the Commission in 1966,* p. 21.

57. Marjan Wijers and Lin Lap-Chew, *Trafficking in Women, Forced Labor, and Slavery-like Practices in Marriage, Domestic Labour: Summary* (Utrecht: Foundation against Trafficking in Women, April 1997).

58. Daniel S. Ehrenberg, "The Labor Link: Applying the International Trading Systems to Enforce Violations of Forced and Child Labor," *Yale Journal of International Law* 20 (1995): 361, 375.

59. International Convention for the Suppression of the "White Slave Trade," May 4, 1910, 211 Consol. T.S. 45, 103 B.F.S.P. 244, Article 2.

60. United Nations Convention for the Suppression of the Traffic in Persons and of the Exploitation of the Prostitution of Others, United Nations Treaty Series, Vol. 96, p. 271, entered into force July 25, 1951.

61. Kathleen Barry, *The Prostitution of Sexuality* (New York: New York University Press, 1995).

62. University of Minnesota Law School, *Creating an International Framework for Legislation to Protect Women and Children from Commercial Sexual Exploitation: Preliminary Report* (Minneapolis: Center on Speech, Equality, and Harm, University of Minnesota Law School, January 1998).

63. See, for example, paragraph 23 in the 1983 *Report of the Special Rapporteur on the Suppression of the Traffic in Persons and the Exploitation of the Prostitution of Others,* which asserts that, "even when prostitution seems to have been chosen freely, it is actually the result of coercion." See also quotes from the testimony given to the Congress of Nice on September 8, 1981, by three "collectives of women prostitutes: "As prostitutes, we are all aware that all prostitution is forced prostitution. Whether we are forced to become prostitutes by lack of money or by housing or unemployment problems, or to escape from a family situation of rape or violence (which is often the case with very young prostitutes), or by a procurer, we would not lead the 'life' if we were in a position to leave it." UN Doc. E/1983/7, March 17, 1983.

64. Micèle Hirsch, *Plan of Action against Women and Forced Prostitution,* April 9, 1996, Council of Europe EG(96), p. 23.

65. Ibid., p. 24.

66. Lin Lean Lim, ed., *The Sex Sector: The Economic and Social Basis of Prostitution in South East Asia* (Geneva: International Labor Organization, 1998).

67. Nancy Erbe, "Prostitutes: Victims of Men's Exploitation and Abuse," *Law and Inequality Journal* 2 (1984): 609, 612–13.

68. John F. Decker, *Prostitution: Regulation and Control* (Littleton, CO: Fred B. Rothman and Company, 1979), p. 230.

69. Ibid., p. 253. See also Charles Winick, *The Lively Commerce: Prostitution in the United States* (New York: Times Books, 1971), p. 117.

70. Neal Kumar Hatyal, "Men Who Own Women: A Thirteenth Amendment Critique of Forced Prostitution," *Yale Law Journal* 103 (1993): 791, 793. The Thirteenth Amendment to the U.S. Constitution prohibits slavery and involuntary servitude.

71. *Report of the Sub-Commission on Prevention of Discrimination and Protection of Minorities,* UN Doc. E/CN.4/Sub.2/1982/20 (1982), p. 8.

72. Declaration on the Elimination of Violence against Women, adopted by the General Assembly 20 December 1993, UN Doc. A/RES/48/104.

73. M. McDougal and F. Feliciano, "International Coercion and World Public Order: The General Principles of the Law of War," *Yale Law Journal* 67 (1958): 771.

74. Geneva Convention Relative to the Protection of Civilian Persons in Time of War, United Nations Treaty Series, Vol. 75, p. 287 (1949), entered into force October 21, 1950.

75. Ibid., Article 27 (emphasis added).

76. Protocol Additional to the Geneva Conventions of 12 August 1949 and Relating to the Protection of Victims of International Armed Conflicts (Additional Protocol I), United Nations Treaty Series, Vol. 1125, p. 3, entered into force December 7, 1978, Article 75(2)b.

77. Kathleen Barry, *Female Sexual Slavery* (New York: New York University Press, 1984), pp. 33–34.

78. *United States v. Sanga,* 967 F. 2d 1332 (Ninth Circuit 1992).

79. Human Rights in Armed Conflicts, Resolution XXIII Adopted by the International Conference on Human Rights, Teheran, May 12, 1968, www1.umn.edu/humanrts/instree/1968a.htm.

80. Common Article 3 to the Four Geneva Conventions of 1949, Convention (IV) Relative to the Protection of Civilian Persons in Time of War, Geneva, 12 August 1949.

81. Linda Chavez, *Systematic Rape, Sexual Slavery, and Slavery-like Practices during Periods of Armed Conflict,* UN Doc. E/CN.4/Sub.2/1996/26 (1996), p. 4.

82. Geneva Convention Relative to the Protection of Civilian Persons in Time of War, United Nations Treaty Series, Vol. 75, p. 287 (1949), Article 147.

83. *Report of the Special Rapporteur on the Situation of Human Rights in the Territory of the Former Yugoslavia,* UN Doc. E/CN.4/1996/63 (1996); and *Report of the Special Rapporteur on the Situation of Human Rights in Rwanda,* UN Doc. E/CN.4/1996/68 (1996), www.unhchr.ch/hurricane/hurricane.nsf/01380868 E99 063778E8025666400339C36?opendocument/.

84. Gay J. McDougall, *Systematic Rape, Sexual Slavery, and Slavery-like Practices during Times of War,* Final Report, UN Doc. E/CN.4/Sub.2/1998/13 (June 22, 1998), p. 13.

85. *Rape and Abuse of Women in the Areas of Armed Conflict in the Former Yugoslavia,* Report of the Secretary-General, UN Doc. A/51/557 (October 25, 1996).

86. Bales, *Disposable People.*

Chapter 4. Slavery and the Emergence of Non-governmental Organizations

This chapter was first presented to the Columbia University Human Rights Seminar.

1. I thank Darren O'Byrne for clarifying this process for me. He develops these ideas in *Human Rights: An Introduction* (London: Prentice Hall, 2003).

2. Anthony Giddens, *Modernity and Self-Identity: Self and Society in the Late Modern Age* (Cambridge, England: Polity Press, 1991), 214.

3. See Adam Hochschild, *Bury the Chains* (Boston: Houghton Mifflin, 2005).

4. Ellen Gibson Wilson, *Thomas Clarkson: A Biography* (York: William Sessions, 1989), p. 17.

5. Anti-Slavery International, "The History of Anti-Slavery International," p. 4, www.antislavery.org/homepage/antislavery/history.pdf.

6. Seymour Drescher, "Women's Mobilization in the Era of Slave Emancipation: Some Anglo-French Comparisons" (paper presented at "Sisterhood and Slavery: Transatlantic Antislavery and Women's Rights," the Third Annual Gilder Lehrman Center International Conference, Yale University, New Haven, Conn., October 25–28, 2001), p. 3, www.yale.edu/glc/conference/drescher.pdf.

7. Quoted in Adam Hochschild, *King Leopold's Ghost* (Boston: Houghton Mifflin, 1999), p. 242.

8. Max Weber, *Economy and Society* (1921; reprint, Totowa, NJ: Bedminster Press, 1968), p. 223.

9. See, for example, the work of Peter Dicken, *Global Shift: The Internationalization of Economic Activity* (London: Paul Chapman, 1992).

10. James O. Finckenauer, "Russian Transnational Organized Crime and Human Trafficking," in *Global Human Smuggling,* ed. David Kyle and Rey Koslowski (Baltimore: Johns Hopkins, 2001), p. 171.

11. As listed in George Ritzer, *Sociological Theory,* 3rd ed. (New York: McGraw-Hill, 1992), p. 131, Weber's criteria for the major characteristics of the ideal-type bureaucracy are:

1. It consists of a continuous organization of official functions (offices) bound by rules.

2. Each office has a specified sphere of competence. The office carries with it a set of obligations to perform various functions, the authority to carry out these functions, and the means of compulsion required to do the job.

3. The offices are organized into a hierarchical system.

4. The offices may carry with them technical qualifications that require that the participants obtain suitable training.

5. The staff that fills these offices does not own the means of production associated with them. Staff members are provided with the use of those things that they need to do the job.

6. The incumbent is not allowed to appropriate the position; it always remains part of the organization.

7. Administrative acts, decisions, and rules are formulated and recorded in writing.

Chapter 5. The Challenge of Measuring Slavery

Epigraph: "The Peculiar Institution," *Scientific American* (April 2002): 4. An earlier version of this chapter appeared as "International Labor Standards: Quality of Information and Measures of Progress in Combating Forced Labor," *Comparative Labor Law and Policy Review* 24, no. 2 (Winter 2003).

1. Chapter 3 explores this theme in detail.

2. The International Labor Organization has decided that a number of Conventions are basic human rights. It calls them core labor standards. They are: Convention nos. 87 and 98, concerning freedom of association and the right to collective bargaining; Convention nos. 29 and 105, concerning the elimination of all forms of forced or compulsory labor; Convention nos. 138 and 182, concerning child labor; and Convention nos. 100 and 111, concerning the elimination of discrimination in employment and occupation.

3. See, for example, the work of Peter Dicken, *Global Shift: The Internationalization of Economic Activity* (London: Paul Chapman, 1992).

4. Mark Findlay, *The Globalisation of Crime* (Cambridge: Cambridge University Press, 1999), p. 47.

5. There is a question regularly asked by a minority of commentators: Are not these slaves better off being cared for by their slaveholders than being turned out to fend for themselves? No one has answered this question systematically, but all anecdotal or qualitative information suggests that slaves are better off when liberated. This has certainly been the consistent view of slaves and liberated slaves that I have met.

6. Ann Majchrzak, *Methods for Policy Research* (Beverley Hills: Sage, 1984), p. 44.

7. Convention Concerning the Prohibition and Immediate Action for the Elimination of the Worst Forms of Child Labour (ILO No. 182), 38 I.L.M. 1207 (1999), entered into force November 19, 2000, Article 3, pt. A.

8. Eugene Webb, D. Campbell, R. Schwartz, and L. Sechrest, *Unobtrusive Methods: Nonreactive Research in the Social Sciences* (Chicago: Rand McNally, 1966), p. 3. Unobtrusive measures are those that have no effect on the research subject, which may include anything from physical trace analysis to archival research. Because slavery is usually hidden, it is often necessary to explore the use of secondary and unobtrusive approaches such as these. Unobtrusive measures are never used alone, but normally serve as complementary techniques allowing some form of triangulation. There is an obvious potential application in the investigation of hidden activities like slavery.

9. Amy O'Neill Richard, *International Trafficking in Women to the United States: A Contemporary Manifestation of Slavery and Organized Crime,* Center for the Study of Intelligence, Central Intelligence Agency, November 1999, http://usinfo.state.gov/topical/global/traffic/report/homepage.htm.

10. This being exploratory, case-study research, I developed a series of guide questions that I attempted to answer for each case in every country and industry. In each of five countries, I used these questions to guide interviews as I

researched types of businesses that used slave labor. See these guide questions in appendix 1.

11. Robert K. Yin, *Case Study Research Design and Methods* (London: Sage, 1994), p. 1.

12. There are many other examples: attitudes that are measurable through human activity but exist only in human minds; self-esteem; and the operational definition and measurement of "love," for example, have occupied many lonely data-crunchers.

13. U.S. Department of State, *Country Reports on Human Rights Practices* (Washington, D.C., 2000–03).

14. U.S. Department of State, *2001 Trafficking in Persons Report* (Washington, D.C., 2001), www.state.gov/documents/organization/4107.pdf.

15. International Labor Office, *Stopping Forced Labour: Global Report under the Follow-up to the ILO Declaration on Fundamental Principles and Rights at Work,* International Labor Conference, Eighty-ninth Session, 2001, www.ilo.org/dyn/declaris/DECLARATIONWEB.DOWNLOAD_BLOB?Var_Document ID=1573/.

16. See, for example, *Report of the Working Group on Contemporary Forms of Slavery on Its Twenty-third Session,* UN Doc. E/CN.4/Sub.2/1998/14, par. 22 (1998), which includes a report sponsored by Anti-Slavery International that reviews slavery conventions.

17. D. Narasimha Reddy et al., *Report on Vulnerability to Debt Bondage Index* (New Delhi: Institute for Human Development, n.d.).

18. Anne Kielland and Ibrahim Sanogo, *Burkina Faso: Child Labor Migration from Rural Areas. The Magnitude and the Determinants,* Terre des Hommes and World Bank, 2002, http://home.online.no/~annekie/Africa_docs/BFEnglish .pdf. See also Anne Kielland and Maurizia Tovo, *Child Labor in Africa: The Facts and the Faces* (Washington, DC: World Bank, 2004).

19. A good example is Alison Sutton, *Slavery in Brazil: A Link in the Chain of Modernisation* (London: Anti-Slavery International, 1994).

20. Human Rights Watch, "U.S. State Department Trafficking Report Missing Key Data, Credits Uneven Efforts," *Human Rights News,* June 6, 2002, www .hrw.org/press/2002/06/us-report0606.htm.

21. Ibid.

22. Lal Bahadur Shastri National Academy of Administration, *Incidence of Bonded Labour in India: Area, Nature, and Extent* (Mussoorie, India: Lal Bahadur Shastri National Academy of Administration, 1990).

23. O'Neill Richard, *International Trafficking in Women to the United States.*

24. There are exceptions, of course. For ethnographic studies of communities of origin for trafficked or smuggled people, see David Kyle and Rey Koslowski, eds., *Global Human Smuggling: Comparative Perspectives* (Baltimore: Johns Hopkins University Press, 2001).

25. Jok Madut Jok, *War and Slavery in Sudan* (Philadelphia: University of Pennsylvania Press, 2001); Binka Le Breton, *Trapped: Modern-Day Slavery in the Brazilian Amazon* (Bloomfield, CT: Kumarian Press, 2003).

26. See www.stop-traffic.org for archived material and details on how to subscribe.

27. Larry Rohter, "Brazil's Prized Exports Rely on Slaves and Scorched Land," *New York Times,* March 25, 2002, p. 1.

28. L. L. Thurstone, "Attitudes *Can* Be Measured," *American Journal of Sociology* 33 (1928): 529–54. Thurstone's ideas were specified most clearly in L. L. Thurstone and E. Chave, *The Measurement of Attitudes* (Chicago: University of Chicago Press, 1929).

29. I defined slavery at its most basic this way: A social and economic relationship in which a person is controlled through violence or its threat, paid nothing, and economically exploited. I noted that, for many academics, the issue of defining slavery took precedence over any other concerns, while among practitioners working in non-governmental organizations or the ILO, the definition was merely incidental. One of the challenges was that a large number of definitions were in use. I explore this problem further in chapter 3 and in "'No One Shall Be Held in Slavery or Servitude': A Critical Analysis of International Slavery Agreements," *Human Rights Review* 2, no. 2 (January 2001), coauthored by Peter Robbins, and in chapter 3 of this book.

30. Garbage in, garbage out.

31. I had, at least, a notion of this process. I wrote my doctoral thesis on Charles Booth, who in the late nineteenth century had "invented" the poverty line and "discovered" the "precise" extent of poverty in Victorian London. His methods of investigation and aggregation were not unlike those I used, and his amazement at subsequently being touted as a world expert on poverty presaged my own similar experience. In 2001, I found that one academic commentator had designated me the "Charles Booth of the twenty-first century."

32. See "The Social Psychology of Modern Slavery," *Scientific American* (April 2002).

33. Publishing in a popular journal meant other responses came as well. One informant explained that we have all been secretly enslaved by television; a U.S. prison inmate asked to be added to the estimates of those enslaved.

34. Stephen Devereux and John Hoddinott, "Issues in Data Collection," in *Fieldwork in Developing Countries* (Boulder, CO: Lynne Reinner, 1993), p. 36.

35. See chapter 1 of my book *Disposable People: New Slavery in the Global Economy* (Berkeley: University of California Press, 1999).

36. Variables were drawn from United Nations, *World Statistics Pocketbook,* Sales No. E.95.XVII.7 (New York: United Nations, 1995); the International Corruption Index assembled by Transparency International, www.transparency international.org/surveys/index.html; "Human Rights Abuses by Country," a table compiled by the *London Observer,* 25 October 1999; Amnesty International, *Amnesty International Report 1999* (London: Amnesty International, 2000); and my own database for slavery and trafficking. In calculating the regression, I included, through several iterations, all the various types of information I had collected on the world's countries. For example, while I doubted that the number of television receivers per thousand persons in the country of origin was a

significant predictor of slavery in a country, I still treated it as a predictor until it was excluded statistically by the regression procedure. The factors listed in the chapter, then, are those that "survived" and were denoted as statistically significant predictors of the incidence of slavery in country.

37. Linear regression estimates the coefficients of the linear equation, involving one or more independent variables, that best predicts the value of the dependent variable.

38. R = .781; R squared = .610; adjusted R squared = .584; standard error in the estimate = .7422. Information on infant mortality, population pressure, proportion of workforce in agriculture, and threatened species is taken from United Nations, *The World Statistics Pocketbook;* information on governmental corruption is taken from the International Corruption Index, assembled by Transparency International, 1999; information on trafficking from a country is taken from my own estimates.

39. Robert B. Smith, "Why Human Development Varies by Region: Exploring Correlates and Causes" (manuscript, Social Structural Research, Cambridge, MA, 2003).

40. Human Rights Watch, "U.S. State Department Trafficking Report Missing Key Data, Credits Uneven Efforts."

41. Using the World Bank's classification of countries according to whether they have a high international debt loading, I treated this as a dichotomous variable and looked at its relationship with my measure of the incidence of slavery. A Pearson's correlation of .439 was significant at the .01 level. In a cross-tabulation, the Chi-square for the relationship between the two variables was 43.39, also significant at the .01 level.

42. Jack Gibbs, *Sociological Theory Construction* (Hinsdale, IL: Dryden Press, 1972), p. 62.

43. Findlay, *The Globalisation of Crime,* p. 224.

44. Interview by author with an Interpol antitrafficking official, London, March 2002. I promised anonymity to this individual.

45. Anne Kielland and Ibrahim Sanogo, *Burkina Faso: Child Labor Migration from Rural Areas. The Magnitude and the Determinants,* Terre des Hommes and World Bank, 2002, p. 5, http://home.online.no/~annekie/Africa_docs/BFEnglish.pdf.

46. Economic Community of West African States, *ECOWAS Plan of Action against Trafficking in Persons (2002–2003),* p. 8, www.iss.co.za/AF/RegOrg/unity_to_union/pdfs/ecowas/10POAHuTraf.pdf.

Chapter 6. Globalization and Redemption

1. See particularly Martin Albrow, *The Global Age* (London: Polity Press, 1996).

2. Ibid., p. 88.

3. See, for example, the work of Peter Dicken, *Global Shift: The Internationalization of Economic Activity* (London: Paul Chapman, 1992).

4. Albrow, *The Global Age,* 129.

5. Ibid., p. 83.

6. See Roger L. Ransom, "The Economics of Slavery," in *Conflict and Compromise: The Political Economy of Slavery, Emancipation, and the American Civil War* (Cambridge: Cambridge University Press, 1989), pp. 41–81.

7. It is remarkable how often this phrase is repeated in the world press. Because general notions of slavery require it to involve legal ownership, when slavery is uncovered it is rarely described as such. Most commonly people are "held in slavelike conditions" or, perhaps, forced to work with no remuneration for years under a threat of violence in "virtual slavery."

8. See, for example, Samuel Cotton, *Silent Terror: A Journey into Contemporary African Slavery* (New York: Harlem River Press and Reader and Writers, 1998); or David Hecht, "Where African Slavery Still Exists in the Eyes of Many," *Christian Science Monitor,* February 13, 1997, p. 6.

9. Kevin Bales, *Disposable People: New Slavery in the Global Economy* (Berkeley: University of California Press, 1999), p. 81.

10. On the disappearance of slavery in Sudan at the time of World War II, see T. Hargey, "Festina Lente: Slavery Policy and Practice in the Anglo-Egyptian Sudan" in *Slavery and Colonial Rule in Africa,* ed. M. A. Klein et al. (Cambridge: Cambridge University Press, 1998), p. 256.

11. Confidential source, personal conversation with the author, 1995.

12. *Sudan Democratic Gazette* (London), no. 114 (November 1999): p. 2.

13. Shannon Field, "The Pivotal Role of Oil in Sudan's Civil War," *Sudan Democratic Gazette* (London), no. 114 (November 1999): 10.

14. See, for example, the "Gospel Plow" Website, which includes reports on the Sudanese civil war and instructions on how to arm "Christian warriors" in the United States, www.frii.com/~gosplow/index.html.

15. "After Ten Years: A New OLS Chief Has a Forward-Looking Relief Policy," *Sudan Democratic Gazette* (London), no. 114 (November 1999): 6–7.

16. Found on the Website of Christian Solidarity Worldwide: www.csw.org .uk/inter-agency_paper_on_sudan.html.

17. C162 Worst Forms of Child Labor Convention, 1999, International Labor Organization, www.ilo.org/public/english/standards/ipec/ratification/convention/ text.htm.

Chapter 7. Human Trafficking

Portions of this chapter first appeared in "Globalization and Slavery," *International Dialogue* 1 (Summer 1999).

1. The 1910 Convention for the Suppression of the White Slave Trade made it a crime for "any person who, to gratify the passions of others, has by fraud or by the use of violence, threats, abuse of authority, or any other means of constraint, hired, abducted or enticed a woman . . . for immoral purpose." International Convention for the Suppression of the "White Slave Trade," May 4, 1910, 211 Consol. T.S. 45, 103 B.F.S.P. 244, Article 2.

2. United Nations Convention for the Suppression of the Traffic in Persons and of the Exploitation of the Prostitution of Others, United Nations Treaty Series, Vol. 96, p. 271, entered into force July 25, 1951.

3. See chapter 3 for more information on the Anti-Trafficking Protocol.

4. Protocol to Prevent, Suppress and Punish Trafficking in Persons, Especially Women and Children, Article 2, Statement of Purpose, pt. a.

5. Protocol to Prevent, Suppress and Punish Trafficking in Persons, Especially Women and Children, Supplementing the United Nations Convention against Transnational Organized Crime, G.A. Res. 25, annex II, UN GAOR, 55th sess., Supp. No. 49, at 60, UN Doc. A/45/49 (Vol. 1) (2001), Article 4, Scope of Application.

6. Provincial Court of Vienna, Judgment Hv 6306/98, 25 June 1999, quoted from *Angelika Kartusch/Katharina Knaus/Gabriele Reiter,* Bekämpfung des Frauenhandels nach internationalem und österreichischem Recht, December 2000, pp. 225–27.

7. In this section I have drawn extensively on Angelika Kartusch, *Reference Guide for Anti-Trafficking Legislative Review* (Vienna: Organization for Security and Cooperation in Europe/Office for Democratic Institutions and Human Rights, 2001).

8. These cases are drawn primarily from Richard Bourdeaux, "Journey into Sex Slavery: Traffickers Are Luring Migrant Women and Girls Fleeing Poverty into Forced Prostitution in Europe: Italy Is Enlisting the Victims to Fight Back against the Pimps," *Los Angeles Times,* August 17, 2001.

9. Protocol against the Smuggling of Migrants by Land, Sea and Air, Supplementing the United Nations Convention against Transnational Crime, G.A. Res. 55/25, Annex III, U.N. GAOR, 55th sess., Suppl. No. 49 at 65, UN Doc. A/45/49, Vol. 1, 2001, entered into force January 28, 2004.

10. This section is adapted from A. A. Aronowitz and M. Peruffo, *Smuggling and Trafficking in Human Beings: The Phenomenon, the Markets That Drive It, and the Organisations That Promote It* (Turin: United Nations Interregional Crime and Justice Research Institute, 2001).

11. Internal trafficking also occurs — in many countries, possibly to an even greater extent than transnational trafficking. It is the subsequent exploitation, and not the crossing of international borders, that defines trafficking in human beings.

12. S. Adamoli, A. DiNicoli, E. Savona, and P. Zoffi, *Organized Crime around the World* (Helsinki: European Institute for Crime Prevention and Control, 1998), p. 17.

13. A. A. Aronowitz, "The Phenomenon, the Markets That Drive It, and the Organizations That Promote It," *European Journal on Criminal Policy and Research* 9 (2001): 171.

14. Ibid.

15. Kevin Bales, "Testing a Theory of Modern Slavery" (paper presented at "From Chattel Slavery to State Servitude: Slavery in the Twentieth Century," an event held at the Gilder Lehrman Center for the Study of Slavery, Resistance,

and Abolition, Yale University, New Haven, Conn., October 22–23, 2004), www.yale.edu/glc/events/cbss/Bales.pdf.

16. Anne Kielland and Ibrahim Sanogo, *Burkina Faso: Child Labor Migration from Rural Areas. The Magnitude and the Determinants,* Terre des Hommes and World Bank, 2002, p. 32, http://home.online.no/~annekie/Africa_docs/BF English.pdf.

17. Aronowitz, "The Phenomenon, the Markets That Drive It, and the Organizations That Promote It," 163–95.

18. A. Bajrektarevic, *Trafficking In and Smuggling of Human Beings—Linkages to Organized Crime—International Legal Measures: Statement Digest* (Vienna: International Centre for Migration Policy Development, 2000).

19. Ibid., p. 17.

20. A. Sipaviciene, "New Routes in Trafficking of Migrants: Case of Lithuania" (paper presented at the international conference "International Migration Challenges for European Population," Bari, Italy, June 25–27 2000).

21. Quoted in Kevin Bales, "The Social Psychology of Modern Slavery," *Scientific American* (April 2002), www.mit.edu/people/etekle/Index.

22. See page 59 for an explanation of the two types of debt bondage.

Chapter 8. Understanding the Demand
behind Human Trafficking

1. Bridget Anderson and Julia O'Connell Davidson, *The Demand Side of Trafficking,* pt. 1: *Review of Evidence and Debates on "The Demand Side of Trafficking"* (Bangkok: Global Alliance against Trafficking in Women, 2002), p. 18.

2. See, for example, H. Ai Yun, "Foreign Maids and the Reproduction of Labor in Singapore," *Philippine Sociological Review* 44, no. 1 (1996): 33–57; B. Anderson, *Doing the Dirty Work? The Global Politics of Domestic Labour* (London: Zed, 2000); Anti-Slavery International, "Child Servitude: Children Working as Domestic Servants" (ASI submission to the United Nations Commission on Human Rights Working Group on Contemporary Forms of Slavery, 1996); L. Coser, "Servants: The Obsolescence of an Occupational Role," *Social Forces* 52 (1974): 31–40; David Kyle and Zai Lian, *Migration Merchants: Human Smuggling from Ecuador and China,* Working Paper No. 43 (San Diego: Center for Comparative Immigration Studies, University of California, 2001); A. Macklin, "Foreign Domestic Worker: Surrogate Housewife or Mail Order Servant?" *McGill Law Journal/Revue de droit de McGill* 37 (1992): 681 ff.

3. For a fuller explanation of this transformation, see Kevin Bales, *Disposable People: New Slavery in the Global Economy* (Berkeley: University of California Press, 1999).

4. Anderson and O'Connell Davidson, *The Demand Side of Trafficking,* pt. 1, p. 23. On attitudes toward gender, race, and sexuality, see, for example, J. O'Connell Davidson, *Prostitution, Power, and Freedom* (Cambridge: Polity, 1998); J. O'Connell Davidson, "The Sex Tourist, the Expatriate, His Ex-Wife,

and Her 'Other': The Politics of Loss, Difference, and Desire," *Sexualities* 4, no. 1 (2001): 5–24; S. Kruhse-Mount Burton, "Sex Tourism and Traditional Australian Male Identity," in *International Tourism: Identity and Change,* ed. M. Lafabt, J. Allcock, and E. Bruner (London: Sage, 1995); J. Seabrook, *Travels in the Skin Trade: Tourism and the Sex Industry* (London: Pluto Press, 1996); R. Bishop and L. Robinson, *Nightmarket: Sexual Cultures and the Thai Economic Miracle* (London: Routledge, 1998). On Western women who practice sex tourism, see J. Sanchez Taylor, "Tourism and 'Embodied' Commodities: Sex Tourism in the Caribbean," in *Tourism and Sex: Culture, Commerce, and Coercion,* ed. S. Clift and S. Carter (London: Pinter, 2000).

5. See, for example, Anita Chabria, *His Own Private Berkeley,* November 25, 2001, http://fpmail.friends-partners.org/pipermail/stop-traffic/2001-November/001756.html.

6. See chapter 1. See also my article "The Social Psychology of Modern Slavery," *Scientific American* (April 2002).

7. Ideas about what the consumers of trafficked people are looking for could be introduced into antitrafficking public education messages and might alert potential victims to the nature of the risks they face.

8. Quoted in Maria-Pia Boethius, *The End of Prostitution in Sweden?* Swedish Institute, October 1999, found at http://www.sweden.se/templates/Article_2295.asp.

9. For example, the trafficker might use the AIDA model of marketing, which aims to generate awareness, interest, demand, and action on the part of the consumer.

Index

transnational, 84. *See also* organized crime; trafficking in persons
cultivated demand, 158
cultural context of trafficking, 138–39, 148–50
cultural relativism, 37

dam construction, 20
"dark figures" of crime, 93
Davidson. *See* O'Connell Davidson
"deaf Mexican" cases, 164
deaths of trafficking victims, 147–48
debt bondage, 149; definitions, 47, 108; environmental destruction, 20; farmers, 67; forms of, 189n14; governmental reports, 100; India, 1–4, 16–17, 20, 32–34, 88; laws, 16–17; redemption debate, 119; three dimensions of slavery, 58, 59–62; vulnerability scale, 98
declarations: definition, 190n2; discrimination against women, 64
demand, 154–71, 204nn7,9; extinguishing, 164–67; prostitution, 167–69; reducing, 167–71
demographic research-guide questions, 175–77
deregulation of markets, 113
Devereux, Stephen, 104–5
Dinka tribes (Sudan), 118–19
discrimination against prostitutes, 54
dispersed economic activities. *See* economic activities
diversification strategies, 77–78
diversity through globalization, 114–15
document forgery, 133–34
domestic service, 161, 171, 192n20
donations, 173
Douglass, Frederick, 117

eastern Europe, 143
economic activities: business analysis, 108–9; civil wars, 120; dispersal, 78–79, 89–90, 113; globalization, 112–25, 155–56; research-guide questions, 177–79
Economic Community of West African States, 110
economic control, of victims, 53–54
economic costs. *See* costs
economic definition of slavery, 72, 85, 199n29
economic growth, 18–19

Economic, Social and Cultural Covenant (1966), 48–49, 51
ECOWAS. *See* Economic Community of West African States
education provision: costs, 15; Freedmen's Bureau, 6. *See also* public awareness/education
Egyptian slave codes, 28
elaborated forms of slavery, 115
elasticity of demand, 170–71
emancipation. *See* freedom
Emancipation Proclamation (U.S.), 5
employment agencies, 143
enforced prostitution. *See* forced prostitution
environmental destruction, 19–21, 153
erga omnes obligations, 42
escaped trafficking victims, 148
escort unit, trafficking operations, 144
estimates: extent of slavery, 102–4, 200n37; testing theories, 105–6; trafficking in persons, 135–66
ethnic appearance factors, 142
Europe: child apprenticeships, 13; global trafficking, 79; redemption of slaves, 117–18; slave markets, 29; trafficking estimates, 135–36. *See also* eastern Europe
evil: definition, 25–27, 189n2; globalization of perceptions, 37–38; human rights defined, 27–31; slaveholders, 24–27; slavery defined as, 34–37; victims' definition, 27, 31–32, 34–37
exoticism, 162–63
expert reports, 98, 100–101, 102–3
exploitation: definition, 47–48; trafficking victims, 133–35, 146–47
exploiting unit, trafficking operations, 145

farming: debt bondage, 67; demand for trafficked people, 159–60; Ivory Coast cooperatives, 82; non-slave farming, 22–23
Findlay, Mark, 90
fishing industry, 10–12
forced labor: definitions, 92, 191n10; information sources, 90; lived experiences, 109; Slavery Convention definition, 44–45, 50–51
forced prostitution, 62–65, 67–68, 194n63. *See also* prostitution

117973

Text: 10/13 Galliard
Display: Galliard
Illustrator: Bill Nelson
Compositor: BookMatters, Berkeley
Printer and binder: Edwards Brothers, Inc.